Dispatches from

Behind the Wheel

DISPATCHES FROM

BEHIND
THE WHEEL

THE COMPLETE ZINE SERIES

REVISED AND UPDATED

WRITTEN AND DESIGNED BY
KELLY DESSAINT

PILTDOWNLAD #10

A Lyft Driver's Log

PILTDOWNLAD #10.5

Notes from an Uber/Lyft

PILTDOWNLAD #10.75

From Uber/Lyft to Taxi

PILTDOWNLAD #11

The Thin Checkered Line

phony lid books

©2019 Kelly Dessaint

ISBN: 978-1-930935-44-0

First Printing, December 2019

Phony Lid Books
PO Box 410005
San Francisco, CA 94141

phonylid@gmail.com

•••●●● ━━━━━━━━━━━━━━━━━━━━━━━ ●●●••••

A Lyft Driver's Log was originally published in June 2014. "It's Not About the Mustache," "Top Ten Questions I Get Asked as a Lyft Driver," "The Cult of Lyft: Inside the Pacific Driver Lounge," "How to Get Kicked Out of a Lyft Lounge," "The Pacific Drive Lounge is My Honey Boo Boo" and "A Lyft Playlist" were originally posted on Medium.com.

Notes from an Uber/Lyft was originally published in Dec. 2014. "For Whom the Uber Tolls," "The Other Uber Driver," "The Chump" and "Peep Show for an Uber" originally appeared on idrivesf.wordpress.com. "A Day in the Life of an Uber/Lyft Driver" was selected as featured content on Medium.com under the headline, "A Day in the Life of a Rideshare Driver in San Francisco." "To Uber or Not to Uber" was reprinted in the *Utne Reader*. "My Uber Breaking Point" originally appeared on Disinfo.com. Part of "Emperor Caveat" was published as "The Power Sex Couple" on Broke-AssStuart.com. "For Whom the Uber Tolls" was first posted on idrivesf. wordpress.com and selected for their Freshly Pressed blog. A longer, more pedantic version of "My Rating Weighs a Ton" originally appeared on Rideshare Dashboard.

From Uber/Lyft to Taxi was originally published in September 2016 and contains expanded, unexpurgated versions of the "I Drive SF" column that first appeared in the *San Francisco Examiner* between May 2015 and July 2016. "Is This a Lyft or Do I Need To Pay You?" and parts of "It's A Cabbies Life for Me" were first posted on BrokeAssStuart.com. The Late Night Larry stories were transcribed via iPhone during various weekly barbecues at the National Cab yard.

The Thin Checkered Line was originally published in Nov. 2018. Some sections first appeared in the *San Francisco Examiner*, including most of "Felicia the Freeloader," "A Taxi-Driving Hero Ain't Nothing to Be," "When I Was a Green Pea," "The Poor Man's Taxi Driver," "The Taxi Driver's Worst Enemy," "Hell Is Other Cab Drivers," "Canary in the Coal Mine," "Tub Thumping for a Lost Cause" and "Requiem for Valencia Street." The versions herein have been expanded and updated.

All photos and graphics by Kelly Dessaint and Irina Dessaint. Except for: Cover by Trevor Johnson. Next:Economy photos courtesy of O'Reilly Media. Photo of Driver 8 and Kelly Dessaint by Lauren Smiley. Cover of "The Thin Checkered Line" by Trevor Johnson. Photos on pages 8-10 by Christian Lewis.

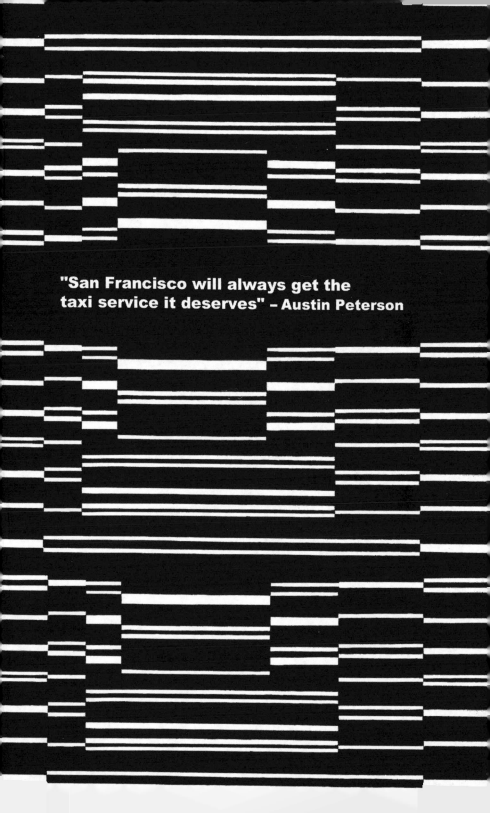

"San Francisco will always get the taxi service it deserves" – Austin Peterson

TABLE OF CONTENTS

Introduction 14

A Lyft Driver's Log 17

Webster & Sutter 21
Be More Than a Number in Eight Easy Steps 24
St. Patty's Day Weekend 27
Downtown Traffic 32
It's Not About the Mustache 38
No Cabs to Cole Valley 41
SFO to Ethiopia 45
The Cult of Lyft: Inside the Pacific Driver Lounge 51
How to Get Kicked Out of a Lyft Lounge 54
The Pacific Drive Lounge is My Honey Boo Boo 55
The Prime Time Hustle 60
Work All the Time 64
A Friday Night Cut Short 66
Second Home Game 76
Something about Kate 81
A Lyft Playlist 84
In Town from a Swing State 87

Notes from an Uber/Lyft 95

Emperor Caveat 99
To Uber or Not to Uber 106
A Day in the Life of an Uber/Lyft Driver 116
The Wrong Bush and Mason 126
Gun on the Street 129
Top Ten Things I Get Asked 137
For Whom the Uber Tolls 140
The Other Uber Driver 143
Peep Show for an Uber 146
My Rating Weighs a Ton 147
Infinite Douchebaggery 149
The Polk Gulch Vortex 155
The Chump 158
Another Wasted Night 159
The Leather Man 166
My Uber Breaking Point 170

183 **From Uber/Lyft to Taxi**

187 It's The Cabbie's Life for Me
191 The Road to Legitimacy
196 My First Taxi Shift
202 Taxi Driving as a Public Service
204 The Displacement Narrative
210 The Incurable Madness of Taxi Driving
211 Is This a Lyft or Do I Need to Pay You?
213 The Danger Dog Incident
216 Playlists, Profanity & Other Trade Secrets
218 On the Recitation of the Waybill
221 The Picky Couple
222 When Nature Calls, Business Picks Up
225 The View from a Taxi
229 Guilty of Driving a Cab
230 What's in a Passenger?
236 Adventures in Late Night Cabstands
238 Marching Backwards into the Future
248 Aiding and Abetting Passengers' Vices
251 Late Night Larry on Hope
253 The Patron Saint of Late Night Drunks
255 Cogs in the Wheels of Corruption
257 A Good Night Comes at a Price
262 Late Night Larry on Pukers
262 I Drive a Taxi So You Don't Have To
264 The Perils of Shopping on the Black Market
266 When We Talk About Uber/Lyft
269 A Hell Ride into the Peninsula
271 Late Night Larry on Orgasms
274 When the Driving's Over the Real Slog Begins

disrupt the

The Thin Checkered Line 279

The Way of the Taxi

Cab to the Yard 283
Gridlock is My Business 289
The Slumlord of Haight-Ashbury 291
Felicia the Freeloader 296
A Taxi-Driving Hero Ain't Nothing to Be 304

A Story with Wheels

When I Was a Green Pea 306
Looking for a Story 311
Personal Economics 315

Navigating the Uber Effect

The S.H.I.T.S. 322
Just Another Manic Mantra 323
Fear and Loathing on Talk Radio 326
The Poor Man's Taxi Driver 330
The Uber-iquity of Convenience 333

The Death of Cab Culture

The Taxi Driver's Worst Enemy 339
Hell Is Other Cab Drivers 343
Canary in the Coal Mine 345

San Francisco Has Never Been What It Used to Be

The New Scourge 347
Tub Thumping for a Lost Cause 351
The World's A Mess - It's in My Cab 355
Requiem for Valencia Street 357

disruptors

INTRODUCTION

PRIOR TO EMBARKING ON THIS WHOLE DRIVING FOR HIRE SAGA, I never could not have imagined the cesspool of absurdity that awaited me. Back then, I just wanted to earn a few bucks doing something out of the ordinary, make a zine about the experience and move on with my life.

That was five years ago.

At the time, I was writing a memoir about a traumatic period in my life. The process was extremely painful and I figured a one-off zine about driving people around San Francisco would be a perfect distraction. People might even dig it enough to buy a few copies.

As I was finishing the first issue of Behind the Wheel, though, it became apparent that this social and economic phenomenon could not be fully encapsulated in just a 60-page zine. The story was bigger that I ever imagined.

In 2014, San Francisco was in the midst of a huge transformation. The latest tech boom had led to hyper-gentrification, glaring income disparity, a homeless epidemic and the wholesale dismantling of the city's legacy as a bastion of diversity and counterculture.

Driving the streets and talking with a wide array of passengers, I had a front row seat to the spectacle. The story almost wrote itself. I just had to take notes.

The only real hard part was deciding on a compelling layout. To this end, I borrowed heavily from Futurism and De Stijl designs, which seemed to convey the architecture of motion and a sense of the "the new."

Since working for an app was so virtual, I wanted to do something totally analogue. I even considered typing the zine out on my Olympia manual like with previous issues of Piltdownlad, but that seemed overkill, especially with a zine about technology. Nevertheless, I typed the street names for the hand drawn maps interspersed among Lyft's computer-generated feedback reports.

Following the release of "A Lyft Driver's Log," I immediately began work on "Notes from an Uber/Lyft," chronicling my transition to Uber.

Unlike the whimsical nature of the first issue, the tone in the second was markedly negative, representing how disgruntled I was becoming. There were still plenty of stories about the people who got in my car, but I didn't shy away from the exploitative nature of "ridesharing."

In the early days, the vast majority of San Franciscans, excluding cab drivers, were enamored with Uber and Lyft. Nobody was talking shit yet, besides me.

When the price wars started in the summer of 2014, drivers began quitting en masse and voicing their displeasure. But their rants were confined to private Facebook groups and/or obscure online forums. The public was still oblivious and more than happy with the services provided by the two companies.

As one of the early naysayers, my barbed critiques of Uber and Lyft generated a great deal of attention. Naturally, the excerpts I posted online were more popular than the actual zines. And despite my plan to avoid the digital realm, I began writing original content for the web.

My post about the vulnerability of drivers operating without support from Uber, "For Whom the Uber Tolls," was selected by Wordpress for their Freshly Pressed blog. After Medium featured "A Day in the Life of a Rideshare Driver in San Francisco," the editor of Disinfo.com contacted me about contributing to their site.

Along with the usual publications that reviewed zines, I sent a copy of "Notes from an Uber/Lyft" to the *UTNE Reader*. They reprinted the chapter "To Uber or Not to Uber" in their December issue.

Once my posts making fun of Lyft loyalists ("The Cult of Lyft") and blasting Uber customers ("Your Uber Driver Hates You") made the rounds and ellicited a firestorm of vitriol from drivers, I stoked the flames further with "How to Fix Ridesharing: Kill Lyft," "The Rideshare Paradox" and "Why I Uber On."

These hit pieces would eventually inspire a Lyft driver/blogger in Boston to post several excerpts on his site in a three part series under the title, "Kelly Dessaint: The Most Hated Person in the World of Lyft."

When the post "Night of the Living Taxi: The Epic Rideshare Fail of NYE 2015" went semi-viral, Joe Fitzgerald Rodriguez interviewed me for the *San Francisco Examiner*. Shortly afterwards, he recommended me to the Editor in Chief for a weekly column about driving for Uber.

At that point, I was driving a taxi and writing for Broke-Ass Stuart's website.

"I Drive SF" premiered in the *Examiner* on May Day, 2015.

Since I was limited to 700 words, many of the pieces were heavily condensed. When I was ready to do a third issue of Behind the Wheel, it only made sense to publish the longer versions and include the naughty bits that were too risqué for the newspaper.

"From Uber/Lyft to Taxi" was a mostly uncensored document about the first two years of my cab driving career.

It took me two years to finally finish the fourth installment of Behind the Wheel. With the "Thin Checkered Line," I tried to fill in the holes left from the third issue and present my outlook on the taxi versus Uber/Lyft conflict.

Much in the same way that the upbeat tone of the first zine was followed by a less than positive reality check in the second, the fourth issue served as a grumpy rebuttal to my previous exuberance of driving a taxi.

After five years, it was time to bring the Behind the Wheel series to an end. I can't keep making zines about driving. Besides resuming abandoned projects, there are new ones I want to start.

So for now, this part of the ride has come to an end.

Kelly Dessaint
October 2019

$7

PILTDOWNLAD

NO. 10

From the trenches of San Francisco's
gig economy, a Lyft confessional

BEHIND THE WHEEL
A LYFT DRIVER'S LOG
SECOND EDITION
REVISED AND UPDATED

BEHIND THE WHEEL:
A LYFT DRIVER'S LOG

Webster & Sutter · 21

Be More Than a Number in
Eight Easy Steps · 24

St. Patty's Day
Weekend · 27

Downtown Traffic · 32

It's Not About the
Mustache · 38

No Cabs to
Cole Valley · 41

SFO to Ethiopia · 45

The Cult of Lyft · 51

How to Get Kicked Out of
a Lyft Lounge · 54

The Pacific Driver Lounge
is My Honey Boo Boo · 55

The Prime Time
Hustle · 60

Work All the Time · 64

A Friday Night Cut
Short · 66

Second Home Game · 76

Something about
Kate · 81

A Lyft Playlist · 84

In Town from a Swing
State · 87

except when it is …

PILTDOWNLAD #10

THE NEIGHBORHOODS OF
SAN FRANCISCO

or at least the ones referred
to most frequently in this zine

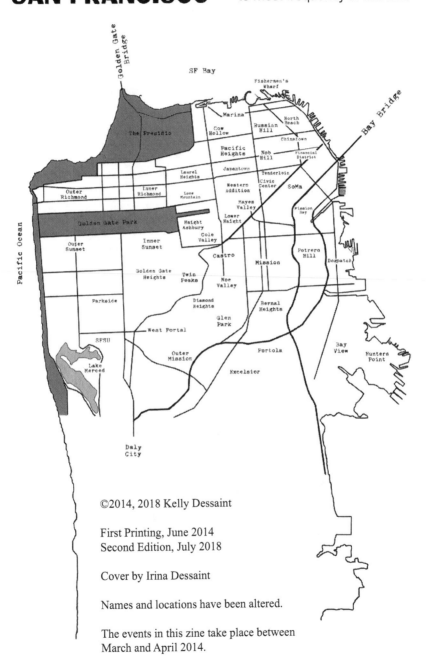

©2014, 2018 Kelly Dessaint

First Printing, June 2014
Second Edition, July 2018

Cover by Irina Dessaint

Names and locations have been altered.

The events in this zine take place between
March and April 2014.

AND WEBSTER **3.12** **SUTTER**

I'M TAKING AMANDA FROM THE MISSION TO SUTTER AND WEBSTER.
She's friendly. Sits up front. Tells me all about her wedding next summer in Martha's Vineyard. I don't know what to say. I'm only perpetuating the conversation out of courtesy. But it's awkward. We are from different worlds. I'm an LA native, in the Bay Area to reinvent myself. She's from Boston. Moved to San Francisco last year. Does PR for a start-up in SoMa.

"I got married in Vegas," I tell her, but agree that it must be a real hassle to organize a large event.

I turn left onto Laguna.

"Do you live in the city?" she asks.

"No, Oakland."

"Oakland's supposed to be hot now."

"Oakland's all right. It's not San Francisco though." When people make a big deal about the East Bay, I feel obligated to be positive. Still, it's like getting congratulated for being a runner-up. "I prefer San Francisco," I tell her. "Maybe one day my wife and I can afford to move into the city... if the rents ever go down."

"Don't you make decent money driving for Lyft?"

"Not enough to live in San Francisco! They say you have to earn over a hundred grand to live in San Francisco now. You can't make that driving for Lyft. Transporting people is a numbers game. You can only get so many rides in a given amount of time. I've only been at this a few days, but I've figured that much out."

"Then why do it?" she asks.

"I don't know... To meet interesting people?" I laugh.

"What's the most random thing that's happened in your car?"

"I just started driving. Not much has happened so far. Just a lot of drunk people."

"What's that like?"

"It's all right. Sometimes the smell of alcohol is so overwhelming it's lodged in my olfactory memory banks and doesn't go away until I get home and start drinking myself."

"Do I smell like alcohol?" she asks.

"No," I lie. I don't want to give her a complex, but her breath, like that of every other passenger whose been drinking, fogs up the windows. I turned the defroster on shortly after picking her up.

As we approach Geary Blvd, I worry that I've already passed Sutter, unsure if it's before or after Geary. I've been watching the signs, but I'm still learning my way around town. I doubt myself all the time. More than I should. For the past several weeks I've been studying the AAA map pinned to my bedroom wall, memorizing the major streets and how they intersect with each other. I occasionally quiz myself to see how much I have learned. I start in the Civic Center, at Van Ness and go east: Polk, Larkin, Hyde... Is it Leavenworth and then Jones? I try going west: Franklin, Gough, Octavia, Laguna... Buchanan? And then Webster and Fillmore? I'm pretty sure that's the order. But after Fillmore, which comes next? Scott or Steiner? And what about north to south, from Hayes Valley to Pacific Heights? I'm fine until I get to Golden Gate, then I can only identify the streets randomly.

"Where are we anyway?" I wonder aloud.

"You're on Laguna."

"Are we going the right direction?"

"I think..."

I know Webster is to my left. In a sudden burst of panic, I turn abruptly onto a darkened street.

"This is a dead end!" Amanda exclaims.

"No, it's fine," I say and then realize she's right. "Oh, you probably saw a sign..." I trail off and make a U-turn.

Conversation is even more awkward after that.

I drop her off. Driving away, I wipe the sweat from my brow. ❖

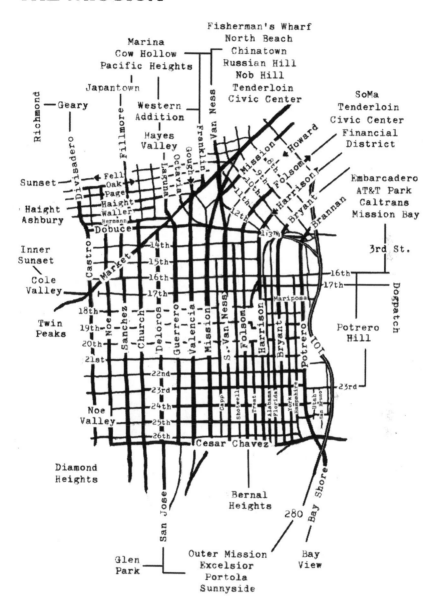

HOW TO BE MORE THAN A NUMBER
IN EIGHT EASY STEPS

1. Download the Lyft app and set up an account using either Facebook or your phone number.

2. Complete your driver information. Go into "driver mode" and fill out basic information about yourself and your car: driver's license number, social security number, address, and license plate number.

3. Watch three five minute welcome videos that explain how Lyft works: the mustache and the fist bump. Cause, you know, it's not as obvious as it seems. The cheerful spokesperson in the video also recommends cleaning your car and removing any personal items from the trunk.

4. Provide your shipping address to receive a welcome kit.

5. Take a test drive with a Lyft mentor. Once you've got your car spotless, go into "driver mode" and wait for a request to meet with a "mentor." When the request comes in, you drive to the pinned location on the map inside the app, meet your mentor and go for a practice Lyft. I met my mentor in Potrero Hill. He was cool. Answered all my questions, like whether I had to wear the mustache. He said yes, but that some drivers put it on their dash because it doesn't fit on their grill. Wink. Wink. Then he took a picture of me, my car, as well as my license and insurance card. The entire process lasted about fifteen minutes. I assume afterwards he filled out a form through the app that indicated whether he thought I would fit in as a Lyft driver. Before we ended

the session, he pretty much told me I was a shoe-in.

6. Wait to hear if you passed your background check. This took maybe two or three days.

7. Final application review. I guess somebody looks everything over and clicks a button that sends the email letting you know whether you've been accepted or not. Since they are almost always on a hiring streak, as long as you don't have a shitty record, you'll most likely get hired.

8. Start Lyfting your way to happiness and financial success!

After 30 rides, Lyft mails you the pink mustache. Talk about incentives!

When I decided to be a part of the ridesharing craze, I went with Lyft because they didn't seem as nefarious as Uber. The "friend with a car" vibe fit my personality more than Uber's pretentious air of a "personal driver." Even though I wasn't too crazy about the pink mustache, I reminded myself that no job is perfect.

What struck me the most about the onboarding process, though, was how haphazard it felt. Like I was dealing with a company that didn't totally have their shit together.

It was mostly little things. The app crashed a few times during the sign-up process. I got some random texts with assorted misinformation. One day I got a text informing me that the state of my insurance didn't match my shipping address. I responded and a guy texted me back with an apology for "the confusing automated message" and let me know my application was fine.

This wasn't that big of a deal, but it gave me the impression that I was applying for a job at an office where maintenance crews were in the midst of setting up desks, chairs and computers while I was forced to present my resume to a bespectacled hipster chick at a fold-up table with a Ritual cup in her hand.

I also couldn't shake the sensation I was signing up to do something that wasn't entirely on the up and up. There was no reassurance from Lyft during the sign-up process other than a promise of a fun-packed adventure making new friends and earning money. Up to $800 a weekend, if I were to believe the Facebook ads. Who doesn't want to make a boatload of money, have fun and make friends?

Still, the vagueness worried me. Besides being a burgeoning start-up, Lyft is also a progenitor of "disruption," an unregulated car service masquerading as a tech company. Lyft drivers are independent contractors. Like taxi drivers. But while taxi drivers lease their vehicles from a cab company and benefit from regulated insurance and permits, a Lyft driver uses their own car. The whole ridesharing deal exists due to a loophole in the law. Therefore, we don't have permits

to do business at the airport. We have no permits to park at cabstands, which is where people often need to be picked up. We have no permits to drive in the taxicab lanes, which would be extremely useful, as anybody who's ever driven down Market Street knows.

As I keep driving, I can't help but ask myself, Is the risk really worth the money? Not only do we use our own vehicles, we use our personal auto insurance. Which does not cover you while driving for hire. At all. Whatsoever. So why even bring it up? Why take a picture of our insurance cards? Why not just focus on Lyft's policy instead, to reassure potential drivers that they're covered no matter what happens out on the road?

I'm supposed to feel all warm and fuzzy inside about driving for Lyft, but it's been five months now since I signed up and the haunting sensation that I'm on my own out there hasn't gone away. I've never been to Lyft's HQ, so again, this is all just a fantasy, but I keep picturing an office with several young techies working furiously behind monitors, a few playing ping-pong, some delivery guys flattening Ikea boxes to fit in the recycling bin outside while an intern tries to make the copier work... If a company like Lyft is just getting off the ground and they're still getting their servers to work efficiently, building a passenger and driver support team, handling the legal shit, the government shit, the money shit, the PR shit, the building twenty fucking Ikea desks shit, all the while continuing to develop the app, you gotta wonder, as a driver, who's got your back?

Lyft wants drivers and passengers to feel like they're part of a revolution in transportation, but those Kumbaya, happy-go-lucky feelings won't mean much when you smash into the back a out-of-state Subaru stopping short on Russian Hill for a view of the Bay Bridge. Or when you run over a jaywalking hipster on South Van Ness as you tap the screen of your phone to accept a ride request. Or lose control of your vehicle while performing an illegal U-turn in the middle of Broadway to pick up a group of drunk Marina bros. Who's gonna be on your side when they're towing your car out of the plate glass windows of Centerfolds?

As easy as it is to become a Lyft driver, all you can do is hope you never have to face the cold, hard reality that as much as Lyft wants you to love them, they don't love you back.

But hey, there's always that pink mustache to cheer you up! ❖

ST. 3.15
PATTY'S DAY
WEEKEND

My first weekend driving for Lyft. I hit Philz on 24th in the Mission for a large Jacobs with cream and light sugar. St. Patrick's Day is on Monday, so everybody's celebrating early. It's seven p.m. and the sidewalks are already crowded with people in green costumes. My intestines twist as I anticipate the night's madness. I take an extra Ativan. I'm about to turn the app on and go into driver mode when the Wife texts me. She's been reading the Facebook group for new Lyft drivers and warns me about pukers. Says other Lyft drivers are stocking up on barf bags.

"That's just fucking great," I text back. "My two least favorite things: drunks and people who celebrate another culture's holidays." Tap send and notice the number I'm texting is for Lyft support. They'd just sent me a message about my hours. Oh, fuck. I make a screenshot. Send it to the Wife. Add, "Just texted this to Lyft. FML." Get an LOL back.

I spend the next few hours in a caffeine and Ativan induced blur, ferrying semi-intoxicated and exuberant passengers to and from different bars and restaurants across the city. Most are in party mode, indifferent to my serpentine driving. I try to maintain an equal level of enthusiasm. I answer all the usual questions:

"How long have you been driving for Lyft?"

"Do you make good money?"

"Are you from the city?"

"How do you like Oakland?"

"Where's your mustache?"

I have a punk and post-punk soundtrack playing in the background, the volume on low. I skip the hardcore tracks and make a mental note to remove the five Bad Brains albums from my iPod, as well as Discharge and G.B.H. That stuff is great when I'm racing to a pinned location, but somewhat awkward during those quiet moments with non-communicative passengers.

At 11 p.m., the air outside is a frigid 54 degrees. But with two or more warm bodies in the car, I'm often overheated. I roll down the windows when I drop off passengers to cool off and fill the car with fresh air. I keep the defrost on all night.

I'm cruising through SoMa. At 11th and Harrison, I get a request. A big-haired blonde gets in the backseat.

"Hello, Shauna." I always address passengers by their first name to make sure the right person is getting into my car. "How's it going?"

"Fine. Can you take me to Berkeley? I'm by the Ashby Bart station."

"Sure thing."

Cruise down 8th Street to I-80 and head across the bridge. Try to make small talk. She's more interested in staring at her iPhone. I skip a Sonic Youth track. Galaxie 500 comes on next. I let it play. "The King of Spain" segues into "Darklands" by Jesus & Mary Chain. I skip a few punk songs. Turn off the stereo. Transition from I-80 to Highway 24. I take the Claremont exit. Head down Telegraph to Ashby.

When I pull up to her place, Shauna offers me five dollars.

"Sorry, it's all I have…"

I refuse the cash. According to the Lyft FAQ, we're not supposed to take cash tips. Tell her she can tip through the app. She says she doesn't know how. I agree it's complicated. Stare at the fiver for a hot minute before she folds it back into her purse.

"Take care now," I yell after her.

I find a parking space next to the Bart station. Call the Wife.

"Hey, I'm in Berkeley."

"Did you get any pukers?"

"No."

"Then come home. Don't risk it!"

"I don't want to stop driving yet. I'm supposed to go another hour."

"You think you'll get rides in Berkeley?"

"No idea. Maybe I'll just stay parked here and see what happens."

"Pick me up! I wanna go for a Lyft ride!"

"Okay, I'll head towards home. I'll text you when I'm outside and you can request a Lyft."

I go back online and head down Telegraph. Two blocks later a request comes. Guy named Davis. I hit accept. Look at the address. It's near the university. I use navigation to get there. The streets are deserted. On the corner at the pinned location I spot a couple waving at me. I pull over.

"Hey! Where's your mustache?" Davis gets in the back with the girl.

"I haven't earned it yet."

"Seriously?" the girl wants to know. "You have to earn the mustache?"

"They don't just give them away. You have to give thirty rides before they send you one."

"That makes sense," Davis figures. "I suppose everybody would want one for their car, even if they don't drive for Lyft."

I cringe at the thought. "So where we going?"

"Just head up the hill," the girl tells me. "We'll direct you the rest of the way."

I go about a mile into the Berkeley Hills.

"I know it's not far, but we didn't feel like walking all the way up."

"Understandable. This is a steep hill."

As I pull up to their house, which overlooks all of Berkeley with the Bay and San Francisco in the distance, Davis complements my Jetta. "I see you got the tiptronic. Cool."

"Thanks. We leased it originally, but we liked it so much we ended up buying it when the lease ran out."

"Volkswagens are awesome cars."

"Yeah."

"Alright, let's go." The girl drags Davis out of the car.

Slowly make my way down the hill. Pause to catch some views. Call the Wife.

"What the hell happened?" she asks. "I requested a Lyft but I got some other guy so I cancelled it."

"A request came in right after I went back into driver mode."

"Really?"

"Yeah, I think I'm going to drive around Berkeley and see if I can get another fare."

"But I'm all dressed now and ready to go!"

"Okay, I'll head your way and see what happens."

A few minutes later, another request comes in for downtown Berkeley. I pull up next to a gas station and wait. I look at the name in the app on the scratched screen of my beat-up iPhone 4: Timbot. There's no profile pic, so I don't know what to expect. Once I accept a ride request, all I have to go on is an address, a first name and a thumbnail of the passenger's Facebook profile pic. I'm always relieved when people have actual pics of their face rather than something abstract, or a picture of their dog. It's easier to pick somebody up on a crowded street when you know what they look like.

A few more minutes go by. I'm about to call when a scraggly-looking guy approaches my car.

"Hey man, what's up?" He drops his backpack on the floorboard. Makes himself comfortable in the passenger seat.

"Not much. How you doing?"

"I'm cool, you know... been hanging out with some friends."

I smell alcohol, but he seems more stoned than drunk. "That's cool."

"Yeah..." He trails off.

"So, um... where we heading?"

"I'm ready to go home. Or... I can hang here if it's a problem."

"Why would it be problem?" I ask.

"I live in West Oakland." He pauses. "So you know..."

"Do you want to go to home?"

"Yeah. But it's not a big deal or anything. Most Lyft drivers don't like going there."

"I'll take you to West Oakland. Just tell me where to go... I don't know my way around Oakland very well."

"Where do you live?"

"Oakland."

Timbot is a lousy navigator. I manage to find my way based on his rudimentary directions anyway. Get on the freeway. Slayer comes on the stereo. I skip the track.

"Sorry."

"You play fucking Slayer in a Lyft?" Tim asks.

"Well, I usually skip those songs when I have passengers."

"Metal's cool, man."

"I only really listen to thrash."

"You like punk too?" Timbot asks.

"Yeah, punk, post-punk, alternative shit, afrobeat, pysch garage... some rap. I dumped a whole bunch of random shit onto my iPod and just let the shuffle sort it out."

"I've never had a Lyft driver like you before," he says.

"Do you take Lyft much?"

"Every once in a while..."

"Hey, aren't you on 18th?" I ask, as I'm about to pass the exit.

"Yeah! Turn here."

I pull up to Timbot's place. We sit in the car talking for a while about music, going to shows, record stores. He asks if I want to buy some acid.

"I have a friend who studies chemistry at Cal," he says. "It's pure shit."

I take his number.

"We should hang out sometimes," he tells me as he gets out. "Maybe go to a show."

"Yeah, for sure."

I call the Wife back. Tell her I'm on my way home. ❖

 Driver summary

Feedback

★★★★★ 52 ratings

"Very friendly!"

"Great job for the first day!!!"

"Very cool driver! Kelly has a lot of cool stories!"

"Cool guy!"

"Down to earth"

★★★★ and below 4 ratings

"Got lost, car smelled like cigarettes and beer, unsafe driving"

Past ratings	Past week	Past week
Rating	**Reliability**	**Accept rate**
✔ ★ 4.85	✔ 93%	✔ 97%
Awesome	Awesome	Awesome

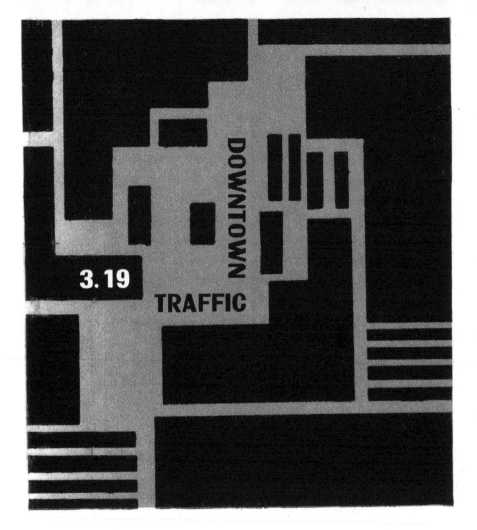

3.19

DOWNTOWN

TRAFFIC

A GAMING CONVENTION IS IN TOWN. SoMa is a madhouse. But that's where the passengers are. It's not easy reaching them on the congested one-way streets. With sweaty palms and white knuckles, I follow the pink navigation line in the app to the pinned locations.

After dropping somebody off at 6th and Folsom, I get a request for Howard Street. Looks like Moscone South. I pull up to the convention center. An older Asian couple gets in. Flux of Pink Indians is playing on the stereo. I hit the forward button. Chumbawamba comes on. I turn the music off. Figure an anarcho-punk set isn't their preferred soundtrack.

They are going to Four Embarcadero Center. Ana sits up front. Asks about Lyft. Like so many others, she wants to know how long I've been driving for Lyft, how much money I make and how many rides

DOWNTOWN

including SOMA, MISSION BAY and the TENDERLOIN

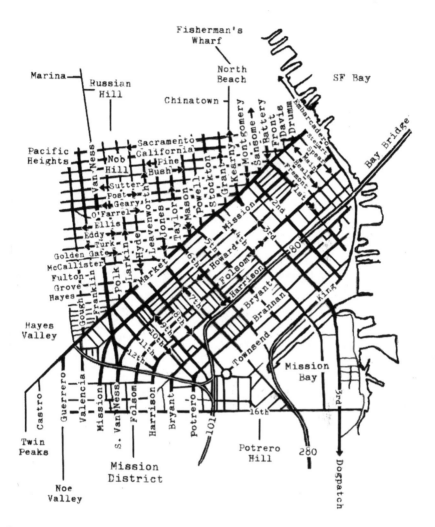

I average... All the usual questions. For some reason, I tell her I had around 75 rides the previous Saturday. I have no clue where that figure comes from. I just blurt it out. In the eight hours I drove, I think I managed 15-20 rides. Ana questions my math. Asks if it's even possible to transport that many people in such a short amount of time.

I am adamant.

She looks at me dubiously.

I feel bad for lying to her, but my brain can't seem to process any other information besides where I'm going, how I'm going to get there and if I'll be able to cross Market. After my first week of doing the Lyft thing, I'm mentally exhausted from trying to remember all the street names, their order, which ones are one-way, how to get from one neighborhood to the next and figuring out Market Street. Before I started Lyfting and the Wife and I were driving around the city trying to learn the neighborhoods, I knew Market would be my Achilles' heel. It's the major thoroughfare, stretched out across the city like the slash from a switchblade. But not all side streets are created equal. Some dead-end at Market while some turn into streets with new names: 3rd becomes Kearny. 6th crosses Market and turns into Taylor. Others traverse Market and don't change at all. Then there are those that zigzag at Market, picking up mysteriously half a block away.

I only have a vague sense of how to Four Embarcadero Center. I drive towards Market. Hope for the best. Try searching for it on my phone, but nothing comes up. I'm probably spelling it wrong. Navigating the narrow streets of San Francisco among Muni buses, taxicabs, cars with out-of-state plates, Google shuttles, delivery trucks, jaywalkers, bicyclists, construction vehicles and suicidal panhandlers, all the while looking out for cops and answering 21 questions about what it's like driving for Lyft requires my full attention. Fortunately, Four Embarcadero Center is clearly labeled with neon lights at street level. I luck out. This time.

I get out of driver mode and leave the Financial District. I need a break from the congestion. I'm sweating bricks.

I pop an Ativan and cross Van Ness before I go back online. Head to the Mission. A request comes in. The Tenderloin. The app says I'm six minutes away. I groan and accept the ride. Head downtown. Ten minutes later, I spot the guy on the corner and pull up.

"Sorry it took so long," I tell him earnestly. "I guess there were no other drivers in the area."

"I'm glad to see you! It's freezing out there!"

Tahir is from LA. Also in town for the convention. Two stops. First, a party store on Post Street where I wait in a tow-away zone and nervously watch a meter patrol car across the street while I finger drum to Iron Maiden. Whenever I think I should take certain tracks off my iPod, I remind myself that I spend more time in the car by myself than with passengers. The song ends. Tahir returns. I kill the tunes. Next stop the Marriott in Union Square.

In front of the hotel, Tahir holds his phone up to my head.

"You don't look like your profile photo at all," he says.

"Really? My wife says it looks just like me."

"It looks like you, but you're not as serious as your picture suggests."

"The guy who took it, my Lyft mentor, didn't give me much of a chance to pose or take a second one. It came out like a DMV photo."

I offer him the regulation fistbump and drive away. Make the mistake of keeping my app in driver mode. End up stuck in traffic on Post between Grant and Kearny for twenty minutes trying to get to Stephanie on Montgomery and Market. When it becomes apparent that I'm not going anywhere anytime soon, I call and tell her she might want to cancel the ride and request another Lyft.

"Something's obviously gone wrong," I say. "A wreck maybe… I'm not moving and I haven't moved for the past ten minutes."

Stephanie doesn't want to cancel though. Instead she walks to where I am parked on Post Street, staying on the line as she approaches. Reports on what she sees: cars, trucks, buses and delivery tucks, none of which are moving. I see her in the distance. She tries to get into another Lyft car a few cars ahead of me, one with a mustache on the grill. The driver chases her away. I wave my arm out the window. She gets in.

"Where's your mustache?"

"Long story."

I can smell the alcohol on her breath. It's early afternoon, and even though she's had a few, she's panicked about being on time to meet her friends on 1st Street.

"I'm really late!" she groans.

Tells me she's going overseas for six months in a few days and meeting up with friends to say goodbye. She's already had lunch with one group of friends. On her way to meet a second now. Has a third event later that night.

"We can do two things," I say calmly. "Wait and hope the traffic starts moving or drive away from the mess and then circle back to 1st Street."

"Do what you have to do. I trust you."

"I'm from LA," I tell her confidently as I head down an alley. "I know my way around traffic jams."

"What brought you to San Francisco?" she asks.

I turn right on Geary. Away from the financial district. As I navigate the congestion and look for a street that crosses Market, I try to entertain this girl. The usual truncated version I've been telling passengers about how the Wife and I moved to the Bay Area because we got laid off from our jobs at Disney is just one of many half-truths I tell people to seem relatable. Stephanie is clearly agitated and upset about being late. If I'm going to keep her mind off the fact that I'm driving far out of the way of her destination, which, from our starting point was only a few blocks away, I need to give her a good story. So I tell her the truth.

"In August, my wife and I had spent ten days at a friend's place in the Mission while she was at Burning Man. Even though we came here several times a year to visit, we'd never been able to spend that much time all at once. We basically did everything we did at home, lie around and watch Netflix, eat cheap burritos and go to thrift stores. But doing all that stuff in San Francisco made it seem more exceptional. We'd always wanted to live here and felt stuck in LA, mostly because of the Disney job. We both worked on an English language-learning program for kids in China that used Disney and Pixar characters. I edited and designs the teacher guides. She was a full time interactive producer. At the time, we were trying to get pregnant. My wife hated working for Disney, but the benefits were phenomenal. We wanted to take advantage of them while we could. In the meantime, we were going to have a lot of fun, travel and go to shows. Cause, you know, once we had a kid, we wouldn't be able to go out as much."

At this point, we are at 6th Street.

I have no choice but to end the ride and hope it doesn't take too long to get her back to Stephanie's destination.

"Then, a month later," I continue, "last September, we came back to San Francisco for a small two-day music festival. We stayed with our friend in the Mission and spent the entire weekend watching bands, getting drunk and doing ketamine. We took Lyft and UberX cars everywhere we went. It was a blast. On Tuesday, after we got back to LA, my wife called me from work and said, 'I have the greatest news...' She'd been laid off. That night, we got wasted, did the rest of the ketamine we'd brought back and decided to move to San Francisco."

"Well, little did we know that San Francisco is in the midst of hyper-gentrification and that rents are higher than we could have ever imagined. So we picked the worst time to move to the Bay Area."

I finally get to 1st Street, which is one-way in the opposite direction. I pull over and point north.

"Just go that way. It should be on the left side of the street."

"I have such a horrible sense of direction," she says. "But I'll try."

Once she's out of view, I get out of driver mode and stay offline until I am deep in the Mission. ❖

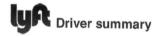 **Driver summary**

Feedback

★★★★★ *44 ratings*

"Awesome driver!"

"Awesome guy super friendly"

"🖼"

"Super patent and helpful. Awesome!!"

★★★★ and below *1 ratings*

Past ratings	*Lifetime*	*Past week*
Rating	**Rides**	**Accept rate**
✔ ★ **4.91**	**125**	✔ **98%**
Awesome		Awesome

IT'S NOT ABOUT THE MUSTACHE

Okay, let's talk about the pink mustache. First, you have to earn the fucking thing. They don't just give 'em away. You gotta give thirty rides before they mail you one.

It's not hard to give thirty rides. By my third day I'd done almost forty. It took another week to arrive, wrapped in plastic in a fancy cardboard box. They included a phone mount and a charger. I left it all in the fancy box and threw it in the corner of my living room with all the other boxes. So what's the big deal? Why don't I "rock the 'stache," as the die-hard Lyfters say in the official Lyft Driver Lounge on Facebook? Or at least place it on the dash, where it looks like what you'd find on the floor after a fluffy convention?

When passengers ask me about it, my answer varies. It depends who's asking. I'll say I forgot it at home. Sometimes I say it's dirty. Or if it had been raining, I say I took it off so it didn't get wet. Or I just came

back from the airport. Once I told these two drunk girls that I'd attached it one day, drove over the Bay Bridge during a wind advisory and never saw it again. After which I pointed out that the mustache came with explicit directions: don't drive over 40 miles per hour. Which of course is impossible to avoid if you live in a city with a freeway.

The real reason, though, is that the pink mustache, despite its nauseating ugliness, has become the perfect symbol for the backlash against all "ride-share" services, not just Lyft, but Uber and SideCar as well.

The term "ride-share" itself is such a completely and utterly outrageous misnomer that it would be laughable if so many people weren't buying into it. The entire concept of the shared economy is based on deception so the founders can avoid regulation. Everybody knows it. The companies know it. They call themselves tech companies, not transportation companies. Particularly when the shit hits the fan. The taxi drivers who protest the loss of their monopoly know it. The state legislature knows it. This whole sharing economy could easily dissipate like a puff of smoke from an e-cigarette with one pen stroke. But instead, they set up what's called Transportation Network Companies to give them a name more appropriate to the paid service they provide. Venture capital firms, of course, don't give a shit. They're just gambling on whether unfavorable laws will be upheld or reversed. Like betting on the ponies, but with politicians and lobbyists. Not to mention that Mayor Lee likes tech. Some of his detractors claim that Big Tech has him in their pocket. He certainly hasn't done much to reel in the tech companies that have begun to infringe upon the rights of San Franciscans. Mayor Lee has pissed off a lot of people.

A few months ago, I began noticing RECALL MAYOR LEE bumper stickers on cabs. It's not clear whether they are protesting the surge of ride-share vehicles or just his policies in general, but it's undeniable that the cab companies and drivers have been hit hardest by the emergence of Uber and Lyft. Cabbies make about 30 grand a year. They lease their vehicles from the cab companies and usually start their shifts 100-150 bucks in the hole. Faced with a major threat to their livelihoods, they have been fighting back. And despite being regarded as less significant than Uber, the Lyft pink mustache is usually on most of the placards waved during protests outside City Hall. Circled and crossed out.

The fact is undeniable: the pink mustache is the ultimate symbol of an unregulated, scofflaw challenger.

Before I drove for Lyft and was just a passenger myself, I got a ride from a guy who had a pink shirt tied up to look like the puffy monstrosity on his dash. He said a taxi driver had ripped the mustache off the grill of his car. Since becoming a driver, I've read several posts on the Lyft Facebook group about cabbies yelling at Lyft drivers and taking pictures of their license plates to report them to insurance companies, or so the posters speculate. No matter what the motives of these cabbies are, it's understandable that they would be upset. And I can hardly blame them. It's one thing to know that these rideshare companies exist, but the pink mustaches most definitely add insult to injury.

That's the thing about symbols:

they can go either way. They mean one thing to the supporters and another to the opposition. There are a lot of Lyft drivers who happily drink the Kool-Aid and parade around town dressed in pink, waving their pink mustaches in the air as a counter protest to the cabbies. They defend their right to not just drive for Lyft but to promote the Lyft brand by brandishing the mustache at any opportunity. It boggles my mind how grown adults can be so proud of something so ugly. Do they not realize how stupid they look on cars? I've spent my entire adult life avoiding the need to wear a uniform and look like a jackass. I see no reason to start now. And the way I see it, I started driving without a mustache, so why not keep going without one? Passengers have a picture of my car and my face prominently on their phone. They know who they're looking for. I can see them and know who I'm looking for. I greet each person that gets in my car by name. Most passengers do the same. There is no need for a mustache to enter the equation.

In fact, I'd say that 90% of the people I've talked to in my car about it say they prefer cars without mustaches. There will always be drunk girls who feel cheated when they get into a car that doesn't have one, but they are easily distracted by something else shiny or bright.

"If you don't want to rock the 'stache, then maybe you're on the wrong team."

I've seen this comment in the Driver Lounge as a response to queries on whether to use the mustache. These Lyft drivers have no qualms about adhering to a group mentality. Most are also major sports fans, as evident in their profile pics and comments during major sporting events. So it makes sense that they would root-root-root for the home team.

But maybe they're right. Maybe I should drive for Uber. Their drivers use a subtle neon blue "U" that illuminates oh so elegantly from their windshield. I have to admit, they look classy as fuck. But I'm lazy. And I don't deal well with change. Also, the owner of Uber is supposed to be a real asshole. Maybe if I were to get called out for not using the mustache, or the mustache becomes a requirement, then I might switch services. I have absolutely no loyalty to Lyft or any other corporation, regardless of how they frame their corporate image.

And, ultimately, that's why I don't use the mustache: because I am the mustache. ❖

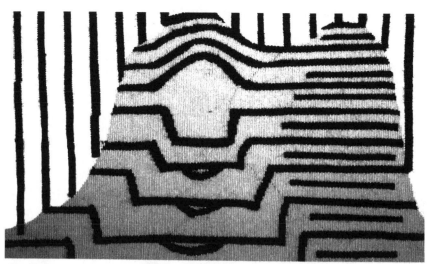

3.25   NO CABS TO COLE VALLEY

PICK UP A GUY NAMED MIKE AT THE SOMA STREET FOOD COURT. Going
to Cole Valley. I drive towards Market under the Central Freeway, per
his instructions. Going to take 17th Street over the hill to Stanyan. I sort
of know the way, but let him guide me. Mike is super mellow. Says he
just got off work. Smells like curry.

"Is this Fugazi?" he asks. "I haven't heard them in forever!"

I turn the volume up a bit.

"Do you work in tech?" I ask.

"No, I'm a furniture designer," he says sharply.

"Oh, sorry. I didn't mean to suggest…"

"It's fine. I assume most people you drive are in tech."

"Not all, but a lot."

"I don't use Lyft that much," Mike says. "But I tried to hail a cab right
before I requested a ride and the goddamn driver wouldn't even open the
door to let me in."

"What?"

"Yeah, he rolled down the passenger window and asked where I was
going. I told him, 'You can't ask me where I'm going before I get in the
car.' I kept pulling on the handle but he wouldn't open it. I stood there
yelling at him on the street, cussing him out while he screamed back at
me. It was idiotic, I know, but they're not supposed to pull that crap."

I find it hard to imagine such a mild-mannered guy shouting at a cab
driver on the street.

"I'm so sick of these taxi drivers! They think they can do whatever they want. They won't take credit cards, when you call to request a cab they don't show up, their cars are nasty, they're rude, they talk on the phone during the whole trip and act like they're giving up their firstborn child by doing their jobs!"

"Damn…"

"I want to support the cab drivers. I really do. I know they're up against the wall with the popularity of Lyft and Uber. But they're just not giving me much of a choice!"

"I'm inclined to give them the benefit of the doubt too," I say. "But cab drivers certainly don't seem to be trying to improve their reputation. I've had so many passengers say the same thing as you. Especially people who live in the Richmond and Sunset who could never get taxis to pick them up, much less drop them off. Now I see taxis out in the Sunset and Richmond all the time. I guess they've figured that much out."

"They still have a lot of work to do if they want to survive."

I drop Mike off. Head into the Lower Haight.

LATER THAT AFTERNOON, I end up behind a taxi with a **RECALL MAYOR LEE** sticker on his bumper. I'd think it was a coincidence, but I've been seeing more of these stickers on cabs lately. Although it's not clear whether they are protesting the surge of Uber/Lyft vehicles or just the mayor's policies in general, the taxi companies and drivers have been hit hard by the emergence of Uber, Lyft and Sidecar—the three biggest on-demand car services.

Before I signed up for Lyft, I considered getting a job as a taxi driver. I read about what it takes to be a legitimate driver. Apparently, cab drivers make about 30 grand a year. They have to lease their vehicles from the cab companies and start their shifts 100 bucks in the hole. Faced with a major threat to their livelihoods, it only makes sense that they would be protesting outside City Hall, carrying signs with the Lyft pink mustache circled and crossed out.

Despite Uber's dominance in the ride-hail market, Lyft is an easy target with its iconic pink mustache. During that fateful visit in September, we got a Lyft from a guy who had a pink shirt on his dash. He said a taxi driver had ripped the mustache off the grill of his car. Since I started Lyfting, I've seen numerous posts on the Lyft Driver's Facebook group about cab drivers yelling at drivers and taking pictures of their license plates to report them to insurance companies, or so the posters speculate.

No matter what the motives of these taxi drivers are, I can hardly blame them. I'd be pissed off too, if I started losing income and these

HAYES VALLEY AND THE HAIGHT

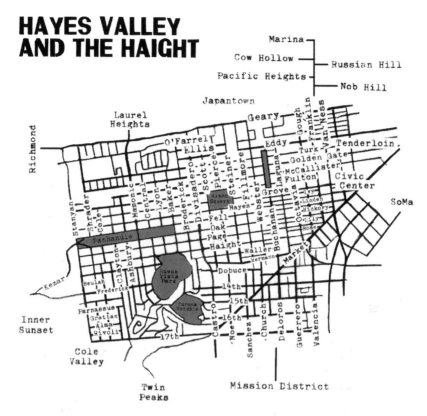

stupid pink mustaches popped up around town, adding insult to injury.

Before I moved to the Bay Area, I had only a vague understanding of what was going on in the city. I read an article about the current tech boom in the New Yorker. I knew tech was a dominant aspect of life in the city. But from the first few weeks we were here, it became obvious we'd stumbled into a city embroiled in a class war. The tech backlash consumes the local news sources we follow on Facebook. Every day there were new articles about Ellis Act evictions, Google bus protests, marches on city hall, protests in the Mission and outside the Twitter headquarters, Google glass wearers getting attacked and old ladies and teachers thrown out of their apartments into the streets.

Recently, a mural went up in Clarion Alley called the "San Francisco Wall of Shame and Solutions." The list of Shames includes the "rideshare" services because they are unregulated by the city and have an unfair advantage over the highly regulated taxis.

All of a sudden, driving for Lyft didn't seem so cool. The prospect of participating in an activity that exists solely through a loophole in the system filled me with dread. I didn't want to be part of the problem. I've lived my adult life with a strong sense of social awareness. I've done my best to not infringe upon the rights of others and fight oppression. But I'm essentially unemployable. A jack-of-all-trades. Master of none. I followed a path in life that led to experiences and opportunities to explore the world around me. I wanted to collect stories, not an impressive resume. The way I figure it, Trader Joe's is my destiny. How else is an overeducated creative type looking down the barrel at 43 with no viable skills besides the ability to occasionally string together a few words into a semi-coherent sentence supposed to pay the bills? While I once held onto the delusion that I could make a living as a writer, I've become more realistic in my old age. But I'm not ready to give up my delusions of grandeur and don the Hawaiian shirt just yet. After looking at the job listings on Craigslist and realizing that I don't even understand what a start-up even does, I sacrificed a little more integrity and went through the process of becoming a Lyft driver. The way I figured it, I'd drive a few nights, see how I feel about it. If I couldn't stomach it, I'd quit.

It's been two weeks now. I'm no less conflicted. As much as I love driving at night in a shiny black car, racing up and down the hills of this jagged city listening to music and discovering extraordinary landmarks at every turn, when I get home, my body and mind are exhausted and drained from moving people around for hours on end and enduring so many meaningless and inane conversations.

THAT EVENING, I get a request for an address on Market in the Castro. Nobody looking my way. Call the passenger. Johnny.

"The app messed up," he tells me. "It gave you the wrong location."

"No worries. It happens all the time."

While on the phone, somebody opens my back door.

"Johnny?" I ask.

"No, Pablo."

"I think you got the wrong car," I tell him.

"Oh, sorry."

"Who was that?" asks Johnny.

"Pablo."

"Who?"

"Nobody. Where are you again?"

"In front of Sparky's."

"Where's that?"

"You must not be from San Francisco."

"No."

"Sparky's is the only 24 hour restaurant in the city. Everybody knows where it is."

Okay. Thanks for the history lesson. "Is it on Church or Market?"

"Church. You can't miss me. I have a cat on my head."

I drive down Church. Johnny is standing between two parked cars wearing a hat that looks like a cat. I can't tell if it's real and don't want to ask. Drive him to his loft in Dogpatch as he rambles about Burning Man the whole way in a coked-out haze of self-importance. ❖

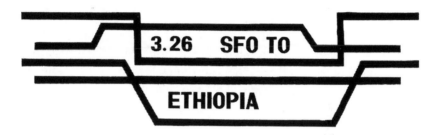

3.26 SFO TO ETHIOPIA

AFTER GETTING COFFEE AT PHILZ, I go into driver mode and cruise through the Mission waiting for a ride request. I've found that when I circle the neighborhood east of Van Ness, I'm more likely to get a passenger than if I were on Valencia, where the other drivers congregate with the taxis and towncars. I can see my fellow Lyfters in the app: little black avatars that disappear when they accept rides or go offline.

My first ping is near 21st and Bryant. Pull up to a freshly renovated Edwardian. Mark comes out with two large duffle bags and a backpack. I open the trunk. Help load his gear.

"Where you off to?" I ask.

"Ethiopia," Mark says.

So SFO, I think as he goes back to get more stuff. An easy thirty bucks.

"Are you flying into Addis Ababa and then doing some backpacking?" I ask to make small talk.

"We're flying into Addis, but from there we're taking a small flight to an orphanage in the mountains."

While we wait for his wife to finish getting ready, Mark tells me they are going to Ethiopia to adopt a child.

"Wow," I say. "That's huge. Are you coming home with a boy or girl?"

He says first they have to fly in to meet the boy, then return in three weeks to finalize the adoption and bring him home. The duffle bags are full of presents for the other kids at the orphanage.

"I got soccer balls," he says with a shrug. "Didn't know what else to buy." His wife joins us. Her backpack doesn't fit in the trunk so they put in it in the backseat. I assume one of them is going to sit up front, which is ideal when going to SFO, since Lyft doesn't have a permit to do business at the airport. If I had a mustache on the front of my car, I'd have to take it off. But they both sit in back, with the backpack between them.

I suggest putting the backpack in the passenger seat. As I drive down Bryant, it's so heavy the car thinks a human is in the seat. Keeps dinging and flashing the fasten seatbelt icon. I strap the seatbelt around the backpack. Hit the freeway at Cesar Chavez.

The couple is nervous, talking in short bursts, mostly going over their itinerary for what I assume is the hundredth time. We make it to the airport in ten minutes. All the traffic is heading north on the 101, going to AT&T Park for the game against the Arizona Diamondbacks.

As I head into the International terminal, I spot an unmarked security car on the right. I cringe, wishing I had insisted one of them sit up front.

I pull up to United. Help them unload their duffle bags and backpacks. Wish them luck. Get out of driver mode and hightail it back to the city before traffic gets worse. I'm stuck for a few miles, until the 280 split that filters out the game traffic.

On Cesar Chavez, I go back online. A request comes in for a Margarita at 26th and Mission. An older Spanish woman with a child waves at me. She has a bunch of paper sacks from Party City. I pull up next to a hydrant. Get out and help them put the stuff in the trunk. They sit in the back. Going to Daly City. I ask whether I should head down Cesar Chavez to I-280. She says San Jose Avenue is faster.

"I'll tell you where to turn."

As I start the ride, I notice she's already input her address into the app, a new feature that's only been active a day or two. I hit navigation and Waze opens and displays the best route. I take Gurrerro to San Jose. Ask Margarita how she likes using Lyft.

She says it's cheaper than taking taxis. I give her some referral cards in case she knows anybody who wants to sign up. They get twenty-five bucks toward their first ride. I get a ten-dollar bonus.

"How long have you been in Daly City?" I ask.

"Not long."

"Where'd you move from?"

"20th and Bryant. We were there for twenty years."

I think about the couple I just took to the airport. That's their neighborhood now. "Were you kicked out?"

"No, the rent just got too high."

We leave the sunshine in the Mission and drive into the fog.

"How do you like Daly City?" I ask.

"It's nice. The apartment is smaller but not as much money."

"San Francisco has become so expensive. It's impossible to live here. I'm in Oakland."

"It's warmer there, no?"

"Definitely warmer than Daly City."

I miss a turn. Despite the stupid navigation. Margarita directs me the rest of the way to her apartment building. One of those ticky-tacky boxes on the hillside.

I park and help with the bags. She tells me it's her grandson's birthday.

"Quantos Años?" I ask in Spanish.

"Eight," she tells me in English.

"Feliz Cumpleaños," I say to the boy.

"Thanks."

A FEW HOURS LATER, I get a request for 5th Ave and Balboa in the Inner Richmond. I pull up to the pinned location. One of the many duplexes and small houses that line the streets south of Geary. Look at the picture in the app. Katie has brown hair and a nice smile. I think she might be friendly and it'll be a fun ride. Perhaps she'll sit up front and chat. I turn on the defroster and make sure the recirculate button is on to pull in the fragrance from the air freshener clipped to the vent. I usually avoid chemical based deodorizers but I had a negative comment recently that said my car smelled like beer and cigarettes. Apparently I picked up the only person that night who hadn't been drinking and smoking.

After three minutes, I call Katie to let her know I'm outside. The Lyft system usually sends the passenger a text or push notification to inform them the car they requested has arrived. But if I've been waiting long, I'll call anyway, just to make sure I have the right address.

I get the girl's voicemail. Sometimes people don't recognize the number, which is the same generic 415 number encoded so neither the passenger nor I have access to each other's personal information. I wait a few more minutes. Finally, I see activity two doors from the street number in the app. Three girls approach my car.

"Where's your mustache?" the first one demands as she slides into the backseat behind me.

"It's in the trunk," I say. That's where it's been since they sent it to me after I completed thirty rides, still wrapped in plastic.

"Then how are we supposed to know you're legit?" a second girl asks and joins the first one in back.

"Why else would he be picking us up?" the one resembling the profile picture points out as she takes the passenger seat. "Hey, Kelly."

"Hello, Katie. How's it going?"

"It's her birthday." Katie gestures to the girl who asked about the mustache. "She's visiting from Seattle and we're taking her out to show her a good time."

I wish her a happy birthday. "Where you guys heading?"

"Smuggler's Cove."

"The pirate bar?"

"Yeah. Do you know where that is?"

"By Van Ness?" I took somebody there during my second week. I don't remember the exact streets though.

"Gough and Fulton. Do you know need directions?" She pronounces Gough like "go" instead of "cough." I can tell she's a recent transplant.

"Yep." I turn around and head towards Geary.

"Where are you going?" she asks sharply. "Why don't you go down Fulton?"

"Sorry."

"You sure you know where you're going?"

"Yes. I instinctively went to Geary, since it's the major thoroughfare."

"Fulton's faster."

"Sure." It's always good to listen to the passenger if they have a preferred route. Most people don't have a preference, but the ones who try to prove their knowledge of the city always tell you which streets to take.

The girls are chatty, talking among themselves and occasionally pulling me into the conversation. Katie promises the others that Smuggler's Cove is free of the usual douchebags you find in the Mission.

I laugh.

"You know what I'm talking about, right?"

"Fucking techies."

"What are techies?" the girl from Seattle asks.

"Tech workers," Katie tells her.

We talk about the tech boom and the hyper-gentrification that's consuming San Francisco.

"What is gentrification anyway?" asks the girl from Seattle.

I tell her the story of two rides I had earlier that day. After I finish my story, sans commentary, Katie points out that before the people with money moved in, the Mission was full of gangs.

I quickly add that while the Mission may have been less inviting before and potentially dangerous, it was still a neighborhood of families with a tight-knit culture who had every right to be where they've been for decades without getting relocated or forced out of their homes to satisfy the needs of hipsters and yuppies looking for some kind of "authentic vibe."

"Before the tech workers moved in," I say, "The Mission was mostly dead at night, except for a few bars and restaurants around Valencia. Sure, you'd see people smoking crack at the bus stops, but now, the entire neighborhood is full of drunken douchebags, techwads, Grubhub delivery guys and bums trying to get a little of the trickle-down. You can't make a trade-off, one bad thing for another, just because one of those bad things is more acceptable or less frightening to you."

"WHAT'S GENTRIFICATION ANYWAY?"

I mention that I lived in San Francisco during the nineties, back when it was full of crazies, misfits, scammers and bums.

"It was a paradise! I was able to live for eight months without a real job and very little money. I did canvassing to make a buck here and there. Back then, nobody seemed to care how much money you made. It was just about surviving in one of the most beautiful cities in the world, soaking up the history and culture of the place. San Francisco was free of bourgeois traps. After all, this is the city where Emperor Norton ruled, where the gay rights movement started and where beatniks, hippies and punks came to find like-minded souls. Now fresh-faced tech workers in designer jeans and hoodies fill the cafes and restaurants. Not all are clueless, but so many of these tech-bros who get in my car don't seem to know anything about San Francisco except where to eat, drink and party. All they talk about is work, money, girls… work, money, girls."

I start to feel I'm getting a little heavy handed with my criticism of the changes in San Francisco. I don't want to bum these girls out. What's that going to do for my rating? I mean, the one from Seattle has no idea what gentrification even is because... I don't know. Perhaps there isn't displacement of poor people by the affluent youth classes in Seattle. But I need to play it cool. And figure out where the hell I'm going.

As I approach Gough, I turn right, but the bar is above Fulton. I end the ride. Turn left on Grove to Franklin. Fortunately McAllister is both ways so I only have to go one block up to get back to Gough.

I drop them off in front of the bar. Katie and her friends pile out.

"Have fun," I say.

They smile. I figure they'll still rate me less than five stars. More so for being an opinionated asshole than making a wrong turn. And why not? Who complains about tech workers while using the apps they create? An asshole, that's who. My iPhone is clipped to the vent above the stereo for the whole world to see. I take advantage of tech, so why do I bitch about the repercussions? Cause I'm an asshole. That's why. Part of the problem. A tech parasite infringing upon the livelihood of decent, hard-working taxi drivers. Yep, that's me.

I probably should have said something like, "Hey, don't forget to give me five stars."

After all, I don't need another potential bad rating. I'm already down to 4.89. But asking for good ratings is a total cheese ball move. Sure, a lot of people think a four-star review is decent, but anything less than five stars and you run the risk of getting deactivated. The Lyft rating system is draconian.

It breaks down like this: 4.9 to 4.8 is "awesome." 4.7 is "okay" and "needs improvement." If your rating hits 4.6, they revoke your driving privileges. So every four-star review drastically impacts your total rating. It may seem innocuous, since four stars are, in the minds of most people who rate things like movies on Netflix or books on Goodreads, pretty good. But that's not how Lyft works. Even though I have a 4.89, the last two percentage points fluctuate daily. Sometimes it's 4.93. Sometimes it's 4.85. It's unlikely I'll be in trouble any time soon, but I constantly worry about my rating. It's more nerve-wracking than whether or not I should put the mustache on my grill. ❖

THE CULT OF LYFT

INSIDE THE PACIFIC DRIVER LOUNGE

When I signed up to be a driver, Lyft added me to a private Facebook group called the Pacific Driver Lounge. It was in the Lounge that I learned there's more to the Lyft experience than just pink mustaches and fist bumps. Lyft wants to cultivate a community between drivers and passengers. Except, only the drivers seem to be interested in participating in that community.

In the Lounge, the faithful worship the pink mustache. They post selfies with the fluffy monstrosities and talk about how they're making a difference in the world by driving for Lyft. They post screengrabs of their pay summaries, showing off how much money they earned, highlighting long drives with prime time tips added ("Score!") and favorable comments from passengers. All of which are followed by hashtags like #fistbumps or #lyftlove.

There are numerous pictures of tricked-out cars. Since Lyft encourages a quirky and fun vibe, many drivers come up with themes for their cars. One guy put a mirror ball in his car and became the DiscoLyft. Another put a karaoke machine in his car and is now the Caraoke. Then there's the RocknRollLyft, where the driver has a guitar and portable amp in the back for passengers to shred on. Or the BatmanLyft. The PirateLyft. ReptileLyft. MomLyft. There's the GameLyft, where the driver has an iPad so his passengers can play Flappy Bird while en route to their destination. It may not be officially called the PornoLyft, but I've heard of a driver who keeps Hustlers and Playboys in the back seat of his car. Maybe there will be a StipLyft one day, where the driver has to remove a piece of clothing each time he takes a wrong turn.

Drivers go this extra mile, at their own expense, for higher ratings, but also to have fun and be part of the Lyft community.

Community is what differentiates Lyft from Uber and Sidecar.

In the Lounge, Uber is referred to as "the dark side."

Cab drivers are the enemy.

The state legislature are a bunch of bullies out to kill the fun.

The worst thing you could do in the Lounge is malign the Lyft brand or you'll ignite a cyber lynch mob.

Like all internet forums, the Driver Lounge is a cesspool of glad-handers, gossip hounds, chicken-littles and a chorus of kool-aid drinking cheerleaders; clueless consumers lapping up a marketing ploy and defending their faith to the bitter end. A handful of participants do 75% of the talking. They maintain the party line and make sure it's all Lyft, all the time. Some of these regular posters are not full-time drivers. They do Lyft to supplement day jobs. So they have plenty of time to waste posting and commenting and making sure the reputation of Lyft is preserved.

While other drivers occasionally use the Lounge to complain about Lyft policies, problems with the app and difficult passengers, more than half of the posts and subsequent comments glorify Lyft and all the wonderful things it stands for.

Since the Lounge is an official Lyft group, the company controls it. But it's mostly self-governed.

There are moderators or "mentors" who patrol the discussions. Posts get deleted if they aren't up to snuff. People get banned for posting inappropriate or non-Lyft related items. (Anything to do with Uber is generally verboten.)

Sometimes discussions get heated and everyone gets upset. People start blocking each other. Discussions can get downright nasty at times, which is all highly entertaining to me.

Over the past few months, I've become obsessed with the Lounge. It's like watching a train wreck in slow motion. I check for new posts daily. I'm not proud of it. Nor am I ashamed. My fascination with the Lounge is akin to some folks' dedication to reality television. We all like to watch people behave without self-awareness.

The Lounge is my Honey Boo Boo.

I have gained some useful information about the driving process by lurking in the group. It's a good place to check the pulse of the city when I'm on the fence about driving in from Oakland to work. Plus, there are so many confusing aspects to being a Lyft driver. The Lyft FAQ can be atrociously vague at times. In the Lounge, however, when these nebulous topics are discussed, you can easily get a consensus or find a few kindred drivers who share your opinion on the matter. Like whether or not it's a requirement to display the mustache, the legality of accepting cash tips, traffic laws and the never-ending speculation on the insurance question.

While the Lyft faithful may dominate the discourse in the Lounge, when the doubters emerge from the shadows, all hell breaks loose.

These are my favorite posts. Or when drivers complain about passengers cussing, being drunk, having dogs, reeking of pot or slamming doors. Some drivers even suggest kicking out passengers they don't like. I always want to point out that in their blind hatred towards cab drivers, they're missing the point of creating an alternative form of transportation. If many of these gung-ho drivers actually listened to why passengers prefer Lyft and Uber, they'd know it's because Lyft users are looking to avoid cabs. But watching these taxi-hating Lyfters slowly morph into cab drivers themselves, it only makes sense that after driving people around for a while, cab drivers might have figured out how to deal with passengers. It's not easy. Every request you accept is a roll of the dice. You never know who's going to get in your car. But hey, trying to appreciate the struggles of the other team requires more self-awareness than you can expect from the Lounge faithful.

Another amusing subplot in the Lounge ensues when a driver is "off-boarded" and removed from the Lounge. Only active Lyft drivers can participate in the Lounge, so drivers who are involved in accidents or altercations are deactivated from the Lyft system and thus removed from the Lounge. This is especially problematic because the most important thing drivers want to know is what happens after an accident. What's covered by Lyft and what isn't? What about deductibles? What happens if our insurance company finds out we've been using our cars as taxis?

Not knowing all these facts leads to a lot of conjecture. Which is ironic because the official word from HQ is that drivers are removed from the lounge to prevent rumors and speculation. But all it takes is one of the Lyft cheerleaders to have an accident, get deactivated and disappear for the rest of the flock to start asking questions. And maybe slowly realize they are taking too much of a risk for a company that is only interested in making money.

Like the mustache, the Lounge is another marketing scheme gone awry. By conning drivers into believing what benefits Lyft somehow benefits them – the expendable workforce – Lyft has assembled an army of corporate shills, a veritable street team... But maybe the Pacific Driver Lounge is what a real community looks like nowadays: a bunch of desperate halfwits working together to promote an exploitative business model that goes completely against their own best interest. And it's just my good fortune that the ensuing shit show is such a hilarious, side effect. ❖

HOW TO GET KICKED OUT OF A LYFT DRIVER LOUNGE: WRITE A BLOG POST

I originally wrote "The Cult of Lyft" for this zine, but then decided the ad hominem tone didn't really fit with the rest of the material. So I published it on my Medium page instead, where the piece languished in obscurity for several weeks.

Until one night, when my judgment was impaired, I posted a link on a public Facebook group for Uber/Lyft drivers, not really expecting much but a few page views. The next morning, though, I checked Facebook and had 77 notifications.

Apparently, someone had reposted the link to the Pacific Driver Lounge, where it was subsequently shared to the other official Lyft Lounges.

Uber drivers were propagating it as well, on Facebook, Twitter and independent driver forums across the web.

The response was overwhelming. I've never been insulted so much in such a short amount of time. Lyft loyalists were outraged. Everyone else did what people usually do on the internet: they talked shit, insulted me, assumed I was a girl, got into arguments with each other and posted memes and wondered how long it would take for Lyft to kick me out of the Lounge.

Some of the comments were pretty funny and I collected a bunch and posted them on my blog. Shortly after that, I was no longer able to access the Pacific Driver Lounge.

This wasn't a surprise. I knew from being a member of the Lounge that people got expelled all the time. And not for just getting into accidents, but for the silliest of offenses, like talking shit about Lyft.

Later that day, Matt Jensen, a community outreach person for Lyft and "Lounge mentor," messaged me through Facebook to let me know that I'd been removed from the Lounge because I'd shared "lounge details" with Uber by posting all the nasty comments about me on my blog.

Someone else from Lyft tweeted at me later that day asking for suggestions on how to improve the Lyft experience. I promptly posted a constructive and very earnest response about some of the problems I'd had with the Lyft platform on my blog. But that was the last I heard from them. They wanted me gone, and away I went.

Oh well.

C'est la vie.

No more Honey Boo Boo for me. ❖

THE PACIFIC DRIVER LOUNGE IS MY HONEY BOO BOO

 James
13 hrs

Check this article out https://medium.com/@piltdownlad/the-cult-of-lyft-part-one-c83af7ece84f

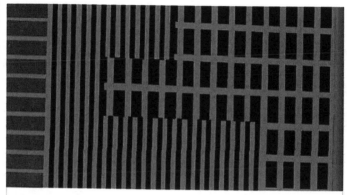

The Cult of Lyft

Inside the Lyft Pacific Driver Lounge

MEDIUM.COM

Like · Comment · Share

👍 18 people like this.

 Carlo Cc Allie Krummel Matt Jensen
13 hrs · Like

 Davis Bullseye, 3-point swish, all net, walk off home run. Boy she didn't leave much for the imagination. Damn, what a summary.
13 hrs · Like · 👍 10

 William On one hand, I hate the cynicism. I chose lyft to be able to have a atmosphere conducive to having a good time.

On the other hand, however, I always wonder whether the one thing that differentiates us will eventually lead to our downfall.
13 hrs · Like · 👍 1

 Carlo Glad to see ur back in the lounge William. 😊💬
12 hrs · Like · 👍 2

 William I owe it all to you man.
12 hrs · Like · 👍 1

Sus lol. This article is amazing. Thank you Kelly for writing it.
I've been a driver for a year: everything written in that article is hysterically true. #NotDrinkingTheKoolaid

Incoming Lyft newbie pompon crew comments.
12 hrs · Edited · Like · 👍 4

Silas HAHAHAHAHAHAHA. Love it!
11 hrs · Like · 👍 3

 Go Hawks Sounds about right, especially the blocking part... Perfect example of one of them:

 Sha-Sha
blocked
1 minute ago · Like

10 hrs · Like · 👍 4

 Mediocre Receiver Wow. And that's why I don't drink kool-aide. Lol
10 hrs · Like · 👍 1

 Keith interesting https://medium.com/.../lyft-its-not-about-the-mustache...
9 hrs · Like · 👍 5

 LuckyLadylyft "The Lounge is my honey boo boo" hahahahaha
9 hrs · Like · 👍 4

 Gürkan Go Hawks lololololol
9 hrs · Like · 👍 1

 Go Hawks I speak the truth
9 hrs · Like

 Bill Cynicism masquerading as insight. Yawn.
9 hrs · Like · 👍 11

 Brittany So funny-
7 hrs · Like

 Peter Well you know what they say about opinions...
7 hrs · Like · 👍 1

 Jeffrey I think I learned more about Kelly than I did about Lyft from that post. We're all responsible for how we handle ourselves in the end, the world doesn't revolve around our needs, tastes, etcetera., and I find it interesting that she views how people choose to express and handle their own Lyft experience as some sort of weird social pressure. As someone who chooses not to go crazy on themes, goes easy on the meetups, and doesn't think of Lyft in messianic terms, I think this gal needs to check herself.
7 hrs · Like · 👍 3

 Marie Lyft fits me. I fit Lyft. I hope everyone finds something that makes them that happy one day. Nothing is ever perfect but you get out of it what you put in.
7 hrs · Like · 👍 5

 Christina Interesting point of view; however coming from a marketing background I have to disagree. Lyft is genius to create brand loyalty (do I have to say duh here?) Whether you agree with method or not (which I do, I like to LIKE my job :P) history has shown that companies who last build brand loyalty!

Plus no luckyladylyft article shoutout? I don't know her, but I'd be perturbed, lol 😬
7 hrs · Edited · Like · 👍 1

 Jennifer This is a beautiful snapshot that pretty accurately calls out this lounge. Loved it.
7 hrs · Like · 👍 2

Jeffrey It's all general examples with little in-depth detail and ad hominem, so really this is all about-self validation and is not terribly expository.
6 hrs · Like · 👍 2

Renée A well-written, albeit cynical read. In a general sense, nearly all of Kelly's observations (good and bad) are accurate. I know nothing is truly private, but nonetheless I feel a bit betrayed. Do we have the right to be miffed that we are the unwitting and nonconsensual subjects of an evidently ongoing series penned by a pseudoprofessional writer who is getting paid for this? Maybe, maybe not. All the more reason to #stayclassy
6 hrs · Like · 👍 3

Missy No. Not that this wasn't written like a first year college book report, but no we serve the public and don't get to be mad when someone calls this The Honey Boo Boo of Facebook groups.
6 hrs · Like · 👍 1

Michael He's clearly right on almost every point he makes. I say let the secret out. Southwest Airlines has dealt with the "Kool-Aid" comments for years. Their culture can be best described as quirky. Yet their employees, for the most part, are very loyal and love their jobs. So who cares if our quirky loyalty to Lyft is revealed...in the end it's what will actually make the company thrive.
5 hrs · Edited · Like · 👍 3

Jeffrey I really don't care what she thinks, but it does suck to be a cynical Godzilla on all the bambis here just trying to have fun earning a buck, even if it isn't her personal taste or way she wants to conduct her life. What's worse it's predictable that she's sitting back thinking "Dance, Monkeys, Dance!" while reading all these comments. Typical and boring for people in their 20's who feel insecure in their own identity. And I say this as someone who would pull this crap myself. https://www.youtube.com/watch?v=n-wUdetAAIY&feature=kp
6 hrs · Like · 👍 2

LuckyLadylyft Kelly Dessaint might as well be tagged...
6 hrs · Like · 👍 3

Bill Kelly's a dude, btw. He, not she.
6 hrs · Like · 👍 7

Sandra Dead on and we are all reacting predictably in response!
6 hrs · Like · 👍 1

Gürkan He should make this whole thread another blog post
6 hrs · Edited · Like · 👍 4

LuckyLadylyft Probably will per your suggestion...
6 hrs · Like · 👍 1

Marie That was his evil genius plan from the get go.
6 hrs · Like · 👍 1

Missy What sets Lyft apart from Uber is its focus on accountability. It's the reason people choose us over cabs and Lyft beats Uber aaaall DAY with its customer responsiveness. That's real, and invaluable and that's what's going to carry is through this battle. Not the gimmicks.

Most Uber patrons I've talked to who avoid Lyft specifically, do so for just the kind of preciousness we promote on the board.

There's an invasiveness to a stranger attempting to be your bestie at 7:00 in the morning on your way to work. Folks feel that and choose Uber.

These are the things that we should be having an open dialogue about on this board without the worry of getting slapped in the face with the banner waving.
6 hrs · Edited · Like · 👍 4

Skot A bit too much "look at the funny circus animals" and mislabeling Lyft culture as a cult. All low-hanging fruit for the average blogger. Still, it ends on a positive note, which is nice. Then again, it likely curls up at the end so it won't come off as a hit piece.
6 hrs · Like · 👍2

 Jeffrey There's a way to be yourself, be a driver with your own style/flavor, still work within lyft's guidelines, and not invalidate and belittle the choices of others that suit them. This ain't it.
6 hrs · Like · 👍3

 Renée Any respect I had for Kelly as a writer after reading the above article quickly vanished after I clicked on the link in Keith's comment. If you missed this inglorious and pedestrian ode to snark (and you get a kick out of biting the hand that feeds you), read on: https://medium.com/.../lyft-its-not-about-the-mustache...
5 hrs · Like · 👍3

 Keith Lying to passengers is SO cool! ☹
5 hrs · Like · 👍3

 Renée You know what else is cool? Misogyny! "There will always be drunk girls who feel cheated when they get into a car that doesn't have [the mustache], but they are easily distracted by something else shiny or bright."
5 hrs · Edited · Like · 👍1

 Keith Yeah super cool....
5 hrs · Like

 Mimi Not amused at all by these 2 articles. What Kelly has FAILED to do with OP article was mention WHY so so many are passionate about the mustache...(whether it's putting food on the table for some, vacation money for others) if you're going to critique the lounge and its members, at least do so from all perspectives and provide an explanation as to WHY so many love LYFT. And the article **Keith** just posted...there's more than one rideshare to drive for...if you can't don the pink stache (TRADE DRESS REQUIREMENT) then please move on...sheesh.
5 hrs · Edited · Like · 👍5

 Gürkan Hate?
5 hrs · Like

 Keith Interesting that she is worried that she would not qualify for other TNCs due to the age of her four year old Jetta, when a 30 second visit to the TNC's webpage would reveal to her that she'd be fine...
5 hrs · Edited · Like

 LuckyLadylyft Articles like this make the private bay area lounge a more comfortable place to share. ..
5 hrs · Like

 Mimi Keith: it's amazing and perturbing to me how much misinformation there is out there...let's not even mention how lazy Kelly was to not investigate before writing these articles.
5 hrs · Like

 Keith Right, Mimi !
5 hrs · Like

 Brian I guess he's gotta get that Web traffic to his blog somehow. Kind of a shame he joined just so he could blog about people in a belittling way, I just wanted a cuddle stache.
4 hrs · Like · 👍1

Marie Kelly just needs a cuddle.
4 hrs · Like · 👍 3

 LuckyLadylyft There should be rules enforced surrounding publishing information from this lounge or writing about this lounge in outside public forums . Like a consequence of immediate removal. Says a lyft driver, not a cult member....
3 hrs · Like · 👍 1

 Marie I thought it was kind of like, What happens in Vegas, stays in Vegas. Ha.
3 hrs · Like · 👍 2

 LuckyLadylyft Lol..hahaha Marie I'm sure you would be fun in Vegas! ☺
3 hrs · Like · 👍 1

 Sus https://www.lyft.com/drive/help/article/1432486
^^ lol. Chug the koolaid! Cheer for Lyft! If you don't, we'll kick you out! Been there, done that, got the T-shirt and back for more.
1 hr · Like

 Lori Did not see the word Kool-Aid once in the article
1 hr · Like

 Brian I just think it's pathetic that there's nothing more worthwhile for him to blog about than what goes on in a group. I'm sure if he had joined the army, he'd write some of the same things. Of course we drank the Kool aid, you have to have passion in your work. I guess the world is so cynical that people are ok with sarcastic exposés .
1 hr · Edited · Like · 👍 1

 Bill Lori:

> The worst thing you could do in the Lounge is malign the Lyft brand. You will soon be facing a cyber lynch mob 👍 🐦
>
> Like all internet forums, the Driver Lounge is a cesspool of glad-handers, group hounds, chicken-littles and a chorus of kool-aid drinking cheerleaders, clueless consumers lapping up a marketing ploy and defending their faith to the bitter end. A handful of participants do 75 percent of the talking. They

48 mins · Like · 👍 1

 Sus And for the record- Drinking the Kool-aid has been a reference to Jones Town, and used by the core original drivers of Seattle to describe the attitudes of the recently on-boarded.
38 mins · Like

 Lori Wow Bill How did I miss that? LOL
36 mins · Like

 Lori Sus it's been used in SF Lyft before there was Lyft in Seattle. Apparently the Kool-alde is contagious
35 mins · Like

Skot Having scanned it again, it strikes me as lazy writing. A lot of snark and glittering generalities and a POV that wobbles between smug superiority and lame shrug. If it was an observation on some other forum it would still be as lazy. 99 out of 100 bloggers could seriously use an editor, and this one is no exception.
33 mins · Like

 Miguel Blah blah blah who cares
15 mins · Like

THE RICHMOND DISTRICT
Including GOLDEN GATE PARK and
SUNSET DISTRICT to Noriega

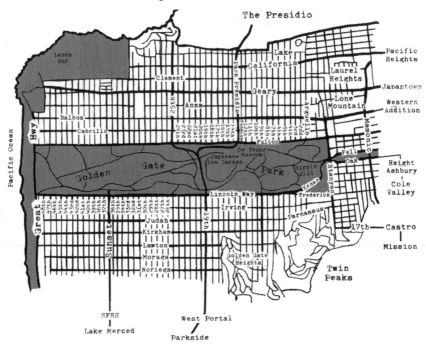

3.28 • THE PRIME-TIME HUSTLE

PULL UP TO A BAR ON 22ND STREET. Girl asks to finish her cigarette.

"Sure. Whatever." I turn up the stereo and keep time to the Feelies on the steering wheel.

Five minutes later she gets in the back. She's about to tell me her destination when another girl approaches my car.

"Hey, are you Kelly?"

"Yeah."

"You're my Lyft."

"Samantha?"

"That's me." She opens the back door and tells the first girl, "You're in the wrong car."

After some momentary confusion, the first girl gets out and Samantha and a friend take her place.

"Was that rude of me?" Samantha asks her friend. They all three know each other. On the way to Grove and Masonic, the two girls talk about how they think the first girl is shallow and superficial. But they don't have many girls to hang out with.

I drop them off and head back to the Mission. At 20th and Guerrero, I pick up Valerie. Going to Russian Hill. She's obviously buzzed and tries to guess what band I'm listening to.

"It sounds 80s," she says.

"You're right about the decade, but if you know who's playing right now, you'll be my favorite passenger of all time."

Down Guerrero, she contemplates the song. I seriously doubt she knows who Ed Kuepper is. But I give her the benefit of the doubt.

"I'll give you a hint," I say. "It's an Australian singer-songwriter."

After she gives up, I have to repeat Ed Kuepper's name three times.

She tells me she was out with friends celebrating. Just got a new apartment. She broke up with her boyfriend and left him the rent-controlled apartment they'd shared since the nineties.

"That's a huge sacrifice," I say. "Break-up rent is always rough, but in a tech boom, it's a motherfucker."

"Yeah, it was a hard decision to make. I wanted out of the relationship."

"So how much higher is your rent now?"

"About three times."

"That sucks," I tell her. "I once stayed in a relationship longer than I wanted to because of rent. But that was in LA, when the real estate market wasn't going nuclear. I can't imagine what it would have been like if I'd had to pay three times the rent to get out. I'd probably still be living in a miserable loveless relationship."

"What can you do?" she shrugs. "Things happen."

LATER, I'm cruising down Brannan. Prime time is at 50 percent when I get a request. Look at the address but don't recognize it. I pull over and zoom into the map. It's near Candlestick Park. As I open Waze to figure out how to get down there, a call comes in.

"Hey, this is Victor. I just requested a Lyft. Wanted to make sure you knew where you were going?"

"Sure. Be there in a few minutes."

I get on the freeway. Their location is seven miles away. It takes me about nine minutes. I park next to a guard station. A few more cars show up. One has a mustache on the grill. A mob of people walks out of the complex. Five guys approach my car. Including the one who requested the ride. Victor tells me they are all going to The Matrix, a club in the

Marina, and they're taking three different cars. Assures me he'll take care of everything and gets in one of the other cars.

I get on the freeway with three dudes in the back and one up front.

"Everybody remember their IDs?" someone asks.

"Oh shit!"

"Can you turn around?"

I take the next exit. Circle around the hill back to the apartment building. Pull up to the guard station again. He grudgingly lets us in. One of the guys directs me towards a parking structure. I pull over and wait.

The process takes forever. I'm idling for ten minutes while the remaining guys talk about their jobs. They seem to work for the same start-up.

"Don't worry," a guy tells me at some point. "We'll tip you."

The app is in prime time. I'm not sure what percentage it was at when I began the ride, but figure I'll get compensated for the hassle regardless of whether they actually tip me or not.

It's a golden rule: people who say they're going to tip do not. Besides, the app is not set up to add tips easily. Most passengers think the tip is already included anyway. (It's not.) Without prime time price surging, I don't think I'd ever get tipped.

Finally, we are on the freeway again. All the way into the city, the guys in back continue talking about work, money, getting fucked up at the club and picking up chicks.

The guy up front has his navigation app open, as if he's testing me. I get off on Octavia. His app says to turn right on Haight. I take Oak to Franklin. We rocket up the hills to the Marina in a squadron of cabs, towncars, Lyfts and Ubers.

Outside the club, one of the guys pulls out a roll of bills.

"What do we owe you?"

"It's all done through the app," I tell him.

"What about a tip?" He flips through some bills. I see mostly twenties. "I want to make sure you're taken care of."

"It's cool. Just tell Victor why the ride took so long." I figure the fare will be astronomical, with the back and forth and all the waiting. I don't want him to think I was the one who fucked up.

I kind of regret not taking the money, but I'm just glad to have them out of my car.

Looking around as I drift down to Lombard: hootchie-mommas and jocks galore. Mental note: stay away from the Marina when the clubs let out. This place is definitely amateur hour.

I head down Van Ness. A request comes in. An alley in SoMa. A very wasted guy and Elizabeth, his sober girlfriend get in my car. She sits up front. Tells me they are going to the Richmond. The guy sits in back. Begins pontificating immediately. He's all over the map with his drunken babble. Elizabeth and I laugh. He keeps rolling down the window. The Richmond is blanketed in fog. Yes, let the cool moist air in, I think and pray he doesn't blow chunks. So far I've managed to transport countless drunks without a single puker. But I know each drunk I let in my car is a roll of the dice.

On Geary, the guy yells out the window at other cars. An older Asian woman at a stoplight smiles back at us. A man waves.

"Hey Kelly," he says after awhile. "Is that really your name?"

"Yeah, why?"

"We thought you were going to be a girl."

"Because my name's Kelly?"

"That and you have long hair. The picture in the app makes you look like a girl. It's very confusing. Sorry. Don't mean to be rude."

"Nah, it's cool. I get that a lot."

After dropping them off, I take my time heading east, hoping for a ride back downtown. Ten minutes later, a request comes in. Andrea gets in the back. Asks if I can take her to Berkeley.

It's 50 percent prime time.

"No problem."

I turn onto Geary and cruise down Laguna to Oak. Hit the freeway. Andrea is super friendly. We talk about what kind of drug addicts we would be. We talk about Woody Allen. We talk about living on the East Bay. She's smart, articulate and friendly. Works at an art gallery in SoMa. DJs at an internet radio station on the side. We discuss the situation with the galleries downtown that are being forced to relocate because all the tech companies are moving into the area and raising the rents. I've been reading articles about it.

"You'd think the start-ups would want something to go on the walls..." I ponder.

"The techies down there just walk right past our place. If we didn't do 3D printing on the side, we'd be out of business."

When I drop her off, I thank her for being such a lovely passenger. Head back over the bridge. It's still prime time.

THE NEXT MORNING, when I get my daily summary, I'm curious how much I made from the ride to the Marina. I ended up going 12 miles. The entire trip took 28 tedious minutes. The base fare was $36 and the prime time tip was $18. I look down my list of my rides and see the one to Berkeley. We went 11 miles in 19 enjoyable minutes. But I guess prime time was at 75 percent because even though her base fare was $32, the prime time tip was $24. So Andrea ended up paying more that the techwads from Candlestick Park, despite wasting my time and being obnoxious, but there's nothing I can do about it. Except take the cash next time. ❖

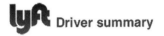 Driver summary

Feedback

★★★★★ *32 ratings*

"He knows his stuff"

"Incredibly friendly, fun to talk to, and most importantly got me home safely and quickly"

★★★★ and below *6 ratings*

"Nice driver. Route ended up being longer than it should have been."

Past 100 ratings	Lifetime	Past week
Rating	**Rides**	**Accept rate**
✔ ★ **4.92**	**174**	✔ **100%**
Awesome		Awesome

4.2 • WORK ALL THE TIME

IT'S ALREADY PAST 10 P.M. WHEN I GET A REQUEST FOR 24TH AND MISSION. I'm only two blocks away. The double-decker bus turns the corner as I roll up. Two guys.

"25th and Grand View." Navim sits up front.

"Where's that?"

"Just go up 25th, all the way."

I ask how they are doing. Navim says he's tired.

"You guys always work this late?" I ask.

"Every day, work, work, work," the guy in the back says, "That's all we ever do." He spends the rest of the ride looking at his phone.

Navim is equally reticent.

"Must be a nice view up here," I say to break the silence as we climb the hill.

"Yes."

That's all I get. After dropping them off, I head back to the Mission.

I need to take a leak. One of the most annoying aspects of doing Lyft is figuring out where to piss after Trader Joe's and the coffeeshops close. There is a green spaceship bathroom at South Van Ness and Cesar Chavez next to a gas station frequented by taxis. One of twenty-five automated, self-cleaning public toilets in San Francisco. The self-cleaning part of the equation, however, is dubious. It smells awful inside. The floors are usually wet and there are often piles of dirty toilet paper strewn about. Along with other detritus like clothes, fast food wrappers, and cigarette butts.

Although there are twenty-four other public toilets around town, the one on South Van Ness is my go-to piss-stop, seeing as how it's in the Mission, my de facto base of operations.

I usually incorporate a pee break with a smoke break and call the Wife. I check in, tell her what's been going on with passengers and then clean my windows. At this point, I'm wiping down my windows three or four times a night. The windows are a constant struggle. My efforts to keep them free of streaks, blemishes and spots are a Sisyphean task in a city full of moisture. All I have to do is drive into the Richmond or Sunset districts and all my work is ruined with one splatter of condensation. And then there's the alcohol infused breath of my passengers that fogs up the inside. I use the a/c and rear defroster as much as the turn signals. Which doesn't help my gas mileage.

After I've buffed out the visible streaks and finished smoking, I get back in my car. I carry cleaning wipes to disinfect my hands. I got the kind with moisturizers. I am a bit of a germaphobe and hate dry skin.

After dropping somebody off at a bar on Divisadero, I cruise through the Castro on my way back to the Mission. Get a request for 18th Street a block east of Castro. Pull up to the location. The sidewalk is crowded. I'm looking for an Asian woman named Edith. She approaches with a man. He has an accent. European tourist.

"We're taking him to his hotel," Edith tells me.

"Which one?" I ask.

"The Stanford Court on California," he says.

Heading to Market, I search Maps to get the hotel's exact location. They start making out. Edith's knees push into the back of my seat. When they come up for air, she asks, "Where are we going?"

"To my hotel," the guy tells her.

"Where are we now?"

The guy has no clue. Suggests random neighborhoods. This only adds to her confusion.

I tell her we are heading to Nob Hill.

The man goes in for another smooch. Again, I feel her push against my seat.

At the hotel, I pull into the driveway.

"Where are we?" Edith asks again.

The man gets out on the right side. She gets out on the left. I end the ride. Her phone chirps. She looks at it while the man beckons her to follow him. She seems disoriented. I hesitate a moment, in case she comes running after my car. Maybe she was just trying to help him get home and had no intention of going up to his room? It's her name on the app. I assume she's local and he picked her up at a bar. He hardly seems drunk. She's wasted though.

The busboys approach them. Oh well. It's their responsibility now.

I follow the driveway back to the street. A taxi is double parked in front of the hotel. The driver glares at me. I turn right on California and head to North Beach. ❖

4.3 • A FRIDAY NIGHT CUT SHORT

FRIDAY NIGHT. I drive into town as the sun falls behind the hills of Marin County. A ribbon of fog wraps around the city. I head to Philz before they close. It's always a major hassle to find parking around 24th. Or any other street in the Mission. It seems like everybody and their brother is driving into the neighborhood to eat dinner and go to the bars, competing with the locals for the few available parking spots. I usually spend ten to fifteen minutes looking for a space.

After I get coffee, I wipe the thick, greasy layer of freeway dust off my Jetta. Go into driver mode.

On Valencia, I pick up two women going to Russian Hill. Vickie sits in the passenger seat.

"When you're in a Lyft, you have to sit in front," she tells her friend in the back.

NORTH BEACH

including CHINATOWN, NOB HILL and RUSSIAN HILL

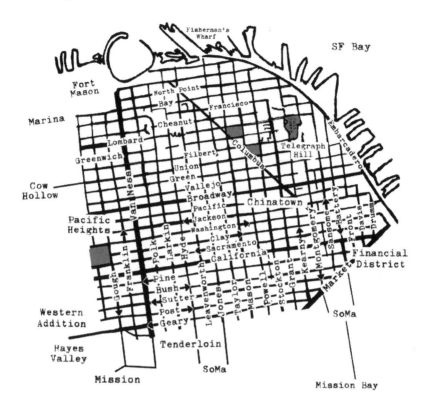

"That's why I usually use Uber," the woman deadpans.

"But Lyft is more fun!"

They're going to a party and deliberating whether they should bring a bottle of wine. Vickie tells me they'll probably want to get dropped off at a liquor store close to their location.

"That shouldn't be a problem." There are markets and liquor stores on practically every corner in Russian Hill.

"Who's going to be at this party?" asks the woman in back.

Vickie turns around in her seat to face her friend. Lists off a few names. They talk about one guy in particular and his propensity to screw as many girls as he can, even though he's such a nice guy.

"He told me that he's just trying to fill a hole since he broke up with Hannah," Vickie says.

They discuss the perils of dating and relationships in San Francisco.

How easy it is for men. While women are outnumbered and looking to settle down. Vickie talks about a wedding she has to attend and the awful bridesmaid dresses.

"I really don't like pink," the woman in back says. "I don't even own any pink clothes. Well, maybe a pair of pink panties."

Vickie laughs. "I always say that same thing." She looks at me. "I hope we're not annoying you with our silly talk."

"No, I hate pink too. That's why I don't put that stupid mustache on my car."

"What kind of car is this anyway? Is it new?"

AFTER MOVING SOME FOLKS AROUND NORTH BEACH, the Tenderloin and Fisherman's Wharf, I get a request in Pacific Heights. Pick up Jonathan on the corner of Buchanan and Green heading downtown to 3rd and Market to meet friends for drinks. He's in his final year of dental school. Says he's tired, but he's making an effort since he rarely has time to hang out. Driving up and over the hills down Gough Street, I tell him about my experiences with dental schools back when I was dirt poor and couldn't afford a real dentist. I ask if he participated in the recent community outreach program that offered free dental work to poor residents. He doesn't know what I'm talking about.

"It was in the news."

I turn onto Market and cut down to Mission. Exposed to the homelessness and depravity of the Mid-Market area, it's hard not to comment on the unfortunate side of the city. I tell Jonathan that before moving to San Francisco, the Wife and I lived in downtown LA for three years. I talk about how we dealt with the street people there, treating them with respect and getting to know them. It was the only way to survive two blocks from Skid Row. Then, as time went by, more yuppies moved in and hired private security teams to roust anybody who sat on the sidewalk. Now downtown LA is no different than SoMa, where the hipsters queue in front of newly opened artisanal restaurants and single-origin coffee shops during the day and at night the club kids form lines around the block while the homeless sleep huddled in doorways.

"Most people on the streets are there because they have no safety net. It's easy to look at street people as less than human, but my mother had Alzheimer's and if she hadn't gone to Alabama to live with my uncle, she could have easily ended up on the streets, lost and confused, doing weird shit like collecting trash. I mean, when we finally realized she had a problem, she'd assembled a menagerie of fifteen cats, three dogs, four turtles, ten parakeets and a homeless family. Had them all living in the garage. I can only imagine what would happen to her if she didn't have somebody to help her."

I pause and realize I've just been pontificating at this poor guy. Something about his bedside manner, I guess. I've always divulged too much information to doctors, or anybody in a white coat, really.

"Well, this is an utterly depressing topic," I say. "You're supposed to be having fun tonight!"

"No, it's reality, you know?"

At 3rd Street, I get in the left lane, even though it's designated for taxis and Muni only. I don't know how else to get to 3rd and Market. I can't drive down Market past 10th Street and, after too many bad experiences, I avoid Union Square and the Financial District like the plague. But I'm behind a town car and figure, if they can use the lane, so can I.

I make the turn. See a cop car. They obviously see me too. I pull over to the curb as if that where I meant to go all along. I'm only half a block from where I was dropping off Jonathan.

The cops get behind me and hit the lights.

"Oh fuck, I'm getting pulled over."

"What should I do?" Jonathan asks.

"Just get out, I guess."

He opens the door and sets one foot on the asphalt.

"Get back in the car!" the cops yell over the loudspeaker.

Jonathan quickly closes the door and fastens his seatbelt. Visibly freaked out, he apologizes.

"Why are you sorry?" I ask. "I'm the one who fucked up! I'm sorry you have to deal with this!"

While waiting for the cop, I think fast. Come up with two options. I can claim to be from out of town, plead ignorance and say I'm just trying to find my hotel. It's tempting in its simplicity, but do I have time to get Jonathan on board? Probably not. That means option two: making the case that I'm exempt from the rule because Lyft is a TNC. I'd read on-line that the state had recently passed a law designating ride-hail services as Transportation Network Companies. The details were confusing and muddled with vague legal jargon, but perhaps it will mean something to the cops. I've had a few passengers swear that I can go where only taxis are allowed. One guy who insisted I take a taxi-only lane was a lawyer.

All I can do at this point is try to talk my way out of a ticket.

The cop approaches my window.

"Never get out of the car when you're being pulled over," he says.

"We don't know what you're doing. Don't want to have to shoot you."

I look at the cop's face to see if he's joking. He looks serious. I'm surprised by how handsome he is: Blonde hair, blue eyes, a chiseled jawline... he could easily be a model.

I try to explain that I'm a Lyft driver and Jonathan is my passenger.

The cop asks for my driver's license. I hand it over. Point out that I thought I could use the taxi lanes since Lyft is a TNC.

The cop is not impressed.

"As far as I understand it, you Lyft and Uber drivers are just picking up people you meet on the internet."

I ask if he'll let my passenger go while he runs my record. He agrees. Jonathan gets out quickly. Pauses to say sorry again. "Good luck!"

I wait for ten minutes with the high beams on my car. Some rubber-necking tourists glance my way but the taxis and busboys outside the Westin pay me no mind.

In the aftermath of the encounter, I realize the music is still playing. A Metallica song comes on. I turn the stereo off.

I'm somewhat horrified at my predicament. The first time in fifteen years that I've been pulled over by the police. In all my 25 years of driving, I've only gotten two tickets. Both for speeding on the highway.

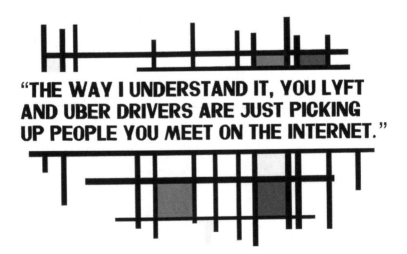

"THE WAY I UNDERSTAND IT, YOU LYFT AND UBER DRIVERS ARE JUST PICKING UP PEOPLE YOU MEET ON THE INTERNET."

The cop returns. Asks me to sign the ticket. I inquire a second time about the legality of Uber/Lyft cars using the taxi lanes. I know it's too late now, but I make one last feeble attempt at justifying my actions. He tries to explain the laws, but I'm distracted by his frosty blue eyes and

POTRERO HILL

Including DOGPATCH and the eastern part of THE MISSION

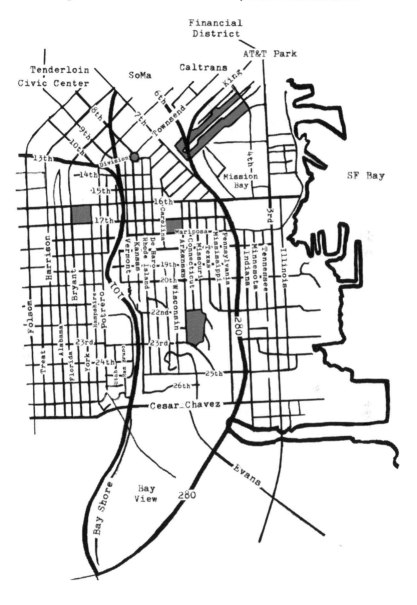

perfect teeth.

I take the ticket and meander like a whipped dog into North Beach. Pull over and call the Wife. Read her the violation code. She looks up the fine. $238. Traffic school will cost about $58. What a drag.

"You should just come home," she says.

"I don't want the experience to get me down. I'm going to drive a while longer."

I pop an Ativan. Head to the Haight. Onto the darker streets. Try to avoid rides until I get my head together. When I go back online, I get a request right away. Pick up a punk rock girl outside Molotov's. Ronnie looks barely old enough to drink. Going to Excelsior. I have no idea how to get there. Put the address into Waze.

Ronnie is from LA. I ask what part.

"San Gabriel."

"Really? That's where I'm from." I say. "Well, Rosemead. What high school did you go to?"

"A private school in Baldwin Park."

"Holy shit! I used to live on Franciscquito Avenue."

"That's where we live!" She puts her hand up for a high-five.

"I swear, I've met more people from LA in San Francisco than I ever did in LA. How long have you been up here?"

"Just a few months ago. Not sure I'm staying though."

"Why not?"

"The techies are bringing me down. All this town seems to care about anymore is apps."

As she laments the state of the city, I offer vague agreement.

"I just thought it was going to be different," she says. "But it seems like if you don't have any money, you can't do anything here."

I tell her that I'm facing the same problems. "My wife and I really wanted to be in the city, but the rents are too outrageous. We ended up in Oakland, which is cool. But it's not San Francisco, you know? Nobody ever left their heart in Oakland."

I pull up to her place and listen as she continues to express her frustrations. She's had a few drinks and needs to vent.

"It's just hard, cause I don't know how to make enough money here. I live in an apartment with five other people. I share a room with my friend. I just want to go to school, but I can't afford to do it here. I miss my friends in LA. I miss hanging out at the Smell…"

"I miss LA too."

"It just seems like everything is happening in LA right now. There's nothing in San Francisco but tech."

"You should check out Oakland. A lot of cool shit's happening there. It's where all the weirdos are now… the punks, the anarchists, the artists, the ragged types, the freaks… The San Francisco music scene, the art scene and the literary scene… they're all moving to the East Bay."

"But I want to live in San Francisco!" she bemoans.

"So do I! But fuck … Do you wanna work in tech?"

"No!"

"Me neither. I just wanna write and make zines and do my thing… I didn't come here to get a job that wouldn't allow me to do anything except work my ass off. But let's face it, if you can't afford the rent, if you don't make a hundred grand a year, you're no longer welcome here. San Francisco is a playground for the rich."

"I just wish it were different. I fucked up coming here…"

"I feel the same way sometimes. This is probably the worst time to be in San Francisco if you're not wealthy."

I don't know what else to say. We sit in silence. The windows are fogged up. I've been idling with a foot on the brake for the past ten minutes. I want to offer some kind of advice to this girl. All I can think of is, "Look, you're young… you have so much ahead of you. Do what feels right. You just gotta stay strong…"

"Yeah, you're right. You gotta stay positive or shit'll bring you down."

We high-five. Say goodbye.

I stay offline and head up Mission, thinking about Ronnie and her woes, which mirror my own. I've been disappointed about the situation in the Bay Area since I got here. Even though I have no interest in tech, as the Wife and I planned our move, I figured there had to be some trickle down economics in play. I had been selling zines and books at City Lights for years. I know several writers and zinemakers who live in San Francisco. Last September, we attended the two-day San Francisco Zine Fest where we met some amazing folks, like the legendary V. Vale of RE/Search and the mail art curator John Held. From a distant perspective, I thought being an artist in San Francisco was still viable. You just have to live in Oakland, I guess.

As much as we love San Francisco, it's not likely we'll ever be able to move into the city. Certainly not driving for Lyft. This is just a way to explore the city, talk to people from all different walks of life and earn a little money. After three weeks of Lyfting I've realized that I'm only making around $16 an hour. Far less than the $35 advertised on Facebook. Of course that $35 an hour doesn't factor in gas, maintenance, upkeep, wear and tear, insurance, bridge tolls and other expenses. I don't even want to think about the taxes. So when I get hit with a $300 ticket, I have to wonder if I'm just wasting my time. Sure, my profits are better than what I'd make at Trader Joe's or any other service job, but still… I need to find something else if I'm even going to afford Oakland.

After I cross 30th Street, I go back into driver mode.

I get a request on 22nd. Four people. Three girls in the back. Stephan up front. He has a bacon wrapped hotdog. It reeks. Mixed with their collective alcohol stench, I hope my gag reflex doesn't kick in. They offer me an option: either take them to the bus station at 6th and Market or drive them over the bridge to Alameda. I tell them it's all the same to me. They ask how much it would cost to go all the way to Alameda.

"30 bucks or so…"

As they deliberate, I say, "Listen, I'm having a rotten night. I just got a three hundred dollar ticket and would just as soon go home. I live in Oakland. So how about this: I'll drive you to Alameda but I'll wait until we're on the freeway to turn the app on, and after we've crossed the bridge, I'll turn it off. Deal?

Deal.

A girl in the back asks me where I live in Oakland.

"Temescal," I tell her.

She says I'm pronouncing it wrong, emphasizing the last syllable when I should pronounce it the Spanish way, with the emphasis on the first syllable. TEM-ES-CAL. Not TE-MES-CUL.

I laugh and say, "Then why are we going to AL-A-ME-DA and not AH-LAH-MAY-DAH?"

She gets defensive. "I grew up on the East Bay and that's how it's pronounced. I swear! I used to swim in Lake Temescal all the time when I was a kid."

"Hey, it's cool," I say. I know she's drunk. "I'm just joking. Thanks for pointing out the proper way to say TEM-ES-CAL."

She continues to insist that her pronunciation is correct even though I am agreeing with her. Her friends tell her that she's belaboring the point. She apologizes. Moves on to my hair. Calls me a hipster.

"A hipster!" I laugh. "Hipsters don't have long hair. They have short messy hair or wear trucker caps and tight pants. My pants aren't tight."

She starts apologizing profusely for calling me a hipster. "I don't even know what a hipster is!"

Stephan, who's finished his hotdog (though the smell is still punching me in the forehead) tells her to chill out.

"You're just drunk and repeating yourself."

"I'm not drunk!"

As we exit the tube onto the island, one of the girls in the back says, "Since I'm sure you've already had your share of tickets for the evening, I recommend driving the speed limit while in Alameda."

"Yeah, the cops like to pull people over for even going two miles over the limit," adds the drunk girl.

I follow their advice. Drop them off at an apartment building and slowly head back over the bridge. I use Waze to find the freeway home. ❖

 Driver summary

Feedback

★★★★★ *41 ratings*

"Awesome guy"

"Nice guy!"

":)"

"Great guy. Awesome driver!"

★★★★ and below *3 ratings*

Past 100 ratings	Lifetime	Past week
Rating	**Rides**	**Accept rate**
✔ ★ 4.91	239	✔ 100%
Awesome		Awesome

"IT CAME FROM SOMA - ATTACK OF THE TECH BROS"

4.9 • SECOND HOME GAME

IT'S THE SECOND HOME GAME AT **AT&T PARK**. But judging from the traffic, it might as well be opening day. SoMa is gridlocked. After getting caught up in the mess once, I try to stay away. It's just not worth the hassle. I look for rides elsewhere.

I'm cruising back to the Mission from Pacific Heights when I get a request for an address in one of the alleys off 5th between Folsom and Harrison. The app recommends I go down Brannan and then up 5th. Traffic is congested at 7th, so I go up to Folsom instead, which isn't much better. I turn onto 5th and hit a wall of cars. Nobody's moving. I call the passenger. Let him know what's going on.

"Game traffic is insane tonight. I'm just a block away." I hope he'll volunteer to walk up to Folsom.

"Don't worry," Stuart says. "Take your time."

Five minutes pass. I'm not getting any closer. Pull into the opposing lane and race towards the light on the wrong side of the street. Turn left onto Clara.

Stuart gets in the front seat. I ask where he's going. Tells me he already entered the address in the app. I start the Lyft. Look at the address.

"Potrero Hill?"

"How do you like the new feature?" he asks. Turns out Stuart works for Lyft. Part of the team that developed the update where passengers can input their destination into the app.

"Navigation is one of the biggest complaints we hear from passengers," he tells me. "We see more negative comments associated with drivers getting lost or not knowing how to get somewhere, so that's why we developed this feature."

I click the navigation option out of respect. Waze opens on my phone.

"I have a hard time using navigation," I say.

"What do you use instead?"

"I memorized the streets."

"Are you from San Francisco?"

"No. I got a map from AAA."

"Interesting."

"I find the forced navigation a little annoying. I downloaded Waze, but I think it's set up wrong. I can't figure it out."

"When we stop, I can show you how to adjust the settings."

Outside his place, while he fiddles around with the app, I complain about various Lyft policies. The rating system for one. The way passengers expect candy and water because other drivers bribe them with treats to get better ratings.

"I have some gum." I hold up the pack of mint Orbit. "But I feel like I get penalized for having a decent car and actually knowing my way around town."

I go off about how I only have access to the New Lyft Driver's Lounge on Facebook, which covers each city in the US that has Lyft, even though I'm in San Francisco and would benefit from other driver's experiences in the city.

"I've only been driving for three weeks, but I've done several hundred rides. San Francisco is its own beast. I should be able to see what other drivers say about it."

He points out that the San Francisco Driver's Lounge has too many nitty gritty details and the people at Lyft are afraid that it would discourage new drivers.

"Yeah, but that nitty gritty stuff is what's important. Maybe I wouldn't have gotten a ticket for turning left in a taxi lane if I'd had somewhere to find out protocols."

"That's an interesting suggestion," he says. "Perhaps they should change it to 50 rides or 30 days, whichever comes first."

"I mean, you can't treat that kind of information as a reward, like the mustache…"

It's obvious I'm wasting my breath. Stuart is just a coder. He doesn't really care about my petty concerns. I thank him for adjusting my app and drive away.

As I head down the hill, I get a request for 3rd and King. Right across from AT&T Park. Not sure how I'm going to pull this off. Head to China Basin anyway. I make it to 4th Street but traffic is at a standstill. I call the passenger to let him know. He asks if there's a better corner to stand on. I tell him traffic is backed up everywhere.

"Well, do your best," he says.

I hang up. A minute later he cancels the ride.

I spend the next forty-five minutes waiting to turn left onto 3rd Street. I'm still worked up over the encounter with the Lyft guy. Pop an Ativan. Blast the music while waiting in the turn lane. Practice my drumming on the steering wheel. The lights changes from green to red and back again. I have the car in park most of the time. When I finally get onto 3rd, I take Townsend as far west as I can before going back into driver mode.

Even though I was supposed to stop driving around 10pm, with the traffic on the bridge, there's no point in even trying to go home.

In North Beach I get a request for the Embarcadero. The pinned location is a parking lot. I assume Suzanne is in the bar across the street. I call to make sure. No answer. Call again. This time she answers. Says she's on her way out. I check the traffic on the freeway. The bridge and all the adjacent streets are still red.

I look around. The bar is packed. I watch the people drink and gesture at each other. The place looks expensive.

I think about the four twerps I picked up a few nights before at the Exploratorium a little farther down the Embarcadero. They were drunk and screaming at each other. Talking about how excited they'd been to check out Google Glass. One guy got invited to buy a pair. He agreed with his friend that fifteen hundred dollars is a lot to pay for them, but he was going to do it anyway. "They're just too cool."

No doubt Suzanne is in tech as well. Ten minutes go by. What kind of self-entitled twit makes somebody wait that long? I look at every person who leaves the general vicinity of the bar hoping one of them is Suzanne. I'm about to call and suggest she gets another car once she's actually ready to leave when I see a blonde woman who matches the picture in the app approach my car.

"Sorry. I had to say goodbye to everybody. You know how it is…"

I say I do, even though I do not. Tell her I'm just waiting to get back across the bridge. "Traffic is backed up due to the game."

She's going to Twin Peaks. Recommends the streets over the freeway. I drive down Market. Iggy Pop's "The Dum Dum Boys" is playing. Droplets of condensation hit the windshield. The fog gets thicker.

I catch every light. After Iggy Pop, "Dum Dum" by the Vaselines comes on. I have my iPod set to play songs in alphabetical order. I turn the volume down.

"Starting to think I should have taken the freeway," I say. "I can still swing down to 101, if you'd like."

Suzanne looks up from the glow of her phone. "No, it's alright."

"Cool. I don't really like the freeway. Not as much to see."

"How long have you been driving for Lyft?"

"About three weeks."

"You like it?"

"It has its moments. Like everything else."

Market opens up once we pass the Castro. The closer to Twin Peaks, the thicker the fog. By the time I'm driving up Burnett, visibility is less than the length of my headlights.

I tell her about my run-in with the guy who works for Lyft and how confounded he was with my take on the Lyft system.

"Most guys who work in tech don't understand anything but code," she says. "Everything is pragmatic and they don't know how to take emotions into consideration."

"If you don't mind me asking, what's it like being a woman in tech? It seems so male dominated. The ubiquitous tech bros…"

"That attitude definitely exists. You hear the dick jokes, the sexist comments and you are expected to laugh along."

"And what, fuck you if you can't take a joke?"

"More or less. Many start-ups are becoming structured now and es-tablishing corporate guidelines. But you still hear stuff. Most CEOs are men. So there are not always decent examples of proper behavior."

"Like the guy who made the comments about street people down-town? Or the guy who called the women in San Francisco '4 to 9ers?'"

"Most of the guys who run start-ups are really good at solving problems. But when it comes to dealing with people, they're clueless."

I pull up to her apartment. She continues talking.

"Before I moved here, I worked in finance in New York and politics in D.C. and I've never felt the need to play along with a groupthink attitude like here in San Francisco. I was surprised. I thought the people who were involved in tech would be more relaxed."

"It's like these guys overcompensating," I say. "After getting picked on for being geeks all their life, when they get their shot at comeuppance, they act like jocks. It's a bad 80s teen movie come to life."

"More like a bad 80s horror movie." She laughs.

"It came from Soma: Attack of the Tech Bros."

She laughs. We say goodnight. I head down the hill. Get on the freeway. Traffic isn't backed up anymore. I'm home in sixteen minutes.

LATER, while relaxing with a vodka and blood orange San Pelligrino, I'm scrolling through my newsfeed on Facebook and read on SFGate that Caltrans had closed several lanes on the Bay Bridge to repair a pothole. Turns out some people were stuck in traffic for two hours trying to get across the bridge.

It wasn't about the game after all. ❖

 **Driver summary**

Feedback

★★★★★ *31 ratings*
"Amazing! Thank you!"

★★★★ and below *3 ratings*
"Great car very comfortable and friendly !"

Past 100 ratings	Lifetime	Past week
Rating	**Rides**	**Accept rate**
✓ ★ **4.93**	**292**	✓ **100%**
Awesome		Awesome

4.18 SOMETHING ABOUT KATE

PICK UP A COUPLE IN THE HAIGHT. Colin's got an English accent.

"What's that you're listening to," he asks. "Some drone-y nineties band? Let me guess who…" Names a few bands.

"Don't disappoint me," the girl says to him.

Finally, he gives up.

"Just tell me the name."

"Died Pretty. They're an Australian band."

"A band you've never heard of," the girl ribs him drunkenly.

Colin gets defensive. Asks if I know of a band from Australia called Something About Kate.

I do not. "Are they recent?"

"Yeah, I saw them in London a little while ago…" Goes on to tell me about their style, how original their lyrics are and that I should definitely check them out.

I say I will and thank him for turning me on to a new band.

"Something about Kate," he says one last time as they get out, feeling somewhat vindicated by the possibility that his music collection might still be bigger than mine.

AROUND TWO A.M., as the bars let out, prime time is fluctuating between seventy-five and one hundred percent. I head to the Mission, hoping to get some fast rides. Hit it and quit it. That's the name of the game with the late night drunkies. Taxis, Ubers, Lyfts, towncars... practically every car on the road is looking for passengers.

A request comes in. 12th and Folsom. The app says one hundred percent prime time. I'm four minutes away. I race down Van Ness.

At the pinned location, a horde of drunks are milling in front of the Holy Cow. I pull up behind a row of double-parkers. Call the passenger to get his exact location.

"I'm right on the corner of 12th," Miguel tells me.

The cars move forward. Pick up their passengers and speed off into the night. I get to the front of the line. A couple climbs into my backseat.

"Hey, you're Miguel, right?"

"WAIT, THIS ISN'T AN UBER?"

His face doesn't match the picture on the app. Not that it matters. So many people have weird Facebook profile pics.

"Yeah, I'm Miguel. Sacramento and Hyde, please."

I take off down Folsom. Turn left on 9th and cross Market onto Larkin. Miguel and his girl are drunk.

"He's taking me back to his place," she tells me after I ask them how their night's going. "And he didn't even have to give me a roofie."

They make-out and giggle.

My phone rings. It's the generic Lyft number. That's weird, I think. Only the passenger I'm picking up can contact me when I'm in driver mode. I ignore it. It rings again.

"Hey, are you calling me?" I ask Miguel.

"Oh, I may be sitting on my phone," he says.

A second later, my phone rings again. I answer.

"Hey, this is Miguel."

"Who?"

"Miguel. I requested a Lyft. Where are you?"

At this point I'm in Nob Hill, straddling the streetcar rails.

"Hold on a second." I turn and ask the guy in back, "Are you sure you're Miguel?"

"Yes! Why do you keep asking me that?" He seems offended.

"Cause this is Miguel on the phone," I say.

"How is that possible?" the girl demands. "Somebody fucked up!"

I tell the Miguel on the phone that I've obviously picked up the wrong Miguel. "Don't worry. I'll call Lyft to sort everything out."

"Wait, this isn't an Uber?" asks the Miguel in back.

At this point, we all realize what has happened. I feel like an idiot. Miguel offers multiple apologies.

"Just email Lyft," the girl tells me. "They'll sort it out."

They want me to let them out of the car and walk the rest of the way.

"I'm not leaving you on the street," I say. "I'll take you home and then call Lyft."

"We still need to pay you for the ride." The girl pulls out her wallet. "I only have four dollars."

I tell them not to worry about it. "What are the odds that two Miguels would be on the same corner at the exact same time?" I wonder aloud.

"It's a very common name," the girl says. "Can you believe he's Argentinian? He doesn't look Spanish at all."

I think about another Argentinian I had in my car the previous week. I thought he was French. "Yeah, I can believe it."

I pull up to their place.

"I have to pay you for the ride." Miguel pulls out a small wad of cash. "How much would this ride have cost?"

I think about the hundred percent prime time.

"About twelve dollars," the girl tells him. "Give him fifteen."

"Fuck that," Miguel says. "Here's twenty."

"Thanks, man. Sorry for the hassle."

I find a semi-legit parking spot and call Lyft. There isn't a prompt for picking up the wrong passenger. I press two. Tell the support guy the whole story in a frantic burst. He must have pulled up a screen with all the details because I didn't have to explain it twice. He can see that the first Miguel caught another Lyft. They refund his money.

By the time I'm done, prime time is down to twenty-five percent. I roll out and try to find another passenger. ❖

 Driver summary

Feedback

★★★★★ *48 ratings*

"Made sure to call me ahead of time so he cluld pick me up on the right side of the street to avoid rain, cool!"

"Such a bright personality"

"So nice! Great!"

"Rad"

"Conversational"

"Great Lyft driver!"

"Great conversation!!!! :-)"

"Thanks Kelly! Good chat :)"

★★★★ and below *3 ratings*

"Picked up wrong person :/"

Past 100 ratings	*Lifetime*	*Past week*
Rating	**Rides**	**Accept rate**
✔ ★ **4.91**	**374**	✔ **100%**
Awesome		Awesome

A LYFT PLAYLIST

Adrian Belew • Agent Orange • The Aints • The Alley Cats Alternative TV • Amebix • Angry Samoans • Anti-Nowhere League Anti-Pasti • Athletico Spizz 80 • The Au Pairs • The Avengers The B-52's • Bad Brains • The Bats • Bauhaus • Big Star Billy Childish • The Birthday Party • Black Flag • The Black Heart Procession • Black Mountain • Black Randy • Blackalicious • Blondie Blue Orchids • Blurt • The Bo-Weevils • The Boys • The Boys Next Door • Brian Eno • The Brian Jonestown Massacre • The Briefs The Brilliant Corners • The Buzzcocks • Camper Van Beethoven

Cat Power • The Chameleons • Cheap Trick • Chelsea • The Chills
Chumbawamba • The Church • Circle Jerks • The Clash
The Clean • Clinic • Cockney Rebel • Coil • The Comsat Angels
The Contortions • Corrosion of Conformity • Cowboys International
The Cramps • Crass • Crime & the City Solution • The Cure
D.O.A. • The Damned • The Dandy Warhols • David Johansen
Dead Boys • Dead Kennedys • Death • Del That Funkee Homosapien
Delta 5 • Delton 3030 • Descendents • Desert Dessions • Devendra
Banhart • The Deviants • The Dickies • Die Haut • Died Pretty
Discharge • Dr. Doom • Dr. Octagon • Dream Syndicate • The Dukes
of Stratosphear • Dungen • Earthlings? • Echo & the Bunnymen
Ed Kuepper • El Rego et Ses Commandos • The Embarrassment
Empire • The English Beat • Essential Logic • Exodus • The Fall
Fang • The Feelies • Felt • Fields of the Nephilim • The Flamin' Groovies
The Flesh Eaters • The Fleshtones • Flipper • Flux of Pink Indians
The Flys • The Freeze • Fugazi • Gang of Four • Gary Walker &
the Rain • GBH • Glaxo Babies • Gogol Bordello • Government
Issue • Grant Hart • Gray Matter • Green on Red • The Greenhornes
Greg Sage • The Gun Club • The Heartbreakers • Holly Golightly
Honore Avolonto • The House of Love • Hüsker Dü • Ian Dury
Iggy Pop • Index • Iron Maiden • J.J. Cale • The Jacobites
The Jam • Jane's Addiction • Jazzateers • The Jesus & Mary Chain
Jim Carroll Band • Johnny Thunders • Joseph K • Joy Division
Julian Cope • June Brides • Khmer Rouge • Killing Joke • King Khan
& The Shrines • King Missle • The Kinks • Kitchens of Distinction
Kool Keith • Kommunity FK • KRS-One • La Dusseldorf • The La's
Laughing Clowns • LCD Soundsystem • Le Tigre • The Leaving
Trains • Lee "Scratch" Perry • Lene Lovich • Let's Active • Liquid
Liquid • Lizzy Mercier Descloux • Loop • The Lords of the New
Church • Los Super Elegantes • Louis Tillett • Love & Rockets • Love
Tractor • Lydia Lunch • Lyres • Madvillain • Magazine • Magnetic
Fields • Mahotella Queens • Marcy Playground • Mark Lanegan
Mazarin • MC5 • MDC • Medium Medium • Megadeth • The Mekons
Metallica • Mick Harvey • Mighty Lemon Drops • Minor Threat
Misfits • Mission of Burma • The Misunderstood • Mo-Dettes
The Modern Lovers • The Monochrome Set • Mulatu Astatke
My Bloody Valentine • The Names • Neil Young • Nektar • Neu!
The New Christs • New York Dolls • Nick Cave & the Bad Seeds
Nico • Nikki Sudden • Nova Mob • Oh-OK • Ol' Dirty Bastard
The Olivia Tremor Control • Opal • Orange Juice • Orechestre

Poly-Rythmo De Cotonou • Os Mutantes • Patti Smith • Payolas
Pere Ubu • Pete Rock & CL Smooth • Pixies • PJ Harvey
Poison Idea • The Pop Group • The Pretty Things • The Psychedelic Furs
Public Nuisance • Pylon • Queens of the Stone Age • R.E.M.
Radio Birdman • Radiohead • Rain Parade • The Raincoats
The Rapture • The Raveonettes • Reagan Youth • The Replacements
Revolting Cocks • Richard Hell & The Voidoids • Ride
Roky Erickson & the Aliens • The Rolling Stones • Rowland S.
Howard • Roxy Music • Sad Lovers & Giants • The Saints • Salvation
Army • Savage Republic • The Scientists • Scott Walker • Screaming
Trees • The Seeds • Serena Maneesh • Shane MacGowan & the Popes
Shocking Blue • Shop Assistants • Siouxsie & the Banshees • Slayer
The Slits • Small Faces • Smashing Pumpkins • The Smithereens
The Smiths • Social Distortion • The Soft Boys • Sonic Youth
Souls of Mischief • The Sound • Spacemen 3 • Spencer P. Jones
Spiritualized • The Stems • Stiff Little Fingers • The Stone Roses
The Stooges • Straitjacket Fits • Subhumans • Suburban Lawns
Suicidal Tendencies • Suicide • Supergrass • Swell Maps • T. Rex
T.S.O.L. • Talking Heads • The Teardrop Explodes • The Telescopes
Television • Television Personalities • That Petrol Emotion
Thee Headcoats • Thee Milkshakes • These Immortal Souls
Thin White Rope • Thrill of the Pull • Tom Verlaine • Tomorrow
The Triffids • True West • Tubeway Army • U.K. Subs • U2
The Undertones • United States of America • Vaselines
The Velvet Underground • The Verve • Vic Godard & The Subway Sect
The Wake • Wayne County & The Electric Chairs • The Wedding
Present • The Weirdos • Whipped Cream • Wild Swans • Wipers
Wire • Wolfgang Press • Wooden Shjips • The Wreckery
Wreckless Eric • Wu-Tang Clan • X • X-Ray Spex • XTC
Yo La Tengo • Youth Brigade • Zero Boys • Zounds
The 13th Floor Elevators • 100 Flowers ❖

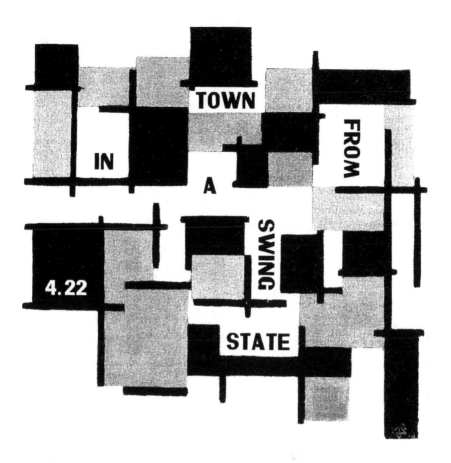

TOWN

IN

A

FROM

SWING

4.22

STATE

THESE DAYS, MY WORKWEEK STARTS ON TUESDAY. Even with two days off, I'm still exhausted. I get coffee and take a couple tourists downtown.

Immediately after dropping them off at the Omni, a request comes in. The pinned location is on the corner of 4th and Howard. Next to Moscone Center South. I drive down Howard looking for a guy named Walt with sandy hair. Nobody matching that description looks my way as I idle in the taxi lane. I call. Get voicemail. A taxi pulls up behind me. I circle back around and pull over in front of the convention center again. Nobody. Call again. This time he answers. I try to get his exact location. Says he's by the Moscone Center next to a small driveway. I turn onto 4th. Pull into what looks like a driveway. Nobody. Call again. He says he has a blue backpack. I circle back around. Still nobody. Then I spot him across the street on the northwest corner of 4th and Howard. He's with another guy. They are next to Moscone Center West. I notice badges hanging off the lanyards around their necks. Goddamn conventioneers.

Obviously unaware that there are two buildings at the convention center. One is South and the other is West. Those designations are important when picking somebody up on one-way streets during rushhour.

I'm in the left lane on Howard, west of 4th. I wait until all the traffic passes. Make an illegal maneuver I like to call the sneaky sidewinder and pull up next to the guys on the corner.

I apologize. Resist the urge to point out to them how to use the app.

They get in the back. I turn off the stereo.

"We're making two stops. First to the Hilton in Union Square, please. 333 O'Farrell."

I look up the address on Maps to get the cross street. Taylor. Perfect. I head down Howard. Turn left on 6th, which crosses Market and becomes Taylor.

Walt and his friend talk about the next presidential election. Say how much they'd like to see Ryan or Rubio take on Clinton.

"One of the advantages of living in a swing state like Wisconsin," Walt says. "My vote actually matters."

The other guy is from New York. He complains about how his state leans democrat because of NYC. "You get out of the city and everybody's republican, but the city makes up most of the votes."

"It's a shame."

I bite my tongue. I want so badly to say, You ever wonder why people who live in cities vote democrat? It's cause we actually deal with each other. We are exposed to poverty and suffering and the struggles of others. We don't live in suburban bubbles. When you're pushed up against other people, you learn some fucking empathy.

But I don't say anything. I can only imagine how bad it would be for my rating to spout off my liberal tendencies, even though I'm supposedly in one of the most enlightened cities in the world. Or one that used to be.

I drop off Mr. New York at the Hilton. Walt is going to the Tonga Room. I head up Taylor.

Walt asks me about Lyft. He is fascinated by Uber and Lyft. Thinks they could easily replace taxis, which he thinks have been regulated and unionized too much already.

"Lyft is capitalism at its best," I say. "Unregulated and outside the law. The government is always standing in the way of innovation! It's like they only exist to limit the advances in technology!"

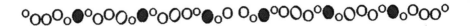

Oh yeah! I go off for a while until I worry my sarcasm is showing.

When I pull up in front of the Fairmont, Walt asks how to finish the ride. "This is my first Lyft."

I tell him, "Just add your review and click submit. Five stars, of course." I smile.

"Of course."

I give him a couple referral cards in case he knows anybody else who wants to sign up.

My next pick up is Spencer on Kearney and Columbus. I get honked at trying to change lanes in the intersection. Pull up next to a guy in front of a porno shop. He doesn't look at me. Wrong person. I call the passenger. Get voicemail. Turn the block for a second attempt. Nobody. Where the fuck are you, dude? Call again. This time he answers. He can't see me. I ask what he's wearing. Spot him across the street. I talk him through finding me.

"Turn around, look to your right... your other right."

Spencer gets in but doesn't put on the seat belt.

"Is that beeping for me?"

"The car doesn't like it when people don't use the seatbelt."

He's going to Folsom and a street between 7th and 8th. One of the glorified alleys that I can't seem to memorize.

He went to Tulane. We talk about cheap rents in New Orleans.

Drop him off across the street from a line of people waiting to get into a place with no sign. I look at a their faces. They don't seem excited about getting closer to whatever they're selling inside.

I drive towards North Beach. Get a request. Montgomery and Sutter. Guy in a suit. Andrew. Going to Marina.

"How do you like living in the Marina?"

"I don't live in the Marina!" he snaps.

I apologize. "I didn't mean to suggest..." I trail off because I don't want to dig a hole any deeper.

"It's alright," Andrew says. "I live in Hayes Valley."

"Oh, that's a great neighborhood. I have a friend who lives on Grove. It's gotten so expensive there..."

He tells me that his rent has just gone up $900.

I express outrage. "How can they just jack up your rent that much?"

"It's only twenty-five percent. We knew it was going to happen for a

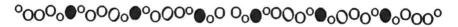

PACIFIC HEIGHTS
including THE MARINA and COW HOLLOW

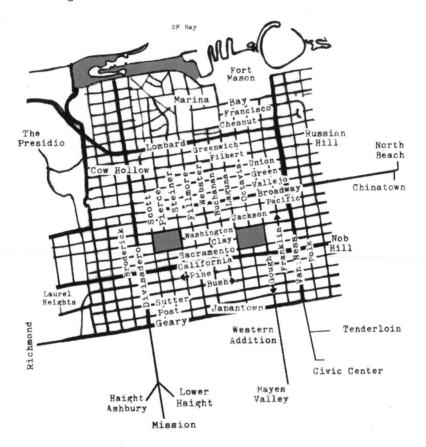

while. Our landlord warned us a year ago."

I do some quick math. He's been paying $3600 for a place in Hayes Valley. Now it's $4500.

"Still…" I can't fathom paying that much money for a place to live.

I drop Andrew off. Pick up Topher. Going to AT&T Park.

He's from Santa Cruz. Works in the peninsula. Says he and his girlfriend are only living in San Francisco for a year or so. "Just to check it out." Tells me that a lot of people who work in Silicon Valley live in Santa Cruz, since it's about the same distance from the tech campuses as San Francisco.

"San Francisco is cool, but it's too congested."

I agree. "It's a lot more congested than it used to be."

A REQUEST COMES IN. At the pinned location on New Montgomery, nobody is looking my way. Get out of traffic and pull into a loading zone a few spaces down. Call. No answer. Wait. Look around. After a few minutes three guys approach. They have a bunch of bags. I pop the trunk.

Two stops. Jeff and the other guy in back are going to Vinyl, a coffeeshop at Divisadero and Fulton. The guy up front is going to Turk and Masonic. They are unmistakably tech workers. They talk shop. Then weddings. Jeff is a Universal Life minister and performs weddings for his friends. Has one coming up.

"I was thinking of wearing Glass during the service so the couple can have a unique perspective."

After that, they discuss the new TV show *Silicon Valley*.

"It was all right," Jeff says. "It's done by Mike Judge, you know the guy who did Beavis and Butthead and Office Space. So you kind of know what you're getting into."

"My friend watched it with Zuck," his friend in back says.

"I actually thought it would be more harsh, since tech has become such a major sore spot here in San Francisco."

"I hear San Fran (sic) has lost its soul. I wouldn't know. I've only been here six months."

"I grew up in the Bay Area," Jeff says. "That's why I came back... to bring some soul back."

I try not to gag. Approach their destination. Pull to the corner. Jeff and the other guy get out.

" I HEAR SAN FRAN HAS LOST ITS SOUL. I WOULDN'T KNOW. I'VE ONLY BEEN HERE SIX MONTHS. "

The last guy makes idle chitchat with me about moving to San Francisco a month before. At his place on Turk, I pop the trunk so he can retrieve the bags. I've gotten good at remembering when passengers put things in the trunk and not just driving off while they yell after me. Shit like that has not been good for my rating. ❖

 Driver summary

Feedback

★★★★★ *60 ratings*

"Love him"

"His hair"

"Kelly told us the most beautiful love story ever. His marriage story is genius, you should ask him."

"RAD DUDE!!!!!!!!!!!!!!!!!!!!!"

"Thanks for being flexible and driving me to the airport!!"

"Great conversation - thanks for the awesome ride!"

"Yay! Kelly was awesome - super nice and fun to talk to!"

"Wonderful"

"Great car great driver great experience!!"

"Great smelling car"

"Awesome"

"Great ride and a great guy, Best driver I've had"

"Gray man at a good time!"

"Kelly is a literary ride"

★★★★ and below *4 ratings*

Past 100 ratings	Lifetime	Past week
Rating	**Rides**	**Accept rate**
✓ ★ **4.91**	**416**	✓ **100%**
Awesome		Awesome

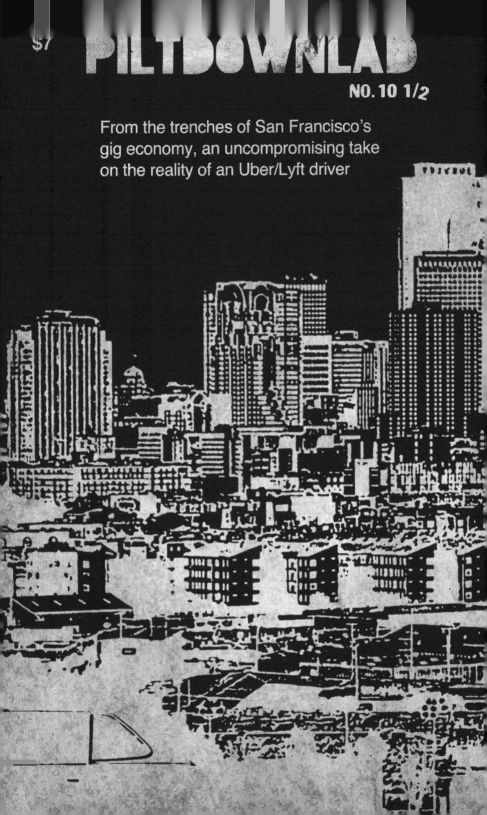

$7

PILTDOWNLAD

NO. 10 1/2

From the trenches of San Francisco's
gig economy, an uncompromising take
on the reality of an Uber/Lyft driver

BEHIND THE WHEEL 2

NOTES FROM AN UBER/LYFT

SECOND EDITION
REVISED AND UPDATED

PLTDNLD

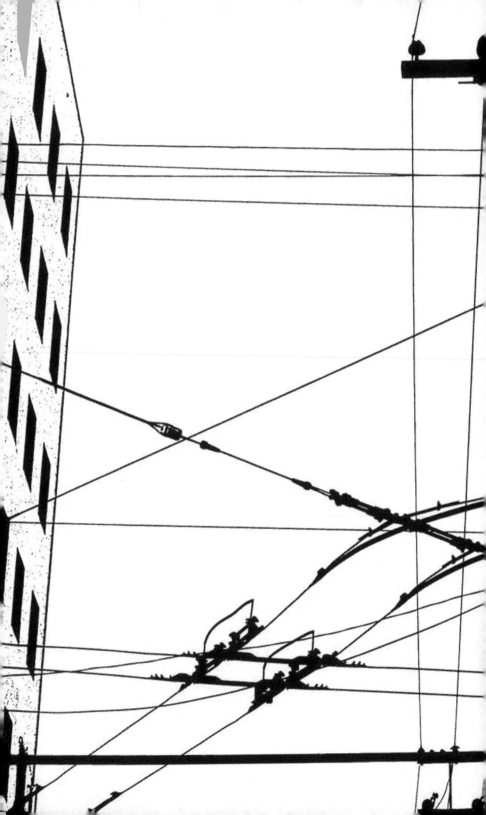

BEHIND THE WHEEL 2

NOTES FROM AN UBER/LYFT

Emperor Caveat • 99

To Uber or Not to Uber • 106

**A Day in the Life
of an Uber/Lyft Driver** • 116

The Wrong Bush and Mason • 126

Gun on the Street • 129

Top Ten Things I Get Asked • 137

For Whom the Uber Tolls • 140

The Other Uber Driver • 143

Peep Show for an Uber • 146

My Rating Weighs a Ton • 147

Infinite Douchebaggery • 149

The Polk Gulch Vortex • 155

The Chump • 158

Another Wasted Night • 159

The Leather Man • 166

My Uber Breaking Point • 170

PILTDOWNLAD #10.5

I DRIVE SF

All photos were taken by Irina from the passenger seat of our Jetta on a peaceful Thanksgiving afternoon in the city and digitally manipulated. Since this zine was originally released, some portions have appeared elsewhere: "To Uber or Not to Uber" was reprinted in *The Utne Reader*, "A Day in the Life of an Uber/Lyft Driver" was published on *Disinfo.com*, and part of "Emperor Caveat" appeared as "The Power Sex Couple" on *BrokeAssStuart.com*

Cover by Irina Dessaint

The events in this zine take place between May and November 2014.

EMPEROR CAVEAT

JULIA IS A **4.2.**

I accept the ride automatically, like I do with all my Uber requests. Just tap the flashing icon on my iPhone as quickly as possible before it expires. Don't even look at the passenger name. Too busy fighting traffic to reach the pinned location.

At a red light, I press the link in the Uber app that opens up the passenger info screen. That's when I notice Julia's rating. In the four months I've been driving for Uber, this is the worst passenger rating I've seen. Even though very few Uber passengers have five stars, they're usually around 4.8 or 4.7. So as I approach Hyde and O'Farrell, I can't help but wonder why Julia's previous drivers have rated her so low.

I pull into a bus stop. Hit the hazards and look around. Nobody in sight. Maybe that's the problem. I monitor all the Facebook groups for rideshare drivers and it's standard policy among commenters that making your driver wait longer than a minute will definitely cost you a star. In the Tenderloin, two stars. At least. I'm lucky I have a space to pull into. Otherwise I'd be double-parked in the flow of traffic, getting honked at by spiteful taxi drivers or possibly rear-ended by a disoriented tourist. I wait five minutes, watching the side mirrors in case a bus approaches. Just as I'm about to cancel the ride, my phone rings.

"We're on Jones, between Eddy and Turk. Uber messed up our address."

A likely story. Probably doesn't know how to use the damn app. Inputting the wrong pick up location is another way to lose a star.

"Okay. I'm right around the corner. See you in a sec."

Fortunately, I don't have to circle four blocks on the one-way streets downtown. Just take a left at Eddy and a right on Jones. Pull up behind a double-parked taxi. A woman and a man wave at me. I unlock the doors.

"Sorry about that," Julia says, as she slides across the back seat. The man climbs in next to her.

"No worries." I pull into traffic. Glance at the taxi driver eyeing me wearily. "The app can be a little janky at times."

"McCallister and Baker," the man tells me. "Do you need the exact address?"

"Nah. We'll sort it out when we get there."

I turn right onto Turk and head towards the Western Addition. I figure they'll give me the silent treatment. Like most Uber passengers. Which, in the ratings playbook, is another lost point.

"How's your night going so far?" the man asks.

"It's cool. How you guys doing?"

"We just came from the Power Exchange," he says.

"Oh yeah?"

"Do you know the Power Exchange?"

"A club?"

"A sex club," Julia says with a hint of derision.

I can't tell by her voice if she's telling me because they'd wandered in by mistake or on purpose. "Really?"

"Yeah. But it was lame," the man tells me. "We were the only couple there."

"Just lots of dudes jerking off," Julia says. "Following us around and asking if they could join in." She laughs. "It was so gross."

"There was that one woman giving a blowjob," the guy points out.

"Ugh. But she was so fat and the dude was covered in hair... I had to turn away."

At a stoplight, I glance in my rearview. They are an attractive couple. She's made up like a three-alarm fire and he's got the international man of mystery vibe down pat. In a club full of dudes looking to wank it to people having sex in public, I can see how they would be popular.

"Was this your first trip to a sex club?" I ask, since they seem inclined to converse and I'm curious.

"Oh yeah. And probably the last." Julia laughs.

"It's not like we were able to do anything," the man says. "Whenever we started making out, the guys would swarm."

"We left after twenty minutes," says Julia.

"I guess that was something we needed to experience so we'd never have to try again," the man tells her.

"I mean, if circumstances were different..."

"Oh, sure... but they'd have to be very different circumstances..."

Their voices go lower. It's obvious I'm no longer part of the discussion. I focus on driving. Watch for errant pedestrians and wobbling bicyclists. I tap my fingers on the steering wheel at the lights. The Pixies are playing on the iPod hardwired into my stereo, but the sound is barely perceptible. I keep the volume low and faded to the front speakers when I have passengers in the car. Nobody likes rock music anymore. It's all about deep house, EDM and dubstep, which I had to google after hearing the term mentioned constantly.

When I get close to the couple's location, I ask which street they're on, Baker or McCallister.

"Baker," Julia says. "About halfway down on the right. Next to that streetlight."

I pull over in front of an Edwardian apartment building and end the ride. "Have a good night."

"You too. Drive safe."

"Take care."

I rate her five stars. Like I do with all my passengers. Unlike most Uber drivers, I adhere to the philosophy: live by the rating, die by the rating.

Back online, I head towards Divisadero. Cruise past the cluster of restaurants and bars where taxi drivers linger. After a few minutes, I get a request for an address between Haight and Page. Another couple. They're ready to go when I pull up. Never even have a chance to look at the name or rating.

"How's your night going?" the girl asks.

"Not bad. What about you guys?"

"Just had dinner and drinks with some friends," says the guy.

"That's cool."

"Anything interesting happen so far tonight?" he asks.

"Well... I just drove a couple home from a sex club."

"The Power Exchange?"

"That's the one."

"Why do you know the name of a sex club?" The girl chuckles.

"It's well known," he responds defensively. "Used to be in SoMa. But they closed a couple years ago. I read that it opened up in the TL."

"You read..." She chuckles.

He laughs.

I laugh. I always do my best socializing with couples. I work well with an audience of two. I tell them the story of a passenger from the night before who'd just moved to San Francisco and got a place at 7th and Folsom, a week before the Folsom Street Fair. "So that was his first impression of the city."

They both laugh.

"What a way to get broken in," the man says. "If you're going to be in San Francisco, you have to be cool with a little public debauchery."

"I just overlook those things," the girl responds.

"I'm the same way," I tell her. "When I first moved here, I was living in North Beach. So yeah... There were drag shows, strip clubs and peep show joints everywhere—that was just part of life in North Beach. And I had a friend who practically lived at the old mom and pop jack shack on Kearney. He was always trying to get me to join him. Even paid my way a few times. But I just kept the quarters and never went into the booth. I was a prude in my younger years."

"Me too," she says.

"How long have you been in San Francisco?" the guy asks me.

"I first moved here in '94. Off and on since."

"That's a long time."

"I'm from LA, so, you know... San Francisco is the great escape."

"What part of the city do you live in?" the girl asks.

"I'm in Oakland now. Priced out of the city."

"Oakland's great. What part?" she asks.

"Temescal."

"Temescal's really cool. You have all those restaurants and shops on Telegraph... Do you know Burma Superstar?"

"I live right behind Burma Superstar."

"Don't you just love that place?"

"I've never eaten there. But my bedroom window faces the back door of the restaurant. I can smell the food all the time. Our life is deeply intertwined with deliveries, smoke breaks and the dishwashers taking out the trash..."

"Oakland is supposed to be San Francisco's Brooklyn," the guy says.

"That's what they say. I've never been to Brooklyn, so..."

"I love Oakland," the girl says. "Such a cool city. Lots of diversity."

"Everything San Francisco has lost is in Oakland now."

"Sometimes just going to Target feels like being at Burning Man," I joke. "Still, it's not San Francisco."

"It's cheaper."

"Not for much longer. The rents in our building have gone up eight-hundred dollars since we moved in a year ago. We're basically living in a construction zone. Whenever a tenant moves out the landlady renovates the apartment and raises the rent. They've been working on the building about half the time we've been there. The unit above us is almost finished but another tenant is moving out at the end of the month."

"Seems like the only people who can afford to live in the Bay Area anymore are the ones who haven't moved in ten years."

"I know. The wife and I moved too much. We made some bad decisions when it came to choosing an apartment. We were subletting a place on Capp Street from a friend. She moved to LA because she was madly in love. We knew there was always a chance she'd want her apartment again, but when we had an opportunity to rent this giant studio in Noe Valley for $1125, we thought, Noe Valley? That's the land of the strollers and brunch crowd. I can't be around a bunch of kids. I have an uncontrollable tendency to shout profanities in public. So we passed on it. Then, a few months later the girl we were subletting from fell madly OUT of love with the guy in LA and came back to San Francisco."

"Sucks."

"Yeah, and that's how you end up in Oakland."

I drop them off and cruise through the Mission, waiting for another request. I fill in the holes of the story I just told in my head. So it will seem more convincing the next time I tell it. I don't know why I'm compelled to lie to my passengers. Perhaps I'm bored of relating the same facts and circumstances over and over. Hopped up on Ativan and Philz coffee, I spend most of my time behind the wheel biting my lip while the people in my backseat carry on conversations. When I do get a chance to talk, it's hard not to unleash a flurry of repressed chatter. Besides asking me how I like driving for Uber, passengers want to know where I live. How long I've been in the city. Where I'm from. Most people I have conversations with haven't been in San Francisco more than a year or two. I get a kick out of telling them about the city in the nineties, when the rents were cheap and the city was actually diverse. But the majority of my stories are not my own. They're based on those I've heard from long-term residents. I can't help but invent a narrative that fits in with the gentrification, displacement and overall cultural shift that's going on

in San Francisco during this latest tech boom. As the ramifications of these changes come to a boiling point, it's a story everybody seems to anticipate. So I perpetuate it.

Since I know the city well from driving its streets and alleyways, I easily come off as a native. And I learn more about the geography and the history each day I'm here. I absorb everything I can about the city. I have no intention of representing myself as some aboriginal San Franciscan, but I'm only around these people five, ten, fifteen minutes tops. That's not enough time to reveal anything authentic about my life anyway.

There is some veracity to my narrative. I really did live here for a while in the nineties. That part is true. I stayed at the Green Tortoise rent free in exchange for three hours of light cleaning five days a week. I spent the rest of my time wandering the streets of the city on foot because I didn't have enough money to take the bus. I sold a little pot and acid to the foreign backpackers at the hostel to make some pocket change for food.

And the Wife and I did consider a friend's studio in Noe Valley around 2009 who was getting serious about a guy in LA. (The Mission apartment was where we housesat for another friend while she was at Burning Man.) Noe Valley wasn't an ideal location, but the real deal breaker was a job. At the time the Wife was working as a contractor for Disney Publishing on an English Language learning program. Just as we were thinking about moving up north, they offered her a fulltime position with a salary you don't walk away from. Not at the height of a global economic crisis. So we gave up on San Francisco. Got a loft in downtown LA. Bought a car. Drove up to San Francisco every chance we could.

A few years went by and then, last September, Disney decided to kill the program. The Wife was laid off and we went back to our original plan to move to San Francisco. Not the smartest decision, given the massive influx of tech workers and subsequent gentrification of every neighborhood in the city.

Looking through Craigslist ads, it became clear right away that we couldn't afford anything in San Francisco. Median rents were around three thousand dollars for a one-bedroom. Tiny studios in the Tenderloin were going for eighteen hundred. There was just no way we could squeeze all our junk and three cats into four hundred square feet. Plus, we had the car. It wasn't even paid off yet. Instead we ended up in Temescal, an up-and-coming neighborhood in North Oakland.

Prior to our move, neither of us had spent much time in Oakland. We drove up one weekend to explore. Stayed at a motel by the airport. In the morning, we went from one end of town to the other. The downtown/ Lake Merritt neighborhood sort of reminded us of downtown LA, but on a much smaller scale. From there we kept going up Telegraph, through the Uptown and Kono neighborhoods until we stumbled upon Temescal. It was obvious from the punk show flyers on the telephone poles, the thrift stores, funky restaurants, coffeehouses and bike shops that we'd found the Silver Lake/Echo Park of Oakland.

We started calling landlords and looking at apartments. Over the next few weeks, we drove back and forth from LA to Oakland trying to find something in our budget. There weren't many available rentals under $1500 a month. Most didn't allow pets or charged pet rent. In our quest for a place that fit our budget, we didn't rule out Berkeley. We even looked at a few apartments on Alameda. But we preferred Temescal. So when the landlord of a small one-bedroom in a Victorian on Shattuck offered us the place without even running a credit check, we forked over the deposit on the spot.

As soon as we got back to LA, we started planning the big move. Based on some rudimentary calculations, our expenses would remain pretty much the same as they were in LA. To supplement the Wife's un-employment checks, I planned to use our 2010 Volkswagen Jetta to drive for the rideshare company Lyft. As least until I found something better.

According to the Facebook ads, Lyft drivers were making up to forty bucks an hour. Of course, once I started driving regularly, I realized that rate doesn't factor in gas, car payment, maintenance, upkeep, wear and tear, insurance, bridge tolls and other expenses. Like the occasional traffic ticket. Or taxes, since driving for Lyft is a 1099 gig. In reality, it's more like fifteen an hour. At best. Still, better than minimum wage. Or what they pay at Trader Joe's and Kinko's. For three months, I did Lyft. And then I found another opportunity to monetize the underutilized seats in my car. ■

TO UBER OR NOT TO UBER

I STARTED SEEING THE ADS ON FACEBOOK AROUND THE FIRST OF MAY:

Drive away with $500—Exclusively for Lyft Drivers

**Drive for Lyft? Make $500 for trying UberX
All it takes is one trip.**

Sign up today!

There was even a pink mustache in the ads. So I knew they were legit. I didn't click right away though. There's nothing easy about easy money.

But the ads keep popping up in my feed two or three times a day. Out of curiosity, I click the link. I'm redirected to the UberX sign-up page. I check to see if my car qualifies. I've always assumed Uber is more selective than Lyft about what models and years qualify for their rideshare service UberX. Before I signed up for Lyft, I'd checked out Uber's site. I remember seeing something about them only taking Priuses. Either I was mistaken or things have changed, because my Jetta totally qualifies.

Still, I don't sign up. The offer is valid through May 31. Since I'm going to LA for my mother-in-law's birthday in the middle of the month, I figure I have enough time before the deal ends. Besides, with how many ads are popping up on my feed, they seem desperate for drivers.

I've always been curious about driving for Uber. Mainly because I hate Lyft's pink mustache. Even though I never attached the thing to the grill of my car or placed it on my dashboard, where it looks like what you'd find on the floor after a furry convention, I generally feel it would be helpful to have something on my car to indicate that I work for a rideshare. Especially when trying to find drunk passengers on crowded streets at night. Uber drivers use a subtle neon blue "U" that illuminates elegantly from their windshields. They look classier. I wouldn't mind putting that symbol on my car.

I've also heard they make more money. One night, while waiting outside The Box on Natoma for my order, I chatted with an UberX driver. He told me he used to drive for Lyft but switched to Uber. Now he's making almost twice the money he did with Lyft. "I get so many requests," he said, "I had to go offline in the Mission to get here before they close."

Since Lyft lowered their rates thirty percent in April, I'm making $200 less a week, driving the same hours. Flush with 250 million dollars in venture capital, Lyft is trying to compete with Uber for a larger cut of the rideshare market. To offset the price cut, they waived the twenty percent commission. At first, demand increased and Prime Time surge pricing made up the difference. But that didn't last long. Since then, the price cuts are having a serious impact on my bottom line. I try to work more to make up the difference, but I can only go so long before exhaustion sets in and I no longer feel safe behind the wheel.

Around the first of the month, when rent is due, things are especially hard. At one point, before the price wars, I stopped getting emails from my credit card company warning me that I was approaching my credit limit. These days, I receive those messages daily. Along with low balance notifications from Bank of America. There are weeks when I can't afford to buy gas until I get my deposit from Lyft on Wednesdays. I go through about $35 of gas during a normal six-hour shift. On Friday and Saturday nights, I used to make around $200 to $250 dollars. Now it's about $150. If there's an event going on, I can hit $200. Weeknights, I make around $100. Tops. Since I spend about the same on gas, I stopped driving during the week to focus on the weekends instead, when there's generally more demand and Prime Time.

As appealing as Uber sounds, I still have reservations about signing up. Based on numerous articles I've read, Uber seems like an unscrupulous company, along the lines of Wal-Mart or Amazon. And Travis Kalanick, the CEO, comes across as an antisocial, libertarian scumbag who'd stab his own mother in the back to get ahead. Probably has a cum-stained paperback of *The Fountainhead* under his pillow that he strokes gently as he falls asleep at night. The name of the company itself, Uber, implies more about the megalomania of Kalanick than the service they provide. And this whole campaign to recruit Lyft drivers is beyond unethical. Participating in it feels wrong. I keep asking myself, Do I really want to associate myself with a company run by a guy who longs for the days of driverless cars so he can get rid of the "middle man," i.e., drivers?

My other concern is the Uber gestalt. Even though they perform the exact same service, Lyft and Uber offer different experiences.

Lyft promotes their drivers as "Your Friend with a Car." Passengers ride up front. Like a friend. Drivers are supposed to greet passengers with a fist bump. Like they would, conceivably, with a friend. Drivers play music and engage the passenger in conversation. Since that's what friends do.

In contrast, Uber's motto is "Your Personal Driver." Passengers ride in the back. They tell you where to go and, after that, there's no implied interaction. Unless the passenger wants to talk, Uber drivers are expected to maintain that invisible barrier between them and the "client."

My Lyft passengers talk to me about Uber all the time. Most people in San Francisco use both apps, depending on price surging, availability or the kind of experience they're in the mood for. I've had numerous passengers tell me that if they're going to work, or in work mode, they take Uber so they don't have to deal with any annoying conversations. But on the weekends, when they're going out, they take Lyft because it's more fun.

I imagine I've talked to, or at least tried to talk to, every taxi driver I've ever had. Unless I was unconscious. If I'm confined in a small space for longer than a minute with a stranger, I can't help but start a conversation.

I can usually make it through an elevator ride, but at stores, I talk to cashiers. At restaurants, I chat with waiters. At bars, if things are quiet, bartenders. On buses and trains, my fellow passengers. I'm a compulsive talker. So as I contemplate the move to Uber, I'm more than a little nervous about whether I can contain my incessant need to gab.

A FEW WEEKS BEFORE THE END OF THE MONTH, I complete the Uber application.

The next day, I receive an email directing me to upload my documents to the Uber website. I scan my license and registration. Send them in. Fill out my background check. Wait. Get a message about emailing a screenshot of my most recent pay statement from Lyft. Send that in. Wait. On May 22nd, I get a text from Uber. My account is active. They're going to send me a phone with the Uber drive app in the mail. I provide my address.

While I wait for my phone, I continue driving for Lyft. One night, in the Richmond, I get a request for an address off Geary. As I idle in front of the pinned location, an UberX car pulls up next to me. He nods in my direction. Both our windows are down.

"What's up?" I ask. "You here for Cathy as well?"

He looks at his phone and says absently, "Yeah."

"Maybe there's a party and they need more than one car," I say, hoping there wasn't a mistake and Cathy hadn't accidentally ordered two cars from different platforms. It's happened before.

"Do you drive for Uber as well?" the guy asks me.

"I signed up for that $500 deal. Just waiting for the phone."

"Oh." He seems disappointed. "I get $500 for referring drivers. Maybe I can check and see if you still qualify for my referral."

At that moment, Cathy cancels the ride. I go offline. "Sure."

He gets out of his car. Hands me his phone. I type in my number and hand it back.

"That's cool Uber gives you an iPhone," I say.

"You can't do anything with it besides run the Uber app though." He shows me the error message on his phone. "The referral didn't work."

"Sorry."

"Worth a shot…"

"Yeah. Well, Cathy seems to have cancelled," I tell him. "Gonna see if I can get another ride before heading back downtown. Good luck!"

I CONTINUE WAITING FOR MY UBER PHONE. It's been almost two weeks since I signed up. The days go by fast as May 31st approaches and the end of the $500 deal looms.

On May 28th, I email Uber about not receiving a phone yet. I receive a message telling me to visit the office on Vermont in Potrero Hill to pick one up. The next day, I head into the city early.

I'm not sure what I expected the office for a rideshare start-up to look like—maybe some folding tables, Ikea desks and chairs, laptops and interns—but I wasn't expecting a circus.

On the corner of Vermont and 16th, there is a sign twirler. I'm momentarily confused because the sign he's twirling seems to be advertising Lyft. His shirt matches the baby blue sign and reads, "$500 and a taco."

I wonder if Lyft and Uber have offices right next to each other.

Directly across the street, under the raised 101 freeway, hanging on a chainlink fence, is a blue banner: "Be more than a number." In the corner is the Lyft logo. As I try to orient myself, a billboard truck rolls by, also in the Lyft colors. "Be more than a number." On the other side: "Get $500 and a taco."

For a second, I think I'm being set up. I knew the deal sounded too good to be true!

On the sidewalk, a group of people are milling around a crowd control barrier. I know from the endless stream of texts I've received from Uber since first signing up that they're hosting referral events for Lyft drivers. Offering $500 and a free lunch.

So Lyft is making a counteroffer of $500 and a taco to any Uber drivers who want to switch to their side. I guess they figure if Uber can poach their drivers, why not play dirty too. But a taco?

Whatever. I keep my head down and stay focused on what I need to accomplish.

Nothing on the front of the building indicates that it's Uber HQ. Just a black awning with the street number, a tinted glass door and a buzzer.

I press the button. A guy with "security" embroidered on a black polo shirt emerges.

I tell him about signing up for Uber but not receiving a phone yet.

He looks confused.

"I can get a phone here, right?" I ask.

"You need to come back tomorrow between nine and twelve."

"I can't get one now?"

"No."

I look at the crowd on the sidewalk. The security guard disappears inside the building. Alright.

I head to Philz for coffee before starting my shift. It's a typical Thursday night Lyfting. Drive a couple to the church that's been converted into a skating rink at Fillmore and Oak. An older couple from North Carolina who introduce themselves as the "Doug and Flo Show!" Take a punk girl to Ingleside. Before I pick her up, I can tell from her profile pic that she's going to be a cool ride. We listen to Subhumans and Buzzcocks as we cruise down 280. Her dog climbs onto the center console to be a part of the conversation. We talk gentrification. Of course.

I call it quits around eleven.

The next morning, I get out of bed as early as I can. A pathetic 10:30. Skip a shower for coffee and a few cigarettes. Then race into the city. I leave Oakland at 11:15 and reach Potrero Hill with twenty minutes to spare. The sign twirler is gone, but the banners are still up. A few people are standing around the taco truck in the parking lot behind the fence.

I press the button at Uber HQ. A different security guard comes out.

"Yes?"

"Hey, I need to get a phone. I came yesterday and they told me to come back today before noon."

"Who said that?"

"I don't know."

"You don't know their name?"

"No. I just need to get a phone."

He hesitates for a moment. "Okay. Sign in on the tablet."

I climb a flight of stairs. At the top is an iPad attached to a metal pole. After typing in my name and phone number, take a seat at one of several folding tables with nine other drivers. I sit down next to a heavyset woman. She asks if I'm a Lyft driver as well. I say yes.

"I need to get a phone before the $500 deal is up," I tell her.

"I'm a Lyft mentor. So I get $1000. I'm going to do my one ride and that's it."

"You're not switching over to Uber?"

"Oh no!" she whispers loudly and leans in close. "I love Lyft. I just want the $1000." She smiles as she sits back in her seat.

The other drivers are all men. Huddled together like compatriots. They're older. Professional. I wonder if they're taxi drivers converting to Uber.

"How long have you been waiting?" I ask the woman.

"About half an hour. The guys over there have been here longer."

A few minutes later, the door buzzer goes off. The security guard tells the person they're closed for the day. It's five minutes to noon. I'm the last in line.

I glance around the room as the woman chats at me about her frustrations with maintaining a high rating despite always offering her customers candy and water.

"I had five stars for the first few months. That's how I got to be a mentor. Since then, my rating's gone down and I don't get as many mentor requests."

"That sucks."

There are five guys and one girl working for Uber. All wearing polo shirts and jeans. There seems to be a distinct look to the Uber employee: white and preppy. I can't help but wonder if they're bummed to be dealing with us drivers. They all have an air of indignation and fear. One guy is walking around like he's pretending to be busy. The girl is filling Uber swag bags with paperwork and U window lights. Another guy is arranging boxed lunches on a table. He gives one to the security guard who takes a seat next to me. The meal actually looks rather substantial. A sandwich, a bag of chips, some pasta salad and a can of soda. Not a bad spread. Better than a taco.

Slowly, the drivers are called to a desk where a guy in a yellow polo shirt meticulously inputs their information into a MacBook. The process takes forever though, as if he was working on an ancient IBM with a bad dial-up connection. Once he finishes adding the drivers to the system, or whatever he's doing up there, he hands them an iPhone. Asks if they have any questions. Some do. He seems to cringe and roll his eyes before each explanation.

At one point, he stops calling any new drivers up to his desk and gets a boxed lunch. There are still about five of us in line. We all watch as eats and clicks away on his laptop. Maybe checking his Facebook. Or sending a tweet.

I feel like taking abstract pictures with my phone of the empty moving boxes and scattered office furniture. It's obvious they just moved into the space. Which is probably a former showroom or an office for a design firm. Seeing as how we're in Showcase Square. Or what's left of it.

Fifteen minutes later, the guy in the yellow polo starts calling up drivers again.

Just as my phone is about to die, I finally get called to his desk. I've barely sat down when he gets up and says, "I'll be right back."

At this point, it's just me and the Uber people in the office. I watch a guy dealing with a massive stack of white iPhones. There must be a thousand phones.

"That's a lot of phones," I say.

"Yeah."

I watch as he attaches them to a MacBook.

"I wipe the content and download the Uber app," he responds.

Another guy looks out the window. "The sign twirler's back."

A few of the Uber folk snicker.

"Has this been going on for a while?" I ask.

"Since we started the recruitment campaign," the phone guy tells me.

"Crazy…" I say.

"What do they care anyway?" a guy wonders. "It's not like you can't drive for both."

The guy in the yellow polo returns to the desk. "Nobody's going for the tacos," he says. "I bet they're all green and moldy."

I laugh along with the Uber workers.

"They're so desperate, it's hilarious."

Hahahaha.

"Lyft is so stupid."

"Why don't they just die already!"

Hahahaha.

We're all having a jolly ole time ripping on Lyft.

"And that pink mustache is hideous," I add.

Hahahaha.

"It's so ugly, I've never even put it on my car."

"I don't blame you," says the guy at the window.

By the time he hands me the phone so I can enter my phone number into the Uber app, we're all good buds.

"Now you have to take a photo."

"Right now?"

"You can do it later, but… here, let me take one with the iPad. It'll come out better."

He has me stand against a wall. I take off my glasses. Slouch down a little since he's shorter than me.

"Did it come out alright?" I ask. "In my Lyft photo, I look like a girl."

"It's fine."

"As long as I don't look like a girl…"

"You don't look like a girl." He shows it to me.

I kind of look like a girl.

"You want some lunch?" He gestures at the table of boxed lunches.

"Nah, I'm cool."

Outside, the line of drivers waiting to sign up is longer. The sign twirler is doing back flips as he throws the sign up into the air and catches it between his legs. Lyft really hired a professional. Not just some street person in a costume. I walk past and he smiles at me.

Holding the Uber swag bag, I feel like apologizing.

Across the street, a few more people are lined up around the taco truck. I head across the bridge to get ready for a Friday night driving in the city.

THAT EVENING, after getting coffee, I turn on the Uber app in SoMa. The interface is entirely different from Lyft. It takes me a few minutes to get a handle on how the process works when a request comes in. Lyft's interface is square. Uber's is round. I touch the screen like I do with Lyft. But the Uber app only gives me a name in a very small font and an address with an icon on the map. The screen of the Lyft app is much bigger. Easier to read. The passenger is designated with a blue pin and the driver's avatar is the silhouette of the front of a car. On the Uber app, the passenger looks like a chess piece. There's no Facebook profile pic. So I don't know what the person I'm picking up looks like. There are also no turn-by-turn directions to the pinned location. I have to zoom in to see where I need to go.

While I'm trying to figure out the app, my personal phone rings. Some weird number in Ohio. I ignore it.

I finally see my passenger is on Townsend. I'm only half a block away. As I cruise down the street slowly, a man and woman wave me down.

"You drove past us twice," she says. "I tried calling you."

"Oh, that was you? Sorry. This is my first Uber ride," I tell them.

They are nice. They sit in the back, as expected. But they're chatty. I tell them about the $500 deal.

"So this ride just made me five hundred bucks."

We talk about the two different services. The guy only uses Uber but the girl takes both, depending on her mood.

"Are you from Ohio?" I ask.

"No, we're from New York."

"Oh." The number that came through... that must be Uber's generic number. But why is the area code is set in Ohio? That's weird. Lyft's is 415. Which makes more sense.

I drop them off. They congratulate me on becoming an Uber driver and making five hundred dollars.

I do a few more Uber rides. It's hard not to keep going. The requests come in one after another. It's obvious Uber is much busier that Lyft. But the disconnect is palpable. Everybody sits in back. After that first couple, nobody else says a word to me. They tell me where they're going and stare at their phones. I even pull my passenger seat forward to give them more legroom. Turn off the stereo.

Unlike the Lyft app, when I end a ride, I can see how much it costs. I'm impressed by the numbers. I know I have to subtract Uber's twenty-percent cut, but still... I like what I'm seeing.

After awhile, the silent treatment gets to me and I switch back to Lyft.

I'm actually relieved when the next passenger sits up front. We have a lively conversation about my Uber experience, going to the office, the stack of phones, the sign twirlers, the tacos and how I just earned five hundred bucks.

"I wouldn't say it was an easy five hundred bucks," I tell him.

"Well, there's nothing easy about easy money," he says.

"Ain't that the truth..." ■

A DAY IN THE LIFE OF AN UBER/LYFT DRIVER

MOST DAYS, I wake up around noon. Usually hung-over. My first thought is always the same: probably should've skipped that last drink. At the time, though, it felt absolutely necessary. Vodka has a way of alleviating some of the physical stress from driving a car all night. At least temporarily.

After several months of driving for Lyft and Uber, my neck is like an open wound. The muscles that run from my shoulder to my jaw are steel rods. I have very little radius when I turn my head left or right. The tension never goes away. It makes my teeth ache. There is a real possibility that I have some dislocated vertebrae. My joints hurt. My right ankle has a creak in it. And I have a chronic case of hemorrhoids. No matter how much ointment I apply, they remain perpetually enflamed. Old age has not only crept up on me, it has run past me and turned around to taunt me.

Besides the physical exhaustion of driving a car in the city, there is also the psychological toll. It's one thing to maintain a diligent eye on my blind spots, the other cars on the road, speeding bicyclists and cavalier pedestrians, but I also have to project a sunny disposition and be accommodating to my passengers. Or risk a negative rating. Not an easy task when I'd rather be committing murder. And yet, with enough Ativan and caffeine in my system, somehow I make it through another shift. Like when the endorphins kick in after a boot to the nut sack, these superficial interactions with complete strangers have a numbing effect after awhile. As long as it's busy and I have enough rides to keep my mind off the grueling process. The slow nights can be torture and I can't wait to get home so I can pummel my brain with alcohol, pills and weed until I stop obsessing over the streets of San Francisco, their order and how they intersect with each of the forty-seven neighborhoods.

My confidence with getting around the city has improved, but my memory is still sketchy at times. This morning I woke up from a dream where I was in the Richmond District and couldn't remember if Fulton was north or south of the park. I lay there half-conscious, certain it ran along the north side of the park, but still checked the map on my iPhone through blurry eyes, just to be sure.

My unconscious plays tricks on me all the time. Another side effect of working until three in the morning. But those are the peak hours for driving rideshare. Even though I'm not an early-riser by nature, I've tried driving during the day. The gridlocked traffic makes getting anywhere in the city such a chore, that it's not worth the frustration. I spend more time driving to the pinned locations than I do taking passengers where they want to go. So I keep driving nights, hoping I'll eventually get used to the schedule.

After opening my eyes and committing to consciousness, I check my email to see if my Lyft daily summary has shown up yet. Sometimes it's in my inbox before I wake up. Other days the email doesn't arrive until the afternoon. These summaries are the only way to find out how much I made the night before driving for Lyft, whether I got any tips and what's happened to my rating. With Uber you know, for the most part, what you've made when you end the ride. And your rating is updated in the app as feedback is left. So at least you're disappointed in real time.

It's soul crushing when my rating takes a dive. I spend my first waking moments wracking my brain trying to figure out what could have gone wrong with my rides the night before. It's not easy making people happy. Even when the ride has gone perfectly, there's never a guarantee that the passenger is satisfied.

After I finally get out of bed, I make coffee and feed the herd of starving cats screaming at my feet. Then a smoke. More coffee. Another smoke. More coffee. Repeat until I'm able to face the day.

I usually don't leave the house until the afternoon. If I'm feeling ambitious, I might leave around three or four. But usually it's closer to five. On the weekends, when I drive until three in the morning, I take off at six. I used to try and make it across the bridge before the toll increases, but I've since given up on saving the extra two dollars.

Before I walk out the door, I go through my mental checklist to make sure I haven't forgotten anything: water, cigarettes, lighter, pills, wallet, house keys, car key, phone and hoodie. Kiss the Wife. Shout an obscenity at the Calico as she tries to sneak through the open door.

Outside, I dust the freeway grime off the car, clean the windows, shake out the floorboard mats and wipe down the seats. A black car is horrible for maintaining an unsullied appearance. Once I've got it looking presentable, I adjust my accoutrements, clip my phone mount and the air freshener to the A/C vents and plug in the charger.

There's usually somebody lined up to take my parking space. People going to the restaurants on Telegraph circle the side streets looking for a place to park from noon to midnight. Sometimes a driver will try to get my attention. Ask if I'm leaving. I just ignore him. Take my sweet time pulling out.

I'm only ten miles from downtown San Francisco. But it can be an epic journey depending on traffic. Since I drive into the city during rush hour, it takes me over half an hour. On a good day. Sometimes, the commute is a grueling fifty minutes. I keep the stereo volume up high.

As I approach the congestion of the I-580 interchange, the first pangs of anxiety hit me. Bay Area traffic is the worst. In my list of grievances with Bay Area drivers, the inability to merge ranks at the top. To be fair, the concept of two lanes of traffic merging into one is mind-boggling no matter what city you drive in. Even though there is a basic rule: one car from one lane, one car from the other lane. Like folding cards into a deck. This method keeps the flow of traffic moving and ensures everybody gets where they're going without creating complete chaos. But while drivers in other cities manage to screw this up, I've never seen cars perpendicular to traffic in a merge lane until I started driving in the

Bay Area. East Bay drivers in particular seem to treat them as a free-for-all. And nobody respects a solid line. I'm constantly shouting over the stereo, "A solid line means you don't change lanes, assholes!"

On the I-80 overpass, I get my first glimpse of the San Francisco skyline. Depending on the height of the clouds and the sunlight, sometimes it seems like I can reach out and poke my finger on the top of the Golden Gate Bridge. Other times it's hidden behind the wall of fog hovering behind the city like a frozen wave.

At the toll plaza, I'm eternally grateful to have a FasTrak. Coming up with the cash each day was a real hassle, not to mention the long lines of cars waiting to hand over their money. But I'm always hot with FasTrak. Can't remember the last time I got a "Valid FasTrak" notice on the screen. I usually get "Low Balance" or "Call FasTrak," which means my account is overdrawn and there'll be another toll violation letter in the mail soon.

After the toll plaza, I begin the ascent onto the new eastern span. There's always some kind of repair work going on as Caltrans tries to fix the construction errors from the original contractor. Each week, a little bit less of the old cantilever bridge is gone as they disassemble it the same way they constructed it seventy-five years ago. Mindful of the cars in front of me, I look out over the water at the mysterious barges that float in the middle of the bay. Traffic on the bridge has a way of grinding to a complete standstill without warning. Especially as we approach the

narrow tunnel through Yerba Buena Island.

On the western span, the view of the city is epic. No matter how many times I've crossed this bridge since first visiting San Francisco twenty years ago, seeing the city spread out on the hills along the bay reminds me why I want to be here so badly.

Straight ahead, on the mountain next to Twin Peaks, Sutro Tower looks out over the city like a sentinel with his hands up in disbelief.

Among the skyscrapers downtown, cranes fill the open spaces. The new buildings grow a little taller each day. I anticipate a glimpse of the Utah Hotel on my left—that gorgeous Victorian anomaly on 4th Street surrounded by the box-shaped condos that have risen up around it.

South of downtown, in the midst of the rolling landscape littered with houses, there is a yellow hill with a few green trees on top, like a jaundiced balding man's head. This is my destination. Bernal Heights. I keep an eye on that hill as I slowly wind my way through rush hour traffic. Bumper to bumper.

Along the raised freeway, billboards advertise tech companies and services like the "world's fastest incentive compensation solution." I'm actually relieved to see one for a new movie release or car insurance.

As I approach the 101 interchange, I pass the 888 Brannon building. Headquarters to major tech firms like Pinterest and Airbnb. There was a time I assumed the room filled with toys and other objects in primary colors on the top floor was a romper room. I thought it was cool these companies had a daycare for the children of their employees. Then I quickly realized this is no doubt a romper room FOR the employees.

I drive over Showcase Square, past the Zynga building, once a cluster of warehouses for artisans and designers. Now it's start-up territory as the design firms are squeezed out of a part of town nobody gave two shits about a few years ago. Despite the boundless affluence behind the brick facades, the streets beneath the freeway are still full of homeless encampments, derelict RVs and destitute men pushing shopping carts full of empty cans towards the local recycling center.

As I approach the I-80/101 transition, I leave enough room in front of me to allow the cars entering the freeway some leeway. Look in my rearview. Some dickhead in a BMW is on my ass cause I'm not going fast enough. Fuck you! Merge, you cocksucker! Merge!

And then, like getting the checkered flag, traffic opens up on the Hospital Curve and it's a race to the finish line: the Cesar Chavez exit, where I fight to get into the right lane so I can turn onto Harrison Street.

Finding a parking place in the Mission is never easy. I'm competing with the local residents and people going to the trendy restaurants and bars. Except I'm happy to park several blocks away. It gives me time to smoke a cigarette and accept the absurdity of what I'm doing.

I've been going to the same coffeehouse for several months and have become friendly with the baristas. If Brian is working, we'll chat.

In the new San Francisco, the only people I see anymore who look remotely interesting are baristas and bartenders. Occasionally, I spot an old rocker dude walking down the street, decked out in tight black jeans and a leather jacket. And think, they must have amazing rent control.

After getting coffee, I smoke another cigarette on my way back to the car. Make sure the volume is turned up on my phone. Go online.

I usually start my day in Lyft mode. Even though Uber is more profitable, I prefer the conversational aspect of Lyft. With Uber, I feel like a servant. Unless there are more than three people, most passengers sit in back, tell me they're destination and then stare at their phones the entire trip. Some folks chat. But the norm is silent rides. Reticent passengers are so common that even when it's just me in the car, sometimes I'll look behind me just to make sure there's nobody there.

A good percentage of Lyft passengers also sit in back and refrain from conversing, but with Uber it's endemic. And forcing a conversation feels weird. Occasionally, I'll glance in my rearview and see them looking in my direction. But what do I say? If something happens on the road, I'll make a comment. If that doesn't lead anywhere, I don't push it. When I get close to a destination, I ask specifics. End the ride. Unlock the doors. Say, "Have a good day/night." Then, in my most sincere tone, "Take care." Which is my standard closer. It's proven to be an effective way to leave things with passengers. Especially the silent ones. My way of exuding respect and bonhomie.

While I always rate my passengers five stars, not all my passengers have been as generous. After six months of driving for Lyft, my rating is a paltry 4.85. My Uber rating is better: 4.93. But I haven't been driving for Uber as long. No doubt it'll sink lower as I do more rides.

Of course, this validates the Wife's theory that my Lyft rating is low because I talk too much and don't have a filter. "You can freak some people out," she tells me when I complain about my rating. "You have a tendency to rant and say crazy shit. For most people, you're a four star driver at best." But I like talking. So I keep doing Lyft.

MY FIRST PING OF THE DAY IS ON FLORIDA STREET. Near 16th Street. One of those old warehouses converted into offices for tech start-ups. Two guys approach my car. One gets in the front seat.

"4th and Townsend," says the guy in back who matches the profile on my phone. "Take a right at 16th, left at Potrero, right onto Division, through the roundabout to Townsend."

"Are you going to the Caltrain station?" I ask.

"Near there. I'll tell you where to go when we get closer."

Even though it annoys me to be told how to drive, I take the requested route through Showcase Square to South Park. Yeah, I know most Uber/Lyft drivers don't know their way around town. A passenger once told me, in his experience, only one driver in ten seems to know the city streets. Another passenger, when I related the previous assessment, said it was an exaggeration. More like three out of ten.

The guys talk about their jobs. The one in back, Frank, wants to leave the start-up where they both work and cash in the stock options they gave him.

"I figure I'll get over three hundred when all's said and done," he says. "That's not too shabby."

"It'll help with the transition."

"I just can't stand that place anymore, but I don't want to cause you any problems in the process."

"Hey man, you gotta do what you gotta do."

Frank continues to complain, reminding himself after every few sentences about the options payout. As we approach the Caltrain station, I ask if they want me to turn onto 4th.

"No, just keep going straight," says the guy up front, directing me to the apartment building across the street. I pull into the curved driveway. End the ride.

The guy's picture pops up on the rating screen.

"Look at that handsome guy," Frank says. "I've really aged."

"Happens to the best of us," I say nonchalantly.

"Don't ever get into start-ups," he tells me.

"I've been driving Uber and Lyft long enough to know that."

He laughs as he climbs out of the car.

I turn right onto Townsend. A request on Market comes in. It takes twelve minutes to pick up Steve, after fighting freeway traffic and the eternal congestion through the Financial District. He's only going a mile away. A six dollar fare. The entire process took thirty minutes.

I head away from downtown and switch over to Uber. Move some folks between the Mission and Hayes Valley. Take a Brazilian couple to the ballpark. The Giants are playing San Diego. Since baseball season started, AT&T Park has become one of my top destinations. When I drive into the city and see the park lights on, I know there's a home game that night. Sometimes a plane with a banner buzzes around the area.

I stay in Uber mode for most of the evening. I'm catching plenty of rides. I drive some students from the California College of the Arts.

Some venture capital douchebags. A girl who works in communications for the delivery service app Postmates. Almost go the wrong way on 4th. A woman gets pissed off at some double-parkers on Fell. On Irving in the Inner Sunset, I pick up this guy who left San Francisco for a year and a half to get away from tech. Then a long ride to the Outer Mission.

Later that night, after the game lets out, I switch back to Lyft. Pick up this guy Jimmy and two of his friends from the ballpark. Drop them off on the east side of Bernal Heights. Or, as Jimmy refers to it as, the Bernal Lows, since the eastern side faces the industrial wasteland along Bayshore. I ask about the recent spate of Smart car tipping in the area that's been on the news. Four cars were pushed over onto their side in one night.

"I think it's funny." Jimmy laughs. "Those cars look stupid."

Heading back down to Cesar Chavez, I get a request for Cortland.

At the pinned location, I wait several minutes. Brian Eno comes on. Reluctantly, I turn the volume down as a girl finally comes out and crawls into the backseat.

"Monica?" I ask.

"She's not ready yet."

"No problem," I say. "I got here fast because I was close. I assume that most cars don't show up as quickly."

"I wouldn't know, I don't live here," she says. Her tone is snotty. She asks me to roll up the windows because she's cold. Okay. It's been one of the hottest days of the year—almost seventy-five degrees—but whatever. She asks to charge her phone. I hand her my charger. When Monica finally comes out, she opens the front door. But her friend beckons her to join her in the back.

"You're supposed to sit up front in a Lyft," Monica tells her.

"That's stupid."

"So… where you guys heading?" I ask.

"The Monarch. Do you know where that is?"

"Yeah."

As I drive down the hill to Mission, they ask if my car is new.

"She thought it was a Mercedes at first," Monica tells me.

"Nah, just a souped-up Jetta," I say, then laugh. "Sorry to disappoint."

Then talk amongst themselves about their friends and their jobs. Monica is a masseuse and her friend is an elementary school teacher.

"Do you have any water?" the friend asks.

"No, sorry," I say.

"Really?" she responds incredulously.

"I'm not lying to you." I laugh, thinking she might be joking.

"Don't all you Lyft drivers carry water?"

"I don't know. Do they?"

"I'd say 99.9 percent of them do," Monica says.

"You're the only driver I've had who doesn't have water."

"I have gum."

They each take a piece.

"It's funny," the friend says to Monica. "I never accept the water when it's offered to me, but the one time I want it, the driver doesn't have any."

She goes off about the lack of water.

"It's not good to carry water in the car," I point out. "I recently read that when plastic gets hot it can cause breast cancer."

"Well, you don't store it in the car. You can keep it in a cooler."

So now I have to get a cooler along with water?

"I've become so addicted to those Starburst candies all the drivers have," Monica says.

"Right? Now every time I get into a car I just expect it."

"We're like lab rats."

They laugh.

When I pull up to the Monarch, Monica gets out. Her friend follows her out the same door, but leaves it open.

"Hey!" I yell after them, but they're already talking to the bouncer.

The sidewalk is crowded with smokers.

"Fucking bitch," I seethe. Put the car in park, get out, walk around and close the door. Curse the clubgoers watching me under my breath.

Drive down Mission. Pull over to stare at the rating screen on my app. I want to one-star Monica so badly, but it was her friend who was the asshole. Still, she shouldn't hang out with such shitty people. I give her three stars so Lyft will never match us up again. Pop an Ativan. Smoke a cigarette.

It's nights like these that make me want to curl up into a fetal position and rethink this whole ridesharing deal. This incessant need to please passengers for a good rating is ridiculous. Why anybody would spend more money than what they already drop each week on gas, maintenance, insurance and car payments is beyond me. Since the Lyft payment platform doesn't make it easy for passengers to include tips on their rides, and Uber doesn't even offer their customers the option of tipping, drivers who give out candy, gum, water and baked goods can only hope for a good rating. What's the benefit in that? Isn't providing a basic service all anybody really wants or needs? In what reasonable universe does somebody get penalized for not handing out treats unless it's Halloween and their porch light is on?

The new San Franciscans are entitled enough already. Lyft and Uber just seem to make it worse by giving them something else to expect. ∎

THE WRONG BUSH AND MASON

I'M CRUISING DOWN FOLSOM. It's Thursday evening and I'm hoping for a busy night. Thursday nights can be very lucrative. Lots of people go to meet-ups and other work-related functions. Throw in a home game at AT&T Park and you're looking at seventy-five to a hundred bucks. In the old days, before the price wars, a Thursday was an easy one-fifty. I usually drive from rush hour to ten or eleven o'clock. If I were driving twelve hours a day, which is a normal shift for a professional driver, I'd be making more money. But that's the thing about Lyft and Uber: the freedom to make your own hours. If I wanted to get locked into a 9-5 gig, I'd get a real job. My commitment to a being a creative is more sustainable to me than money. So I pay the price. The Wife pays the price. Our cats pay the price. And, by doing rideshare, the car pays the price. As it is, I'm five thousand miles past the fifty thousand mile service. But I can't afford to take it to the dealer. The service icon on the dash is a glowing reminder that I am not making enough money driving for Lyft and Uber to afford to drive for Lyft and Uber.

At 5th Street, I get a request for a small gym on 7th Street. Three girls going to the Mission. They sit together in the back. Fill my car with the smell of girl sweat. One of them went to a concert the night before with her boyfriend.

"What was the band called again?" her friend asks her.

"The Electric Sixes. I think."

"Never heard of them."

"They're like a nineties band. Thomas likes them."

"What kind of music was it?"

"I don't know. I want to say… punk rock? It was very loud."

"Ew. That sounds awful. How did you put up with it?"

"You know… Thomas really wanted to go. He had a good time."

"Ah… the things we do for love."

"You took one for the team…"

Drop them off. Turn the stereo back on. Blast The Birthday Party until I get another request on Hayes. Steve sits up front. Points to the tattoos

on my arm. "Is that a sleeve?"

"Yeah." I've long since given up on the pretense of looking professional. I used to wear button-ups that covered my tattoos, but it's more comfortable to drive in a t-shirt.

"How much does something like that cost?"

I shrug. "About ten grand."

"Wow. That's a lot of money"

"The artist is pretty well-known. Has a two-year waiting list."

"How much does he charge?"

"$150 an hour."

"So that took almost seventy hours?"

"Uhm, yeah?" Sometimes I forget San Francisco is crawling with nerds who can calculate math in their head. Ten grand is a generalized figure. I actually don't remember how much it cost or how many hours it took to tattoo my entire left arm and shoulder. Just that it was a lot of money and some of the tattoos are still not done. "At this point, I'd take the money over the tattoos," I tell the guy.

After taking him to his destination, I go offline. I need a cigarette. Cruise up to Geary and find a place to park. Check in with the Wife. Then head to the Whole Foods on Franklin in Pac Heights.

In my eternal quest to find a convenient place to piss after the coffee shops close at eight, I discovered this Whole Foods with an easily accessible underground parking structure that's rarely crowded. From there, it's a straight shot to the bathroom. Don't even have to enter the store. There are usually several cabs in the lot.

I usually go upstairs for a vegan donut and a bottle of water. That's it. I take pride in only spending a few dollars at Whole Paycheck. The cashiers even make comments about my low-ticket purchases:

"That'll be a whopping... $4.35."

Going back online, I switch to Uber. Get a request at Geary and Taylor. Two men and a woman named Veronica going to Bush and Mason. They're pissed because they'd just tried to get in a cab but the driver wouldn't pick them up.

"There are six of us," Veronica tells me. "So maybe the driver thought we all wanted to get into the same taxi. But we'd ordered two. He wouldn't even roll down his window so we could explain. Just drove away. And the second cab never showed up at all. So I just downloaded Uber on my phone. You arrived two minutes later."

I listen while the three of them rag on taxis. They keep drawing me into the conversation, as if I'm supposed to agree with them. Why, because I drive for Uber? From day one, passengers have regaled me with stories about lackluster cab experiences. The cars are filthy. The drivers are rude. They won't travel to the outer districts. People complain about requesting cabs and waiting half an hour or longer for them to show up. If they show up at all. New converts to the ridesharing phenomenon are genuinely relieved to finally have a better transportation option. In a city where most people don't own cars, Uber and Lyft provide a highly desirable service. So it's understandable, if you're in a rideshare car, that you probably hate taxi drivers.

But I don't see it that way. After driving for several months and dealing with all sorts of idiotic passengers, I've developed a great respect for taxi drivers and their plight. Maybe they act the way they do because people suck and it's just a natural reaction to being on the shit end of the service industry. In some ways, I think cab drivers have it better because they aren't subjected to an unfair rating system. If I don't like how a passenger is treating me, I can't just kick them out of my car. I'd end up with a low rating, which would impact my ability to continue driving.

"Taxi drivers have a right to be pissed off," I say. "To get a license to drive a cab they have to attend taxi school and learn the streets of the city. But with Uber and Lyft, anybody with a smart phone and a semi-functional vehicle can come into the city and take over their profession without even knowing how to get from one part of town to the other. They just rely on GPS."

"But do they teach cab drivers how to be civil with their customers?"

"Apparently not," I concede. "Even the guy at the taxi commission in San Francisco has admitted that cab drivers weren't providing quality service. But that doesn't mean they can't evolve and start improving the experience."

"They could start by showing up when you request a car," Veronica says snidely.

"Taxis are going the way of clock radios and VCRs," one of the men tells me. "They can't stand in the way of modernization."

"Well, I've been doing the rideshare thing long enough to know that we're nothing but underinsured, untrained taxi drivers, with none of the protections and all the risk. Hate on them all you want, call them relics of the past, shortsighted, whatever, but there's more to running a transportation company than just an app. Ridesharing isn't sustainable based on technology alone."

I know my opinion is falling on deaf ears. Fortunately, we're close to their drop-off point. With all the confidence in the world, I pull over at Bush and Jones, two blocks from where they actually wanted to go. I don't realize my mistake until I pass Mason and go, Hey... Wait a minute... I dropped them off at the wrong Bush and Mason!

I try to circle back and retrieve them but I get stuck in traffic. By the time I return to the cross streets they're long gone.

Certain my rating will go down, I watch the app for the rest of the night. But it holds steady at 4.93. ∎

GUN ON THE STREET

I'M STUCK IN TRAFFIC ON 24TH. I can see police cars ahead with lights flashing. A cop is directing vehicles past a crime scene. This taxi driver behind me keeps blowing his horn and pulling into the opposite lane trying to get around me. After several minutes, I lower my window and yell, "The street's backed up! Calm down already!"

Once past the congestion, I find a parking spot on Shotwell. As I'm walking to Philz, people stand on the sidewalk watching the cops. A white girl asks a group of spectators, "Does anybody know what happened?"

She doesn't get an answer. They turn away from her like they don't speak her language. I keep moving.

At Philz, Brian's working the register. He gives me the scoop. Somebody had a gun. He's not fazed by the police activity. Just another day in the Mission. Waves his hand when I offer my card. I drop a few bucks in the tip jar instead. My first free cup of coffee. I'm starting to feel like a regular.

Sometimes I notice Brian has an accent, but I can't quite place it. Today, I inquire and find out he's from New Zealand. We discuss the Dunedin Sound and Flying Nun Records. A customer lines up behind me. I say goodbye.

My first ride is a couple going to the ballpark. They have on Giants shirts and Giants hats. He's wearing a Giants jacket. I picked them up in Nob Hill. As we move slowly through Tenderloin during rush hour traffic, the woman asks me about the pink mustache. Over the past few months that I've been driving for Lyft, I've fielded many questions about the mustache. My answer always varies, depending on who's asking. If they seem pro-Lyft, I'll say I forgot it at home. Or it's dirty. Or, if it had been raining, I say I took it off so it didn't get wet. Once I told these two girls that I'd attached it one day, drove over the Bay Bridge during a wind advisory and never saw it again. But lately, not many passengers even ask me about the mustache anymore.

I point this out to the couple in my back seat and add, "I guess things are moving so fast with ridesharing that people in San Francisco have gotten used to the idea. There's no need to advertise as much."

LATER THAT EVENING, still in Lyft mode, I get a ping for the Street Food court on Division. Edith is a marketing rep for Instacart, a delivery start-up. She's coming from a meet-up with a bunch of delivery drivers. Or, as she refers to them, "personal shoppers."

"You might appreciate this," she tells me. "The Lyft driver who took me to the meet-up actually delivers for Instacart as well. So when I told him where I was going, he went offline and joined us."

"That's cool," I say, feigning interest.

"Do you drive for any other companies besides Lyft?"

"Uber."

"I use them all. They're all pretty much the same."

"But with Uber you sit in back?"

"Sure, there are little differences in the experience. Uber is like the jock type, right? Lyft's more like the quirky drama club kid. And Sidecar are the ones you see in class and forgot they still go to school."

"That's funny." I laugh politely.

"I know. I tweeted it this morning. Do you drive full time?"

"No, just part time."

"You have another job?"

"I'm a fulltime, unpaid writer."

"Neat. Do you have a blog?"

"I mostly focus on print."

"And you like driving for Lyft and Uber?"

"It gives me free time to write and make zines. So it's good for that."

Drop her off in Anza Vista. She gives me her card in case I'm interested in signing up to be a driver. I mean, personal shopper.

Head down Masonic. Get a request for Divisadero and Eddy. Two guys and a girl. Going to Taylor and Geary. From the moment they get in my car, the smell of pot is overwhelming. I make no move to lower the volume on the stereo as Wreckless Eric plays in the background.

"You guys smell good," I joke.

"What?"

"Weed," I say. "You guys reek of weed."

"Oh, check it out." The guy up front pulls out a quart size bag of buds. "Take a whiff of this." Sticks the bag in my face.

"Holy shit, that smells fucking good!"

"Some primo shit." Tells me that he's growing it hydroponically in his apartment in San Jose. Been shopping it around to the dispensaries in the city. Offers to give me a couple buds.

"I don't have anything to put it in though," I say. "Just my cigarette pack. But it'd probably stink up the car for the rest of the night."

"That sucks."

"It smells better than what I have at home."

At Geary, I turn right. Wreckless Eric segues into the Jacobites. As I drive down the street I can't tell if I'm heading towards or away from downtown.

"Am I going the right way?" I wonder aloud.

"I think," says the guy next to me.

"Yeah," the girl in the back says with authority.

I laugh. "I might have gotten a contact buzz from that weed."

"That's possible. It's some good shit. Too bad you can't take any."

"I know…"

Before they get out, he makes a final offer. I pass.

On Geary, I pull over next to the convalescent hospital for a smoke break. There aren't many blocks in the city to park without obstructing a fire hydrant or driveway, but the stretch between Gough and Laguna on Geary is a sure bet.

As I lean against my car smoking, my boots crunch the shattered window glass on the sidewalk. An endless stream of cars, taxis, Ubers, Lyfts and Munis roars past. The ground shakes from the onslaught of traffic.

I definitely feel strange. I know it's unlikely to catch a buzz off smelling weed, but it did smell really good.

Back online, in Uber mode, I get a request for the Kabuki movie theatre on Post Street. Take a guy on in the Lower Haight. As we pass Molotov's, we see a group of guys fighting on the sidewalk.

"Oh, look. Fight!"

I slow down. Two guys are throwing punches at each other. Barely connecting. A third guy seems to be trying to get involved, but his form is just as sloppy.

"Ah, they're just drunk."

"Not much of a brawl. Fuck it."

From there, I pick up Philip on Clayton. He's going to SF Eagle in SoMa. Sits in back. But he's chatty. Manages a coffeehouse on Haight Street. Been in San Francisco for fifteen years in the same rent controlled apartment.

"I'm not leaving that place until I bail on San Francisco. I'm happy to deal with the bad plumbing and the ratchet floor. I came to San Francisco to live in an old house. Not some prefab condo in Walnut Creek."

"The only move you can make in this city is out."

"Honestly, I'm sick of talking about the same old shit, but…"

"It's hard to ignore the reality of what's going on."

"Right? This tech boom isn't going to end anytime soon. The new batch of techies learned from the mistakes of the dot com era."

"And if the bubble did burst, the results would be disastrous for the economy."

"I say let it happen!"

"But we're all dependent on tech. Tech has us by the balls." I point at the iPhone on my dash.

"Hey, I'm no Luddite. I don't fear technology. But I'd gladly give up Facebook and my iPhone if it meant I wouldn't have to deal with all this bullshit. I only use Uber and Lyft because cabs are so bad." He laughs. "I really hate cabs… But these tech companies are out of control."

"Who's going to stop them?"

"The government should fucking protect its citizens from the machinations of capitalism run amok. Tech companies shouldn't be allowed to trample the rights of normal people. Regulate them like any other business. They claim to do no evil, but tech companies are only looking to make billions of dollars. Pure and simple. They don't give a shit about anything else. Money and power. That's all that matters anymore."

"Still… I think this city is stronger than the tech boom."

"I hope you're right."

As we drive past Alamo Square, the fog comes in like sheets of rain.

"No matter how much San Francisco changes," I say. "At least the fog will always be the same."

We talk old San Francisco until I pull up to the leather bar.

"Maybe we'll have a good earthquake soon," Philip says.

"One can dream…"

We shake hands.

I head downtown. Stopped at a red light, I watch a town car pull up to a group of people on the sidewalk. The driver honks.

"Taxi?" he yells out his window.

I can't hear their response but after he drives away, a woman asks her companions, "What was that all about?"

A FEW HOURS LATER, I get a request for Noe Valley. Pull up to the pinned location on Jersey. Nobody around. I wait. In my rear view mirror, about halfway down the block, I see people in the street. Hit reverse.

It's dark and hard to make out their faces. A guy approaches my passenger door.

"Kelly, right? I'm Paul."

"Sorry about that," I say. "Your pin was in the wrong location." I always apologize when passengers input the wrong address, even though it's his fault he didn't notice where his pin landed.

"No problem," he tells me. "I requested the ride for my brother-in-law. He's going to the Marriot Marquis. Can you pop the trunk?"

I get out and heave a suitcase into my trunk.

"Take care of him," an old woman with a heavy British accent tells me. "He just flew into San Francisco from London."

"Sure thing."

The guy is wearing a pilot's uniform. He folds up his coat and places it on the suitcase. Gets in the back seat. As I drive down 24th to Guerrero, he thanks me for giving him a ride. "My name's Steve."

"Kelly. Nice to meet you."

"How long have you known Paul?" he asks.

"I don't know Paul."

"Then how did he know to call you?"

I explain briefly how Uber works.

"So this is your own car?"

"Yeah."

"They don't provide you a car?"

"No."

"That's quite a racket."

"Yeah. And they barely have any insurance, either. So if we get in an accident, we have to pretend to be friends, okay?" I laugh.

My comment doesn't seem to faze him.

"Do you think we could stop along the way to buy some cigarettes?"

"Sure." I pull over in front of a bodega on Guerrero.

As he gets out of the car, he drops his wallet. Dollar bills and pound notes scatter. He struggles to pick them up. When he returns, he gets in the front seat.

"So... what's your policy on smoking in your car?" he asks.

"I'm about to call it a night, so yeah... you can smoke."

"Great." He offers me a cigarette.

"I have my own."

We light up. He tells me about flying into SFO.

"So you just flew the plane that you arrived in?"

"Well, yeah," he says nonchalantly.

Steve is in town for a few days to visit. Works for British Airways. Has a wife and two kids. His mother is staying in San Francisco for a year, helping out with his sister's kid.

I tell him a version of my story. How driving for Lyft and Uber allows me to explore the city, what I think about living in Oakland, etc…

We talk about our wives. The suburb he lives in outside London. I'm thinking something along the lines of *To The Manor Born*, but he assures me it's still urban.

"Not like Oakland, but you know… there are businesses and people."

He asks if I know of any bars around his hotel. I think about it for a moment. "There's The Chieftain. It's only two blocks from the Marriot."

"We should get a pint," Steve suggests.

"Ah, I have to go home. My wife is waiting for me with dinner on the table. I'm not the one on vacation," I tell him jokingly.

I'm approaching 4th Street. Since I can't turn left off Mission, I drive past the hotel, turn around so I can use the hotel's driveway.

Two busboys instantly approach my car. I help them get the suitcase from the trunk as Steve struggles with his jacket. He reaches in his pocket. Pulls out several bills. Hands then to me. I protest, more out of consideration for the bus boys—it looks like he's giving me all he's got—but take what he offers anyway. We shake hands.

As I drive down 4th towards the freeway onramp, I hit forward on the stereo until Black Sabbath comes on. Crank the volume and head across the bridge. ∎

I CUT COSTS ON THE BACKS OF DRIVERS.
CLE UBER
I LOVE SELF-DRIVING CARS BECAUSE I CAN FIRE UBER DRIVERS.
DRIVERS' TIPS

TOP TEN QUESTIONS
I GET ASKED AS AN UBER/LYFT DRIVER

1. How long you been doing Uber/Lyft?

2. Do you like driving for Uber/Lyft?

3. I heard you guys make good money doing. Is this your full time job?

4. Where are you from?

5. Do you live in the city?

6. What's Oakland like? Is it as dangerous as they say?

7. What's the craziest that's happened while driving for Uber/Lyft?

8. Have you ever had anyone throw up in your car?

9. What kind of music is this?

10. Where's your mustache?

FOR WHOM THE UBER TOLLS

IT'S SATURDAY NIGHT. Not even late. A few minutes after nine. I'm at
Mission and 7th. Get a request for an address on Market, a block and a
half away. I take a right on 7th and pull into the far left lane. As I turn
onto Market, a girl in cut-off jeans and a tank top waves me down. She's
practically in the middle of the street. Grabs my door handle before I can
even stop. Climbs in the backseat.

I ask if she's Andrea, the name of the person I'm supposed to pick up.
She mumbles something and rolls down the window. The rider destination has already been added in the app so I start the ride.

"We're going to the Richmond then?" I ask, anticipating a nice long
ride with 1.5x surge. Cha-ching. She says nothing. I look over my shoulder. She's curled up against the door, passed out. I start driving, hoping
and praying she isn't a potential puker. Turn off Market onto Hayes and
then right on Franklin.

As I approach O'Farrell, I get a text from the generic Uber number:
"I'm on 8th and Market across from Chase."

I immediately pull over. What the hell?

"Hey!" I should, in attempt to wake up the girl in my back seat. "I think you got in the wrong car."

Goddamn it, I think to myself, Not again...

She comes to, but her eyes are blurry. She's not all there. It's obvious she's wasted. I don't smell alcohol though.

"You got into the wrong car," I tell her again.

She's confused. "Uhhmmm... I can get out..." She has an accent. As her voice trails off, she looks around. She has no idea where she is.

Oh man... I feel my pulse accelerate as the reality hits me. I picked up the wrong passenger! And she's not even sober enough to share my distress!!

Besides losing a profitable fare, I was hoping to make the $38-an-hour guarantee Uber's offering this weekend. And the only way to accomplish that is by staying online for the entire hour. With the Treasure Island Music Festival and several other events going on in town, business was supposed to be "off the charts," according to the numerous emails I'd received from Uber about it all week. With rent on the horizon, I really need the money from a busy weekend. But I can't just leave this very intoxicated girl on the streets of Western Addition.

"Where do you need to go?" I ask.

She tells me an address on Battery Street. I assume that's what she probably said when she first got in the car. I have her repeat the address a second time, just to make sure. Ask if she's okay.

"Yeah." She curls back up against the door.

I cancel the original ride and tap the fare review link. Select the option "don't charge ... wrong client."

At least the Financial District isn't that far away. If I hurry, I can get her home fast, get back online and maybe still score some of the Uber guarantee for the hour.

As I'm about to pull out, my phone rings. The generic Uber number. It's Andrea, the girl who actually requested the ride. I explain, as apologetically and calmly as I can, that I picked up the wrong passenger. I tell her that I've already canceled the ride and will make sure she doesn't get charged. And that I'll send a follow up email to Uber. She asks what to do next. I tell her to request another ride. Apologize again. All the while, I resist the urge to tell her what really happened. Maybe she's willing to help me? I could use some female assistance. What if I have to drag this girl's unconscious body out of my car by myself?

I don't even want to think about that scenario!

With growing trepidation, I begin my via dolorosa to Battery Street. Fighting traffic and shitting bricks. I can't help but wonder, What if something happens along the way? What if I get in an accident? How do I explain to the cops why there's some random chick passed out in the backseat of my Jetta? Is my conscience really that guilty? Or have I just been reading way too many news articles lately about rapes and assaults and all kinds of horrible situations in Uber cars? I mean, how can I not be paranoid, now that it's happening to me? After all, who am I but some guy in a gypsy cab?

I try to take deep breaths. My fear has become sentient. It's talking to me. Trying to convince me that I do, in fact, really need to freak the fuck out. Yes, I know… This is some serious shit. Best to get it over with as fast as possible.

As I'm rushing through Nob Hill, another ride request comes in. Damn it! I forgot to go offline. I let the request time out. Make sure I'm no longer in driver mode. I don't need to screw up my acceptance rate too.

When I finally reach the address, I heave a sigh of relief. There's even a place to pull over in front of the high rise with a glass lobby and storefronts. Finally, the universe is throwing me a bone. I take another deep breath and wake the girl up.

"Hey! We're here!"

I'm surprised how easily she comes to. But she's still really out of it. I ask if she needs help. She says no. Reaches around the seat and floorboard, seemingly for her purse or phone. It doesn't look like she has either. I notice there are twigs in her hair. I ask if she's okay. She says that she is fine. There's a tinge of annoyance in her voice, like she's sick of me asking. Opens the car door and careens into the street, in the opposite direction of the apartment building.

I yell after her, "You're going the wrong way!"

Fortunately, there's no traffic. She spins around and heads towards the right building.

"Are you sure you're okay?" I call out.

She comes back towards me and reaches for my hand.

"Thank you so much."

"You're going to be okay, right?"

"Yeah."

But I'm not convinced. She walks to the building and struggles to get through the door. A guy eventually opens it for her. She moves aimlessly through the lobby and then gets into an elevator. I can only hope this is where she lives and that she makes it into her apartment. I hesitate before taking off. Tell myself, At least she's safer here than in the Civic Center.

I pull into the first parking spot I can find and contact Uber the only way I can: a support ticket through their clunky website. After clicking through a bunch of drop-down menus that encourage me to check the FAQ before contacting them, I explain in my message what happened, how I picked up the wrong passenger and had to take the girl home. ■

THE OTHER UBER DRIVER

WHILE CRUISING THROUGH THE DUBOCE TRIANGLE, I get a request on Market Street. Pick up a middle-aged tourist guy and his twenty-something daughter. They're in town from Texas. Ron and Lisa. They ask if I know George.

"Who?"

"The other Uber driver," Ron says.

"George was our Uber driver before you," Lisa tells me.

"I don't really know any other drivers," I respond after a momentary hesitation. "We basically stay in our cars."

"George does Uber to support his wife and three kids," Lisa says.

"He never has time to even see them because he drives all the time. Not like you. You're probably just doing this to support your marijuana habit."

"What'd you say?" I ask with an uncomfortable laugh.

She doesn't reply.

"Poor George," Ron goes on. "He probably saw us together, father and daughter, and felt jealous of our close relationship."

Lisa scoffs. "Well, looks can be deceiving.

Ron keeps making small talk with me. They're Airbnbing a place in Telegraph Hill. Spent the day going around town drinking and shopping. I'm taking them to the Macy's on Union Square where Lisa saw a purse she liked earlier but didn't buy.

"It's a tote!" she clarifies.

Traffic around Union Square is always the perfect example of a clusterfuck. On Saturdays, it's the epitome of a clusterfuck.

I point out the traffic when we're two blocks away.

"Don't worry about it," Ron tells me. "We're in no hurry. Long as the purse is still there."

"It's a tote!"

Five minutes later, about a block away from Macy's, I tell him, "It's gonna take forever to get there with all this traffic. Macy's is right there."

I point at the giant sign looming over the street.

"I suppose we can walk one block," Ron says. "Maybe hit up this place over here... Johnny Foley's." He reads the sign on the Irish pub across the street.

I take a left on Powell and a right on Ellis. Go offline and drive away from downtown as quickly as possible. I've made the mistake of trying to get rides downtown on a Saturday before. Never again. Let the cab drivers have the business. They can take all of downtown as far as I'm concerned. Since all the one-way streets are split into taxi and bus lanes, it's designed for cabs anyway, not regular cars.

I go back online after I cross Van Ness. Pick up a guy going to the Haight. Drop him off and track down a woman with an accent and her gentleman friend.

"Oh, is this your bag on the seat?" she asks.

"Bag?"

I reach around. It's a paper shopping bag from a boutique. Look inside. See a scarf and a flask. Instantly realize that girl Lisa must have left it behind. She had several bags when she got in.

"I know who this belongs to," I say.

"What's in the bag?" asks the gentleman. "Lingerie?"

"A scarf."

"Boring. "

I drop them off in the Mission and email Uber. Parked on 24th, I look through the bag for the receipts to see if it has her name on them. There's a stuffed porcupine and a swimsuit bottom as well as the scarf and flask. About $100 worth of stuff. I feel bad. She must be freaking out. She seemed too uptight not to have a cow over losing her hard-earned purchases.

Oh well. There's a link on the confirmation email from Uber to click if you think you might have lost something in a car. Perhaps she'll notice it when she realizes she's one bag short.

I put the bag in my trunk. Smoke a cigarette. I'm about to go back online when my phone rings. The generic Uber number.

"Is this Kelly?"

"Yeah, Lauren?"

"Lisa."

"Right. I have your bag."

"Oh, thank god!"

I get the address for her Airbnb in Telegraph Hill and her phone number, just in case. "I'm in the Mission, so it'll take a little while to get there. I have to drive all the way across town."

"That's fine."

I take Cesar Chavez to Guerrero, cruise to Market Street, down to Franklin, up and over Pac Heights to Broadway, through the tunnel and into Chinatown. I forget to turn on Powell, so I have to circle around on Kearney to Columbus. My phone rings. It's Lisa.

"Just checking to make sure you didn't get lost."

Uhmmm… Is that another stoner crack?

"Sorry. It took a while to get to North Beach from the Mission. I'm just a few minutes away."

Slowly, I head up the hills, dodging several rambunctious taxis and maneuvering around lost tourists.

Lisa meets me outside the apartment building.

"Nice view you got here," I say. Take the bag out of my trunk.

Lisa thanks me and hands me a folded ten dollar bill.

I acknowledge the tip. "Happy to help."

Ten's alright, I think as I make a five point conversion out of the dead end. A twenty would have been even better… ∎

PEEP SHOW FOR AN UBER

Post and Buchanan. Sunday. 7:30 p.m. I'm indling in front of the Japantown Peace Plaza when three obviously drunk guys and a totally wasted chick stumble towards my car. Blonde, Abercrombie and Fitch, nouveaux-tech types. I'm waiting for someone named Raffi.

"Are you our Uber?" a guy wants to know.

"Are you Raffi?" I ask.

"No. Steve."

"I'm looking for Raffi," I say.

"I can be Raffi," he responds with a chuckle.

"Sorry."

The girl approaches and demands to know why they're not getting into my car.

"This isn't our Uber," Steve tells her.

"Why not?" She leans into my window. "You can be our Uber, can't you?"

"No. Sorry."

"C'mon. I'll show you my tits."

I shrug. "Still not your Uber."

"Don't you want to see my tits?" she slurs, then pushes her shoulders together to emphasize what little cleavage she has. Gyrates her shoulders and winks at me like she's Marilyn Monroe. "They're kinda great."

She's a B cup at best. I resist the urge to tell her I'm not impressed, that a pair of double Ds are waiting for me at home.

"Hey!" One of the other guys careens closer and chimes in, "I've seen them and they're fantastic."

"Look," I say. "I'm sure your tits are awesome. But I can only pick up designated passengers. Sorry."

The girl continues to jiggle her goods until a couple approach my car from the other side of Post. This guy looks like a Raffi.

They slide past the drunk girl and climb into my backseat.

The drunk girl continues to shout as we pull away.

"That girl's really wasted," I say, hoping to ease the tension.

"We know," says the woman with Raffi. "They were in the restaurant."

I can tell by her tone of voice that the drunk girl and her rowdy friends had already been a disturbance that evening, prior to attempting to steal their ride.

Heading down Gough to Golden Gate, they tell me they're going home to watch the new *Game of Thrones*.

We discuss the latest season – the wife and I are currently binge-watching an illegal download of the first two seasons – until we reach their high-rise in South Park. ∎

X X X = = = X = 0

MY RATING WEIGHS A TON

Pick up a guy from a burger joint in the Marina. He's carrying a take-out bag. Drive him to Pac Heights. Nice dude. But the smell of his crappy fast food is nauseating. I love a cheap, greasy burger, except trapped inside a car the smell seems to metastasize until my head is swimming in a toxic stew. I have these Febreeze air freshener cartridges that clip onto the vents. I hit recirculate to help mask the odor.

After dropping him off, I roll down the windows. Immediately, I get another request. Drive back towards the Marina worrying about the stench lodged in my olfactory nerves like an act of shame. I'm certain my next passengers will think I'm the one who reeked up the car.

To my surprise, the pinned location is Roam, an artisan burger restaurant on Union. What luck!

Two girls get in the back. I tell the one who requested the ride, "I just picked up this guy from another burger joint and was trying to air my car out. I'm so relieved you're at a burger place too!"

"Sorry," she says snidely.

Uhhh... "No, it's a good thing."

She grunts. Obviously wasted. The stench of secondhand alcohol merges with the lingering cheap burger stink to create a noxious miasma of putridness. And it's only 9:30! I stopped driving the late shift a month ago because I was sick of dealing with the drunkie shit show. And the subsequent hits to my rating.

"Alhambra and Pierce. Take Fillmore."

"Alright." I take off but hesitate before starting the ride on the app. Sometimes I wait until I'm sure the passenger is not going to be a problem. I'd rather lose a fare than risk a low rating.

During the short drive, she talks to her friend about some interpersonal bullshit that makes no sense to me. Drunken advice. The worst kind of advice. How the girl should do this and not do that. But the girl doesn't take too kindly to the counseling. They start arguing. When I pull up to the apartment building at Alhambra and Pierce, they're calling each other bitches.

I try to be cool and end the ride with my usual, "Have a good night." And then, in the most sincere tone I can muster, "Take care now."

That "take care now" is my standard closer. It's proven to be an effective way to leave things with passengers. Especially the silent ones. My way of exuding respect and bonhomie. But I can tell from her repugnant snort that it misses its mark this time. She chases after her friend who is careening down the street.

"Where the fuck are you going, bitch?"

I get out of there fast. Wonder what I could have done differently... I know she was in a foul mood when I first interacted with her. I probably shouldn't have said anything, but how could I have known? There's just no telling with people...

An hour later, just as I suspected, my rating goes down a hundredth of a decimal point. ∎

INFINITE DOUCHEBAGGERY

AFTER GETTING COFFEE AT PHILZ, I'm walking back to my car smoking a cigarette. Pass two guys sitting on a milk crate. The older one says hello. Smiles wide and asks for a cigarette.

I pull out my pack. "Sure."

"I'm drunk," he tells me, stating the obvious.

His equally drunk but surly friend mumbles, "How bout two cigarettes?"

"I have three left. I can only spare one."

He grunts.

The happy one takes a cigarette. Asks for a light. "Where you going?"

"I gotta work," I say.

He laughs. "I'm drunk. Sorry."

"I know. It's alright."

"Where are you from? I'm from Mexico."

"Los Angeles. Which used to be Mexico."

"Alright." He laughs heartily.

We shake hands. The sullen guy grunts in my direction.

I walk back to my car. Wipe off the freeway dust. Clean the windows. Go into driver mode.

A request comes in. 17th and Valencia. I head down 24th. At South Van Ness, the light is green. My signal is flashing. Zounds on the stereo. I keep the beat on my steering wheel as I wait for the pedestrians to cross. A car in the middle of the intersection is turning left. We both have traffic lined up behind us. I glance in my side mirror. A girl in a Sentra looks distressed. No doubt wondering if she's going to make the light. I'm wondering the same thing as I monitor an endless column of pedestrians.

Mr. Left Turner's face is full of determination. I'm already pulled as far to the right as I can go without entering the crosswalk. Who's going to make it first? Me or him? The crowd is thinning. The last pedestrian, an old lady with two oversized bags, is almost in the middle of the street as the number next to the flashing red hand ticks down.

Seven seconds.

Six seconds.

I'm ready. So is Mr. Left Turner. The girl behind me inches closer to my bumper. Once the old lady is a few feet from the curb, I'm going for it.

Four seconds.

Just as I'm about to remove my foot from the brake and take off, a guy in raw denim jeans and a hoodie, staring at his iPhone, enters the crosswalk. Three seconds to go. The old lady is about to step on the curb as the guy slowly makes his way across the street, never once looking up from his phone. The familiar Facebook logo is emblazoned across the front of his hoodie.

Two seconds.

Mr. Left Turner charges through the intersection, beating Facebook boy to the middle of the street as the light turns red. Not exactly the safest maneuver, but at least he got through the light. My front end is blocking the right lane on South Van Ness. We're all waiting for Techie MaGoo to finish sauntering across the street.

"Show some fucking hustle," I mumble. "Motherfucker."

I curse his pants.

I curse his hoodie.

I curse his very existence.

Of course, he can't hear me with earbuds blocking out the world and sealing in the oblivion.

I fantasize about hitting the gas. Just plowing into the crosswalk and taking out this self-entitled douchebag. I contemplate whether I can generate enough speed to get him airborne… I'd really like to see him fly through the air, flip off the grill of my car, smash into my windshield, roll over the roof and tumble to the pavement with two broken legs and several cracked ribs. Maybe then he'd realize he doesn't own the world just because he makes over a hundred grand a year at some bullshit start-up and still dresses like a middle-schooler.

Once the thechie is out of harm's way, the cars move past, flashing me dirty looks, like I'm the asshole who screwed up traffic.

Fuck, I hate that guy!

Even though people get run over by cars all the time, there's a strong tradition of jaywalking in San Francisco. It's part of the pedestrian culture of the city. People who've lived in LA and San Francisco will always marvel at the difference between walking in the two places.

In LA, you don't jaywalk. Period. Besides possibly getting a ticket, you'll get run over. Walking in LA is a blood sport for drivers. You have to look both ways fifty times before you cross on green in case some dickwad in a Porsche tries to outrun oncoming traffic.

In San Francisco, the accepted practice is to cross once there are no more cars coming, regardless of whether the light is red or green. The stoplights here are brutal. Even when there's not a single car on the road, the lights play out their pattern. And it's usually chilly. So standing on a corner waiting for a walk signal is absurd. But these new transplants, in their infinite need to feel authentic, take this San Francisco custom of jaywalking and incorporate it into their general attitude of entitlement.

Some days it feels like the whole city is full of assholes…

After driving a girl from her place in a SoMa alley to a posh Victorian in Pacific Heights where she works as a nanny, I pick up two jock-looking dudes on Union. Can't tell which one requested the ride based on the profile pic. They look alike. Abercrombie and Fitch types. Going to the Tenderloin. Except they call it TenderNob, which doesn't change the fact that it's still the Tenderloin.

One guy is telling the other about a recent breakup.

He reassures him that it was a good call dumping the girl. "That bitch was crazy!"

"I need to get my stuff back though, but I can't face her."

"You should hire someone from TaskRabbit to do it."

"That's a great idea!"

After dropping them off, I get a request for Russian Hill. Robert calls to make sure I can drive to SFO. I assure him it won't be a problem.

At the top of Francisco Street, I wait for him to emerge from a Spanish Colonial apartment building. As he approaches, I help put his bag in the trunk. What the fuck. I'm feeling generous. He sits in the back. Spends the next twenty-five minutes on his phone talking about hiring "rock stars."

"We need rock stars!" he says emphatically to the guy on the other line. Since he's getting on a plane, this is his last chance to give a pep talk. He keeps saying, "But is he a rock star?" and "Oh yeah! Now that guy's a rock star!"

As I pull into the airport, I end the ride and take my phone off the clip. I've heard some rumors on Facebook that airport security can monitor rideshare cars through the GPS in the apps. It sounds farfetched, but I don't want to risk a ticket. Even though Lyft and Uber have told us we can drop off at the airport, just not pick up, drivers still report getting harassed by airport officials. It's so confusing. I don't know what to believe. All I'm sure of anymore is that you can't trust Uber or Lyft.

I interrupt the guy's conversation and ask which airline he's using. Head to the United terminal.

Once the guy's out of my car, I move slowly past a line of taxis circling back to the arrivals section to pick up passengers. Look at the price on my phone. $28. Rides to the airport used to be around $40. Now they're $25 or $30, depending on the starting point. Which makes the dead head ride back to the city even more painful. Especially in traffic.

I crank the Psychedelic Furs. Take 280.

After a smoke break in Mission Bay, I switch back to Lyft. A group of preppies cram into my car. They're heading to the Richmond. I take Mission to 9th, cross Market and head up Larkin to Geary.

"What's your favorite book?" the guy up front asks me as we pass City Hall. "Tell me fast. Don't think about it."

"*Last Exit to Brooklyn*," I respond.

"Never heard of it. Have you read *Atlas Shrugged*?"

"Yeah, in college."

"*Atlas Shrugged* is the greatest book ever written."

I laugh. "You're joking, right?"

The guy looks at me straight-faced. "No. Why?"

"Because Ayn Rand, or Oink Rand, as I prefer to call her, was a lousy writer and her entire lousy philosophy was all just a pathology based on childhood trauma after her family lost their shit during the Bolshevik Revolution. Have you read *We The Living*?"

"No."

"Well, that book, which is actually her most entertaining book, even more so than *The Fountainhead*, describes her experiences as a child. It explains a lot about who she really is as a person. If you can get past all the anti-Bolshevik propaganda."

"I've only read *Atlas Shrugged*."

Of course you began and stopped there, I think. Because you just want to fulfill every stereotype of the young libertarian worker invading San

Francisco. I try to be nice during the rest of the ride, despite his many attempts to instigate more discussion of Objectivism and Libertarianism. I can tell he's the kind of guy who enjoys starting arguments.

"Look, if I'm anything, I'm a socialist. Okay? And I'm about twice your age, so you ain't converting me to shit at this point."

He shuts up.

Now I just have to worry about whether he has any influence with the girl when it comes time to rate me.

After cruising the Richmond waiting for a ride back downtown, I get a request for a guy who drives for Lyft. It's easy to recognize other Lyft drivers from their profile pics. We all have the same green foliage background. But Gene's given up on Lyfting. Got himself a real job in Walnut Creek.

Originally from Concord, he's drunk and confrontational. Trying to be funny. But I'm in a foul mood. Don't feel like playing along. When I tell him I'm from LA, he makes a crack about how SoCal people are shallow and superficial.

"What makes you think that?"

"Everybody knows it!"

"I'm from LA, born and raised in a shitty neighborhood east of downtown. There's nothing superficial or shallow about where I come from. And I can assure you that most of the people I grew up with are not like the transplants and Hollywood crowd."

"Still," Gene snorts.

"How would you like it if I called everybody from NorCal a preppy tech douchebag?"

The girl in the back laughs. She's from Cleveland.

"The only difference between LA and the Bay Area," I point out, "Is that we say 'totally' and you guys say 'hella.' We're all Californians."

"But we're more spiritual up here," Gene insists.

"What are you talking about? LA is full of cults! Ever hear of Scientology? The Manson Family?"

"Yeah, I guess you're right…"

What's with Bay Area people talking shit about LA? I wonder to myself. Everybody I know from Southern California loves San Francisco.

"Look, California is California. We're all fucking crazy. In LA, we're crazy from the sunshine. While up here you guys are crazy from being drunk and stoned all the time!"

"Still, we've been through some shit!"

"What, Loma Prieta? Ever hear of Northridge?"

"Okay. Okay."

"Granted, that shit with the Nimitz freeway was real fucking gnarly."

"My father was on his way home from Richmond when the upper deck collapsed," Gene says. "He helped pull people from the rubble."

We sit silently for a few moments.

"I think there are more hippies in Northern California," the girl says.

"Oh, definitely," Gene agrees.

"And people here are thin skinned and sensitive," she adds.

"LA folks are too," I say. "I think that's part of being Californian."

"So what made you want to move to San Francisco?" she asks me.

"San Francisco is one of the few places Angelenos can go to reinvent themselves. It's not easy for somebody from California to acclimate to other parts of the country. When I'm in another state, I feel like I have to apologize for being from LA. We carry the stigma of being Californian everywhere we go. You don't just leave your cultural identity behind, even if you don't feel like you have one. New Yorkers are New Yorkers no matter where they live. People born in the South are forever Southern. The same with Texans and Midwesterners. We don't have this same kind of loyalty to place in California since our parents or our grandparents are from somewhere else. But I'll always be Californian, whether I like it or not, because nobody will ever let me forget it."

After dropping them off, I think about calling it a night. Decide to do one last ride. Go back online. A request comes in immediately. I pull up to the pinned location, AsiaSF. The "gender illusionist" club is quiet. Nobody around. Just some drunk kids leaning against the wall. When I glance in their direction, the guy stands up and helps a girl to her feet. They move to my car.

"Wallace?" I ask through my window before I unlock the doors.

"That's me." The guy is huge. He falls into the backseat behind me and the car shakes. The girl gets in on the other side. Pushes Wallace into an upright position. He leans his head against the door. Rolls down the window.

I keep my window down as well. The smell of alcohol and food is overwhelming.

"Is he going to be alright?" I ask the girl before driving away.

"He'll be fine."

They're going to Crocker-Amazon. A long ride on the freeway. Wallace seems like he's about to blow. Sweating profusely and coughing. I drive fast while trying to avoid potholes. Besides Wallace's occasional hiccups, the ride is completely silent. The stereo is off. I don't force a conversation. Just nervously glance in my rearview mirror.

A few blocks from their destination, cruising up Geneva, I hear, "Oh shit!"

I pull over immediately. But I'm not fast enough.

Wallace catches the first surge in his hands. I reach behind my seat and open the door. He gets the rest out onto the bike lane. I give his girlfriend some tissues. She cleans him up as I drive the final three blocks to their apartment.

I go offline. Call the Wife.

"Well, it finally happened..."

At least he didn't puke all over my seats. ∎

THE POLK GULCH VORTEX

It's the busiest Saturday night in a long time. With the price cuts and so many new drivers, the market is oversaturated. Most nights there are too many drivers and not enough passengers. Even on the weekends. But tonight is busy, busy, busy... It almost feels like the old days. Almost.

Surge pricing is in effect for Uber. Lyft is in Prime Time. The rates are fluctuating from seventy-five to two times percent higher than normal all over the city. There's hardly time to think. Drop one passenger off, pick up another. A couple from Western Addition going to 8th and Market. A girl from the Nema building to the Page on Divisadero. A guy from the Haight back to SoMa.

Outside Butter, I pick up three girls dressed in costumes going to the Richmond. All the way there they sing Mandy Moore songs. As I race up Franklin, one of the girls tells the other two:

"Did you know that Hayes valley is surrounded by projects?"

"What?" the other two gasp.

"Yeah. I have a friend who's from San Francisco. Been here like six years. She told me."

"Well they'll eventually tear them down, right?"

"Oh, I'm sure. But can you imagine?"

"That's just, like, so hard to believe. Cause Hayes Valley is so nice."

"I know!" the other two shout in unison and then break up in giggles.

After dropping them off at Trad'r Sam on Geary, I hear the faint rumblings of Dead Kennedys and turn up the stereo.

"Win! Win! I always play to win! Wanna fit in like a cog! In the faceless machine!"

At 15th Avenue, I get a request on Clement. Two couples going to Haight and Central. Wasted on sake bombs, they smell like food and booze. One of the guys in the back almost pukes, which I don't realize until his girlfriend says, "That was a close call!"

"Should I pull over?" I ask in a panic. Since my last experience with a puker, I'm on high alert.

"I'm fine," the guy says.

"You sure?"

"Yeah. It passed."

From the Haight, I race to a ping at 5th and Harrison. Transport two girls to South Van Ness and Mission. I spend more time driving to pick them up than taking them the nine blocks to their destination.

At two times surge, I'm taking a couple to Western Addition. The guy is new in town. Beth is pointing out landmarks along the way. As I wait for the light at 16th to cross Market, he asks her about the Lookout.

"Is that a gay bar?"

"Well, this is the Castro," she says

"They should put disclaimers on gay bars," he declares.

Beth says nothing. I wonder if she regrets getting mixed up with a homophobe. Or at least thinks what I'm thinking, What about the massive rainbow flag on top of the building? This is San Francisco. You'd have to be blind to mistakenly walk into a gay bar.

After driving a girl from Laurel Heights to a bar in the Marina, I get caught in a Polk Gulch Vortex…

First, I pick up passengers on Union. Drive them to Polk Street. Get a request a few blocks down the street. Take a group of girls from a nightclub to an apartment in Pac Heights. As I pull away, I get another ping for Polk Street. Drive back. Take two very drunk guys to Bar None on Union. Then a ride back to Polk. A group of girls going to North Beach. Then some out-of-towners back to Polk. Pick up a couple going to the Marina. I'm cruising down Lombard when I get a call for Chestnut. Two girls going to Playland on Polk and Pine.

Sometimes it can go on like this for an hour or more. Until I log out of driver mode and head to another neighborhood far away from Polk Street. But sometimes even the Richmond isn't far enough.

I drop a couple off at 7th Avenue and California. As soon as I go back online, I get a request for Polk and Sutter. Head down Geary. I'm seven minutes away. But the lights are on my side.

The moment they get in my car the girl is screaming, "I need pizza!"

He name is Virginia. She and her companion, the guy who actually requested the ride, Will, reek of alcohol. I can almost see the fumes come off their bodies like cartoon stink lines. My back window is completely fogged up.

"Turn that up!" Virginia commands me when she hears the Bush Tetras playing in the background. "Too Many Creeps."

"Louder!" Virginia yells. Then turns her attention back to Will, who's almost unconscious. "I know the best place downtown for pizza! And it's open late!"

Next, she's telling me about the pizza joint. As we drive down Polk, she hangs out the window and yells at the pedestrians. "PIZZA!"

I'm hoping that since they're hungry, they won't throw up. After they scarf the crappy pizza from that joint on Mission, they might just puke their guts out. But as long as it doesn't happen in my car, I don't give a fuck.

"We're getting pizza!" she yells at a bag lady in a crosswalk. "PIZZA!"

On Mission, I pull up next to a taxi.

Virginia harasses the driver. "What's so Luxurious about Luxor?"

I glance at taxi driver who looks at me, the iPhone lit up on my dash and the drunk girl in my back seat. Shakes his head.

Virginia yells at his two passengers, "Who takes cabs anyway? What's wrong with you people?"

I cringe. Stare straight ahead. The light turns green. Cab speeds off.

At 8th Street, Virginia yells, "Stop right here!"

I slam on the brakes. The pizza place is on the opposite side of the street. I try to flip a bitch but don't quite make it. Have to back up. An SUV speeding towards me down Mission swerves to make the light.

A girl yells out the window, "DUMBASS!"

"FUCK YOU!!" Virginia yells back at them.

I groan.

Virginia and Will get out of the car. She lets out a battle charge. "PIZZA!"

They take off down the sidewalk.

After 1 a.m., each request is a roll of the dice. I decide I've pressed my luck enough for one shift. Call it a night.

I stop by the Safeway on Market in the Castro for a bottle of vodka and a six-pack of San Pellegrino. I have to pee badly. Not sure if I can hold it until I get home. Check to see if the green spaceship bathroom on Market is available. As I get close to the wall that separates the parking lot from the sidewalk, a pair of legs are protruding through the open door. Somebody is passed out or dead. Their spread-out legs prevent the sliding door from closing. A few people are milling about nearby, pointing in her direction. I decide to hold it. ∎

THE CHUMP

I'M IDLING IN THE BIKE LANE ON VALENCIA WITH MY HAZARDS FLASHING, waiting for Glen. For the past five minutes. Pulled to the right to avoid disrupting the flow of traffic, I cringe each time a bicyclist has to swerve around my car.

A couple step between two parked cars. Are they...? No. The woman holds out her arm at a passing cab. It stops on a dime. They climb in the back and disappear.

Where the fuck is Glen?

I'm inclined to split, but I'm giving Glen the benefit of the doubt. I've already called him and he assured me that he's on his way out. So I wait, like a chump, grateful I'm not in a worse position. But it's been... six minutes now.

What's wrong with this guy? I swear, some passengers can be real assholes. Not only do they request a ride and then make you wait, they don't want to take more than a few steps to get in your car. So you have to make sure you get as close to their pinned location as possible and block traffic waiting for them to mosey outside. Otherwise... otherwise, what? They rate you low.

Uber passengers are definitely worse than their Lyft counterparts. Uber passengers make you flip a bitch to pick them up on the opposite side of the street. They send you into awkward driving situations without a single concern for what it's like to drive a car in this city. And they make you wait. It's become an epidemic. Assholes like Glen.

Where the fuck are you???

Fuck you, Glen! You fucking scumbag dickhead motherfucker!

Oh, is that him with the girl over there?

I look at them imploringly. Please be my passengers…

Nope.

Fuck! Fuck! Fuck! Man, I fucking hate Glen! I wish I hadn't called him and had just canceled. But I'm such a chump. So I keep waiting.

Another Uber car pulls up behind me. Hey, fellow chump. I wonder how long you'll have to wait. Well, fuck! His passengers are ready to go.

Just as I'm about to hit "cancel-no show," Glen shows up with a chick. They climb in the back.

"Sorry for the delay," the girl says, sweetly.

"No problem," I mumble.

Heading downtown, listening to them discuss their lame-ass jobs, I hate them even more. And myself, for playing along with their self-entitled douchebaggery.

This is the last time, though. From now on I'm not waiting longer than two minutes. Three at the most. Maybe four. If it's not a busy street. ∎

ANOTHER WASTED NIGHT

SATURDAY NIGHT. Not feeling it. The sky is overcast. It's cold. 6 p.m. feels like 10. Even though we're in the middle of summer. I'd much rather stay home with the Wife and watch *Game of Thrones.*

Despite my laziness, I get ready to drive. Dust off the car. Cross the bridge and stop by Philz for a large Jacob's. In Lyft mode I get my first request. Two guys. One chugs a beer as he walks to my car. Off to the Great American Music Hall to see Dark Star Orkestra, the Grateful Dead cover band. We talk about the Dead, LSD, pot and the TV show *Silicon Valley,* which one guy thinks is awesome but makes him question whether he should be living in San Francisco.

"I work in tech. But I'm not part of the whole scene."

In all the chatter, I miss O'Farrell. End the ride. Do a right-right-left to get them to the front of the venue. The sidewalk is jammed with Deadheads. A cloud of pot smoke hanging overhead wafts into my car.

A request comes in for Larkin and Bush. An English couple going to the Buckshot.

"We don't know the exact address," the guy tells me. "I can look it up on my phone…"

"Don't worry about it. I know where the Buckshot is."

"You don't need to put it into your satnav?"

"No. It's just a straight shot from here."

I head down Gough to Geary.

"Most Lyft drivers don't seem to know where they're going."

"I've heard that."

He tells me about London taxis and The Knowledge, the test all London black cab drivers must pass in order to drive a taxi in the city.

"It's been called one of the most difficult tests in the world," the guy says. "Like having a detailed map of London imprinted in your brain."

"Lyft is the complete opposite," I say. "All you need is a smart phone. And the mustache. The brand."

"I noticed you didn't have one."

"Not many drivers use them anymore."

"Really?"

"Well, if you drive for both Lyft and Uber, like most rideshare drivers, it's not practical to have a mustache."

"Why does it matter if you have a mustache or not?" the girl asks. "Do they make you shave it?"

I laugh. Wait. "What?"

Her boyfriend chuckles. "Oh, no. He means the pink mustache they put on the front of their cars."

"That's a mustache? I thought they were wings."

We all laugh. Drop them off. Get a request for a Kelly on 22nd Avenue. I wait outside her place for several minutes. On the corner is a Russian deli. A few blocks down is the Holy Virgin Cathedral, the largest Russian Orthodox Church outside Russia.

Kelly finally comes down. Cute blonde. Short skirt. All dolled up.

"Hey, I'm Kelly."

"Me too!."

We laugh.

"Where you heading?" I ask.

"Inner Sunset."

"Hmm. Do you want to drive through the park or take Stanyan?"

"Just take Stanyan."

"Yeah, that sounds good." The park is faster but it seems weird sometimes to be trapped inside a car driving long stretches of darkened roads surrounded by wilderness. I prefer to drive girls, especially when they're travelling alone, on well-lit streets.

"Hold on," she interrupts our discussion about our mutual name. "I have a FaceTime request."

"Where are you?" a guy on the other end asks.

"I'm in a cab on my way!"

"Hurry up! And bring some girls."

"I'm a girl!"

"No, we need more girls! What about Karen, is she with you?"

"No. Just me."

"Bullshit. Tell Karen to come along."

"Seriously, she's not with me. What's wrong with you?"

"Are you in a club?"

"No. I told you, I'm in a cab."

"Then what are all those lights?"

"They're streetlights, dumbass."

"Which club is that?"

"I'm on Geary! Look, I'm on my way. I'll see you in..." she looks at me in the rearview.

I hold up five fingers.

"I'll see you in fifteen." She taps her phone furiously, as if to poke out the guy's eyes. "I swear. Idiots. Why am I even going over there?"

"Well, it's Friday night."

"Gotta do something, right?"

After dropping her off, I'm cruising down Kirkham. Waiting for a ping. Prime Time is at twenty-five percent. I'm about to switch over to Uber and check out the surge when I get a request for an address on 11th Ave. I arrive as a taxi is unloading and a Prius is picking up. Must be a house party, I think. A girl on the sidewalk waves me down. Asks me to wait and runs back inside.

She returns with a guy and a girl, deposits them in the back of my car and says, "Don't worry. They won't puke." Then to the couple, "Tell him where you're going."

They recite different addresses at the same time like dutiful children.

"You got it?" she asks me.

All I heard was something about 10th Avenue. "Sure."

We take off.

"So uhhh..." I glance in my rearview. They're obviously wasted but I don't smell alcohol on them. "Where you guys heading again?"

"I'm going to Edgewood Avenue," the guy tells me. He has an accent. "It's close by... I think."

"What's the name of the street again?"

"Behind the university."

"Which university?"

"I'll show you." He leans forward. Looks out the windows. "Where are we now?"

"11th and Judah."

"Take Judah."

"Do you mean the medical center down the street?"

"What medical center?"

"Never mind." I head towards UCSF.

As I drive down Judah, he kisses the girl. They disengage and he has a sneezing fit. After numerous explosions, I offer him a Kleenex. He refuses. Keeps sneezing.

"You better just take one." I hand him the tissue.

As I turn onto his street, I ask for a number.

"It's on the corner up there."

I pull over. The guy says something to the girl in what sounds like an unfamiliar language. Kisses her again and gets out.

I turn around. "Where are you heading again?"

"Can you just drive please? Thanks."

I take off slowly. When I get back to Judah I ask, "Left or right?"

"I don't know."

"Didn't you say something about 10th?" I ask.

"Yes. Please, can we go to 10th Avenue?"

"Okay. You got a street number?"

"I'll just tell you when to stop."

I go a few blocks and ask again for a number.

"Uhhhmmm… 16… 20."

"Alright." I pull up to 1620 10th Avenue and look over my shoulder. The girl is sprawled out in my back seat, her eyes practically rolling around in her head. She didn't seem that wasted a few minutes ago. She's young. Probably a student at SF State. If she's drunk, she didn't buy the booze.

"Do you need help getting inside?" I ask.

"Yes. Thanks."

I end the ride and park. Get out. Open the back door. She takes my hand. I help her to her feet.

"Don't worry, I'm married," I say as I put my arm around her shoulder.

"Oh, you're married?"

Just when she seemed completely oblivious, the concept of marriage brings her back to reality.

"Yeah and I'm about twice your age."

I'm only telling her these things because I'm uncomfortable with my hands on a young girl. I want to seem, at the very least, fatherly.

She isn't steady on her feet. But she's moving. I direct her to the door.

"Do you have your keys?" I ask.

She pulls a set from her pocket. There are three keys on the ring. I find the one that looks most like an apartment key. I'm about to put it in the lock when she pulls away.

"What's wrong?" I ask.

"That's not my house!" She careens down the sidewalk.

"Are you sure? Let's try the key at least." I yell after her.

She stumbles.

"Oh shit!" I run to catch hold of her before she falls into a tree.

"That's not my house," she tells me.

"But that's the number you gave me!" I try to keep my voice down but I'm beginning to panic.

"It's somewhere…" She looks up and down the street. "Around here."

"You don't know where your apartment is?"

"No!" She starts to cry.

"Okay. Let's just get back in the car. Don't worry. We'll find it."

I help her into the passenger seat. She cries harder.

"Is there somebody you can call?" I've already ended the ride so I can't call the number associated with the app. Not that it would do any good. The girl who requested the Lyft didn't seem to know where she lived. "Do you have a roommate?"

"She's out of town."

"There's nobody else?"

She pulls out her phone, opens it and then throws it at me. "Oh god!" Bursts into tears again.

I pick up the phone. The text app is open. Looks like she's been drunk-texting some guy named Tony. The last message is a jumble of letters. The text equivalent of slurred words. "Ljkhdlgkalskdglakhdlgkhalkh."

I search for something that might have her address in it. I look in Maps. I check her contacts. Her phone number has a New York area code. I look in the settings. Nothing. I search her recent calls for a "mom" or "dad." But then pause... it might be premature to get family involved. It's 1:30 in the morning. 4:30 on the East Coast. I don't want to cause trouble if I can avoid it. She's just a kid who's probably taken a drug she's too inexperienced to deal with. I can only imagine her parents freaking out if they get a call at four in the morning from some guy in a gypsy cab informing them their daughter is too fucked up to remember where she lives. Not that I have a clue what else to do at this point...

"Let's just drive a little while and see if anything looks familiar."

I figure 10th Avenue is still our best bet. I drive south at a crawl. She's looking on the right side while I look left.

"Do you remember the color?" I ask. "Or the..."

Oh, who am I kidding? Every fucking house in the Sunset looks the same. There might be subtle differences in the exterior paint, but at night, it's almost impossible to make much of a distinction.

"That's it!" she yells.

Oh, thank god! I pull over.

"No. It's not."

"What? Are you sure?"

I move a little further down the street.

She starts bawling again.

Oh, come on... "Look, what's wrong?"

"I need to get out. Can you pull over please?"

I stop, expecting the worst. She opens the door and leans out.

"I'm such a bad person," she moans.

"Why, cause you're fucked up?"

"No, I did a bad thing."

"You just need to go home and sleep it off. Everything'll be alright in the morning."

"I'm a bad person."

"You're not a bad person. C'mon. It's okay."

"Gaaaahhhh," she cries. Gets out of the car. Stumbles down the street.

"Oh fuck!" I chase after her. Try to convince her to get back inside. "Just relax, okay? You'll feel better in the morning. Trust me." I don't know if anything I'm saying is helping her anxiety. "Everything's going to be fine." I don't know what else to tell her.

She looks at me, her eyes filled with tears. "Really?"

"I promise. You'll feel so much better in the morning. Trust me. I'm old. I know about these things."

"Gaahhh…" She wraps her arms around me and buries her face in my chest. Sobs uncontrollably.

Oh, fucking hell! I think. This is not good!

Here I am, on a dark street with a very young, extremely wasted and distraught girl who obviously needs comfort. I want to call the Wife to deal with this situation so badly I actually contemplate the logistics of how fast she could get here from Oakland, knowing full well it's not even remotely possible.

I put an arm around the and pat her head. "It's okay. It's okay." I try to sound reassuring. Look around. Curse my luck.

"I'm such a horrible person," she mumbles into my tear-drenched shirt.

"It's gonna be alright. Let's just find your place, okay?"

"Alright."

It takes another few minutes of reassurance before she releases me from the bear hug. I lead her back to the car. Help her inside. We drive a few blocks. I turn around. Head back the opposite way. She looks out the right side. I look left. At least we've switched sides.

"That's it!"

"You found it?"

"No."

We drive some more.

"There!"

"Are you sure?" I'm not feeling optimistic anymore.

"Yes, that's it!"

"Really?" I help her out of the car. Drag her to the door. Say a quick prayer. Put the key in the door handle. Please work…

The key turns. I heave a sigh of massive relief. "We found it!"

I unlock the door. There's a flight of stairs. Oh, shit! I hadn't thought about what I would do when I actually got to her door. There's no way I'm going inside this girl's apartment. I figure if she passes out on these stairs, she might wake up with a sore neck, but at least she'll be safe.

"Alright." I hand her the keys. "Now just go inside and go to sleep."

She lingers. Doesn't seem to want me to leave.

I feel like I've inadvertently befriended a lost kitten that I'm trying to shoo it away.

"What's your name?" she asks.

"Kelly."

"Thanks, Kelly."

"Okay. Good night." I close the door. "Lock the door, okay?"

As I walk away, she watches me through the curtain over the glass door. I close the outside gate and turn around. She's staring at me. I get in my car. Glance back. She's still looking through the glass. I wave goodbye. She waves back.

I drive down the street. At the end of the block, I turn around. Head back to Judah. As I pass her place, the curtain is closed.

On Irving, I pull over and smoke a much-needed cigarette. ∎

THE LEATHER MAN

I DON'T USUALLY DRIVE ON WEDNESDAYS ANYMORE, but it's getting close to the end of the month and I need to make rent. Even if it is hard earned, I can clear sixty or seventy bucks for the night. Anything helps these days.

I'm late getting out the door. To save time and avoid traffic, instead of going to the car wash in Berkeley, I hit the one on 10th and Harrison in SoMa. In the bay next to me is a black Navigator with TCP stickers. Probably an UberSUV. The guy's in a suit and tie. While I'm wiping down my car, I smell weed. Glance in his direction. He's smoking a blunt. Okay. I prefer a little Ativan to calm my nerves, but whatever works, dude.

After Philz for coffee, I get my first ping while driving down Hayes Street. Pick up a couple on Page, across from a Baptist church. They sit together in the back.

I ask about the church, whether it's still active. The man says they have services on Sunday and Wednesday evenings.

"But isn't it Wednesday?" I ask.

"You're right."

We glance at the church. It looks abandoned.

During the drive to Davies Symphony Hall, the woman worries about whether or not they'd locked the back door when they left.

From there, I catch a ride to SFO. Four kids from LA in town for a conference. The company they work for is based in the Peninsula but they manage the LA office. They complain about the cold weather and how they can't wait to get back to LA.

Back in the city, two friends have a faux-fight in my backseat:

"You're an intelligent, thoughtful person," one girl says to the other. "You can't possibly believe that."

"Don't tell me I can't be dumb!" she responds.

Drop them off in Cow Hollow. Get a request for The Brixton on Union. Sarah's going to the Outer Sunset. Tells me she's exhausted after a hectic week.

"And we're only halfway to Friday!"

"Where do you work?" I ask.

"Google."

"In Mountain View?"

"Yeah. But I'm just a contractor."

"You take the shuttle?"

"Yeah and I feel really guilty about it."

"I didn't say anything!" I laugh.

She laughs too. "I know. Believe me, I was conflicted about it when I took the job. I even thought about taking Caltrain instead. But the shuttle is so much cheaper."

"You have to pay to ride the shuttle?"

"As a contractor, yeah. Only employees ride for free."

"That's crazy."

We talk about how the Google buses have become the latest symbols of displacement.

"I've lived in this city for six years," she declares. "I went to State. And I've worked as a waitress and bartender for the past two years, living in a tiny bedroom in a house with six other people. This is the first job I've ever had that isn't in a bar or a restaurant. It's kind of nice working in an office. Plus, I'm finally making enough money that I might be able to get a place with only one roommate."

LATER THAT EVENING, I get a request for the corner of 18th and Hartford in the Castro. A group of guys standing on the sidewalk. Four middle-aged looking dudes and a younger man dressed all in leather with a leather cap. As James, the one who requested the ride, leans in and asks if they can all ride together, the leather man gets in my front seat. Looks at me intensely as the others climb into the backseat.

"I know you're only supposed to carry four people at time," James says. "But I'll give you a good tip."

"Sure. Just play it cool."

James crawls on top of the others. "Don't worry. We'll keep a low profile."

They all seem very drunk. Except for the leather man. As the four guys writhe and laugh in the backseat, we discuss the difference between Victorian and Edwardian houses.

"I'm still trying to figure out how to tell them apart," I tell him.

Because most houses in San Francisco were built immediately after the earthquake and fire in 1906, as the Victorian period ended and the Edwardian began, there is a lot of crossover and ambivalence between the two styles.

"I know the difference," he says. "I live in a Victorian. That's why I'm glad they're building those ugly towers for all the techies. I don't want them coming for my place."

"Hey!" one of the guys in the back yells and then laughs.

"Do you want me to stop?" I ask.

"Oh!"

"We're fine, driver!"

The leather man complains about the whitewashing of the city. The influx of frat bros, sorority chicks and families invading the Castro.

"It's only a matter of time before people start referring to the Castro as Noe Valley adjacent," he says. "I swear, if I hear one more tech apologist talk about how San Francisco is always changing and it's a city of transformation, blah blah blah… I'm going to lose it! Before, all kinds of people came to San Francisco. Now it's just straight, middle-class, boring ass white people."

"The Castro doesn't seem like the Castro anymore." I glance in the rearview. It's hard to tell what the men are doing back there. Just lots of movement and grunting. "I remember in the nineties the whole city was pretty much Castro adjacent."

"You know why there were so many queers in San Francisco in the nineties? Loma Prieta hit and the transplants abandoned the city. They all went back to where they came from. But we had nowhere to go. I'm from bumfuck Kentucky. I'm not going back there. Ever! They're going to sprinkle my ashes in the Bay when I die!"

I don't know what to say. I'm constantly struck by how similar these stories of displacement are, the fear of eviction and the struggle for survival. Particularly among those who were marginalized in their hometowns and came here to be a part of something meaningful. They believed in the promise of San Francisco as a place to fulfill dreams. And now, as the city is transforming so rapidly and becoming a playground for white, middle class suburbanites, they are faced with the tragedy that you can not just lose your dreams in San Francisco but become just as marginalized here as in the places they abandoned…

As the murmuring and grunting in the back seat reaches a crescendo, I accidentally miss the turn.

"Just stop here," the leather man commands.

"You don't want me to turn around?"

"No, this is fine."

While the four in back disengage themselves, James struggles to wiggle out the door so the rest can get up.

"We just committed several vile acts in your back seat," he says.

"Wouldn't be the first time," I joke.

The guy in the middle holds out his hand. "Wanna smell my finger?"

"That's alright."

"You sure?"

"Pretty much."

"Okay."

I say good night. Go back online. Wait for another request.

MY UBER BREAKING POINT

Hello Lyft, Old Friend

IT'S WEDNESDAY AFTERNOON. The sky is pissing rain. I'm swerving through the Marina on my way to pick up Tina, trying to avoid crater lakes and double-parkers. Turn onto Van Ness. With rush hour traffic from Lombard on my back, I pull into a driveway a few doors down from the pinned location. Tap the arrive bar on the Lyft app and tap again to confirm that I've actually arrived. Ian Dury comes on the stereo. While I wait for Tina, I bang my fingers against the steering wheel along to the beat.

Just as the song ends, a girl emerges from the high-rise apartment building and dashes through the downpour towards my car. I turn down the music as she jumps in the front seat.

"I tried to get as close as I could," I say. "But this is the only driveway."

"That's alright." She slides the seat all the way back with authority and props her Uggs on the dashboard.

"So we're going to…?" I ask.

She doesn't respond.

"Oh, right." This is a Lyft. I've gotten so used to driving for Uber the past few months, I keep forgetting how the Lyft app works. Passengers generally input their address when requesting a ride. I close out another window. Expand the map screen to figure out her destination. "SoMa?" Still nothing.

"Okay then…" I reverse slowly, watching traffic through the windows of a parked car.

I've just started driving for the day. Tina is my second ride. Despite loading up on Philz coffee when I began my shift, I haven't got my head into the game of moving folks around the congested city yet. As aggravating as it may be, I usually drive rush hour. The traffic is horrible, but at some point, surge pricing, or prime time, in Lyft parlance, usually kicks in, which is the only time you're guaranteed to make more than the bare minimum.

I decide to follow the suggested route in the app. Although I can't read the street names underneath the thick red lines on the map, I can tell the app wants me to go down Broadway to The Embarcadero. Not my preferred route to SoMa from Russian Hill during rush hour, but I follow the app's advice anyway. Lyft passengers always seem to want you to follow the in-app navigation. Even if it's the less efficient route. Whatever. It's their $1.35 a mile.

Tina coughs and snorts. I glance in her direction. Yoga pants, hoodie, thick sweater and a scarf wrapped around her face like a fashion-conscious anarchist. She stares into her phone, which erupts with a woman's voice enthusiastically describing how to melt butter for the quickest fudge recipe on the internet. Then she watches another step-by-step video recipe. In between videos, she snorts, coughs and hacks.

"Are you okay?" I ask.

"I'm sick." Hacks. "Sorry."

As I approach The Embarcadero, I immediately regret following the directions in the Lyft app. What was I thinking? Rush hour is bad enough. Throw some rain in the mix and it's a clusterfuck. Traffic is completely gridlocked. We're barely moving. At twenty-seven cents per minute, I'm wasting both my time and Tina's time. With the Bay on my left, the only way out of this mess is to take a right on Washington. But I'd still have to traverse the Financial District, where the streets are no doubt backed up as well. Fuck! I should have known better than to follow the directions in the app. Had I taken Hyde, even if it were just as clogged, I'd at least have a few more options. Now that I've screwed myself, I can only push through until I get to Mission Street.

Besides her constant coughing, hacking and sneezing, Tina is silent as she continues to watch recipe videos, send texts, write emails and listen to her voicemail. She makes a few phone calls on speakerphone so I can hear every word of her inane conversations. Apparently, a coworker smells funny. Her roommate leaves dirty dishes in the sink. A client doesn't know how to use the print function on his MacBook. I want to blow my brains out.

Why is this girl in the front seat anyway? Didn't Lyft recently send out a press release telling users if they don't want to interact with their drivers, they can just sit in the back seat? I guess she didn't get the memo. It never ceases to amaze me how easily people will conform to the traditions of a gypsy cab service just to avoid taking the bus. Or paying a taxi fare.

Fuck, I hate Lyft. As I sit in suspended awkwardness next to Tina, feeling like we're both going to explode from the tension, I begin to wonder if I really have reached my Uber breaking point. I thought I had, but now I'm not so sure… This isn't the first time I've bailed on Uber. Except in the past, I'd do a couple Lyft rides, realize how exhausting it is pretending to give a shit about the people I drive for even less money and quickly flip-flop back to Uber. This time, though, I don't have a choice.

As much as I'd like to say I quit driving for Uber because of their lies, the inability to protect passengers from physical and sexual assault while insisting that their background checks are superior to taxis (a claim that is being challenged by prosecutors in Los Angeles and San Francisco), the false promises to be a kinder Uber, the threats to journalists, the disdain for the disabled, the mistreatment of drivers or the general douchebaggery of their libertarian, cut-throat business practices, Uber made it easy for me to stick to my convictions by charging me $200 for a cracked iPhone 4S.

Back when I first signed up, Uber didn't allow drivers to use the "partner" app on our personal phones. Instead, they issued us iPhones that ran the app (and only the app). And charged us $10 a week in rental fees. Whether we drove that week or not. Eventually they released a version we could download. Most drivers quickly returned the Uber-issued phones to avoid the rental fees. I was ready to send my phone back too, but I'd accidentally cracked the screen. One night, when I got home from driving, I left the phone on the bed and somehow managed to shatter the screen between my ass and the pillow top mattress. It was mind-boggling. I mean, I've dropped phones on concrete before and only ended up with a few scratches. Yet this one couldn't withstand a little pressure?

Fucking Uber and their janky ass phones!

I posted a few queries on Facebook groups for drivers and emailed Uber asking what to do about the damaged phone. But as with all emails to Uber support, the response was as vague and uninformative as the opinions of other drivers on Facebook. I didn't know what to do: take the chance and return the useless phone or spend eighty bucks and get it fixed myself?

With those ten-dollar charges rapidly adding up, the Wife was pissed to no end. She hates Uber. She hates their entire predatory business model. She hates worrying that we'll have to declare bankruptcy if I get into an accident. She hates their exploitation of foreigners (which is rarely, if ever, discussed in the media—journalists prefer to focus on the part-time, middle class workers of the on-demand economy). She hates the Uber passengers who scuff up the interior of our car as they drunkenly climb in and out. She hates the plastic sleeve on the windshield that holds the Uber placard. And she especially hates their crappy phones.

Whenever she saw the thing with its screen smashed into a splintered web of disappointment gathering dust on my nightstand, she reminded me, with increasing annoyance, that I shouldn't be paying $10 a week for something I didn't use. "Fix the damn thing or send it back already!" When the nagging got to be too much—Er, I mean, when I realized she was right, as always—I returned the phone to Uber. Cracked screen and all. Fuck it.

That weekend, disgusted by how Uber is handling the Sophia Liu case, now that the driver has been charged with misdemeanor vehicular manslaughter, I made one of my many grand declarations to never drive for Uber again. I was done! How could I affiliate myself with a company

that refused to accept even a shred of responsibility for the death of a six-year-old child? With all those billions and billions, they can't break off some for a little girl's life? Yeah, I know it would set a precedent and they'd be on the hook for all the other misdeeds perpetrated by Uber drivers. And yeah, the guy fucked up. He wasn't paying attention to where he was going. On those congested Tenderloin streets, you need to keep your eyes on the road. But the way an Uber spokesperson said the driver had no business even looking at his phone when the accident occurred, since he was in between fares, rubbed me the wrong way. As any Uber or Lyft driver knows, the entire process is about looking at a phone. You look at the screen for requests. You look at the heat maps to see where it's surging. You look at the phone to make sure you're online when you go a few minutes without a ride.

As devastating as the situation is, Uber makes it worse by doing everything they can to distance themselves from what they created: an app-based taxi service for non-professional, unregulated and underinsured drivers. It's obvious Uber doesn't care about anything but world domination at the expense of whatever or whoever gets in their way. Whether it be state and local laws, protesting drivers or small children. They are barely concerned with their passengers, much less the public at large. And they don't give one iota of a shit about the drivers.

I just couldn't be a part of their rapacious practices anymore. After putting off the inevitable for too long already, it was time to implement my exit strategy and move on to driving a taxi. As soon as I earned enough money for taxi school, I would finally be done with Lyft and Uber. Then it's the cabbie's life for me!

In the meantime, I started driving for Lyft again. Which wasn't an easy sacrifice to make. At least with Uber there's no expectation of conviviality. The Lyft experience is so pedestrian. Lyft tries to hold your hand the whole time. It's excruciating when you know what you're doing and just want to get the job done. That's why Uber is killing Lyft in the ride-hail wars. They are the bridge between taxis and limos. A premium service at a cut-rate price.

With Uber, there are no illusions. Unless you're an idiot—or believe corporate shills like The Rideshare Guy—you enter the life of an Uber driver knowing damn well you're going to get fucked up the ass. Lyft, on the other hand, is all about a false sense of community and inclusiveness. As long as you play by their rules. I've ever come across a more jingoistic, flag-waving group of kool-aid drinking cheerleaders before I discovered the loyal drivers in Lyft's Facebook driver lounges. These private groups have since been disbanded, as if John Zimmer, the CEO, happened upon them one night and, after perusing the infinite flow of asinine comments by a chorus of gossip hounds and glad-handers, murmured into the glow of his computer screen, "Exterminate the brutes."

Lyft may portray themselves as fun and quirky and the "friendly" alternative, but they're just like Uber. Except when they cut rates and tell drivers it's for their own good, they never fail to mention how we're part of a community. Which makes their version of exploitation so appalling.

I like my evil pure and uncut, thank you very much.

Of course, community comes in handy when you get in an accident and you're forced to crowdsource the $2,500 deductible to get your car fixed. Cause you know, in the "sharing" economy, money if just another underutilized resource.

GoFundMe might as well be a subsidiary of Lyft. Since you don't get as many rides as you do with Uber, you don't make as much money. Yeah, it's great passengers can leave a tip through the app—unlike Uber, which strictly forbids tipping. But hardly anybody tips. And those who do tip maybe add a buck or two to their total. At the most. Occasionally, you get somebody who leaves more than twenty percent. But it's demoralizing to receive my Lyft totals the next morning and see how little I've made and how much more I could have made if I got at least twenty percent in tips to offset Lyft's twenty percent cut of my meager profits.

Each time I get into my car to drive for Lyft, I have to suspend the belief that it's a viable occupation. I never feel like I'm providing an essential service. More like participating in a newfangled pyramid scheme. And perpetuating laziness and the new transplants' fear of public transportation.

Sure, there are some great moments with cool and interesting passengers, but that happens with Uber too. The majority of my passengers talk to me. I think my long hair, tattoos and glasses put people at ease. I'm chill and articulate. Everybody assumes I'm a student. I love to bullshit and discuss San Francisco history and lore. I've had some great conversations while driving for Uber and Lyft. Unfortunately, confabulation doesn't translate to a living wage.

Yet.

When it comes to Uber and Lyft, charm doesn't pay. But I hope that once I get behind the wheel of a bonafide taxi, a charismatic personality will be an asset. And I can unshackle the reins of a tyrranical rating system. It's exhausting trying to make people happy so you can get those five stars.

Based on what I've noticed at the Whole Foods on California, despite the strain of losing fares to these apps, taxi drivers seem more relaxed. Unlike ride-hail drivers, who always look squirrelly and overworked. Maybe all that flexibility isn't what it's cracked up to be. As Uber and Lyft lower their rates, claiming this tactic will lead to more rides, drivers are working harder than ever to make up the difference.

And compared to Uber, Lyft is way more labor intensive. It's all about Lyft Line these days, the cheaper service where different passengers share the same ride going in similar directions. About seventy-five percent of my rides are LyftLines. Which means I'm driving more, doing more pick-ups and more drop-offs, all the while making less than if I were just giving one decent Uber ride. While Uber wants to compete with taxis, Lyft seems to be competing with the bus. It's a race to the bottom. And drivers are rats on a sinking ship.

After a few days of doing non-stop LyftLines, I began to feel like a soccer mom: Pick up one passenger here. Pick up the second over there. Drop off one. Then the other. Repeat. Over and over... The process is rarely easy. The algorithms that determine who gets dropped off first don't always make sense. And despite choosing to use LyftLine, riders can be impatient with the procedure. I had one woman tell me when she got in my car that she was running late to catch the Caltrain. As she sweated me about it all the way to pick up the next passenger, I pointed out that she really shouldn't be using LyftLine when she's in a hurry. Another night, this bossy girl insisted I pull over on Kearney and call the guy I was supposed to pick up next and ask him to walk three blocks to meet us because she didn't want to drive into Union Square. Granted, it would have been a nightmare—this was during Christmas—but while on the phone with him, I got the sense he didn't know his way around the city very well. Sure enough, he got lost. While we idled in a tow-away zone for twenty minutes waiting for him to find us, the girl kept saying, "Why doesn't he just use the navigation in his phone?"

As annoying as LyftLine is, the Lyft app is the worst aspect of driving for Lyft. I can't believe some commenters think the Uber and Lyft apps function the same. They do not! Uber has the superior app. If there's one thing Uber is willing to spend their billions on other than marketing and lawyers, it's app development.

When it comes to interacting with the app, Lyft is like a needy child. You have to tap when you arrive at the pinged location, tap again to confirm you've arrived, tap when the passenger gets in the car, tap to find out the destination, tap once you've reached their destination, tap to end the ride, tap to rate the passenger, tap to go back into driver mode... Tap, tap, tap... All the while dealing with passengers and traffic. The Uber app is a little more intuitive. There's still a lot of tapping, but the process feels simpler.

During my second week driving exclusively for Lyft, I complained about the app to a passenger who happened to work as a software engineer for Lyft. He seemed to be soliciting a critique, so I pointed out all the things I found problematic. His defensive response was typical of how most people who work at Lyft respond to criticism. If anybody wonders how Lyft manages to stay in the ride-hail game, despite Uber's dominance, it's their cult-like stubbornness to admit they are doing anything but the "Lord's Work."

Later that night, when I finally got sick of the Lyft Lines and the shitty app, I switched over to Uber. It was like putting my aching feet into a pair of worn-in slippers. I was able to see where I needed to go easily on the map, which is larger and has translucent lines over the boldly labeled streets. The passengers sit in back. Interaction is minimal and mostly respectful. Hardly anybody uses UberPool, their version of shared rides. And when people do request a ride through UberPool, nine times out of ten, they aren't matched with another rider.

I only gave a few rides with Uber that night, including one to SFO, but the following week I didn't get a payment summary. I went onto their website and blanched when I noticed my account was negative $168.00. I emailed support and, after five or six exchanges, was finally informed

I was being charged a "deposit" on the cracked phone. Plus a few rental charges from the weeks I didn't drive before I returned the phone.

That was the deal breaker.

At the current rates, it would take me several days to pay off the debt. All the while, shelling out what little cash I have left for gas, car washes and bridge tolls. There was just no way I could justify the expense. I kept thinking of all the things I could buy with $200. Like a couple used tires to replace my bald Michelins. Or a cheap break job before I have to fix the rotors as well. Both of which I desperately need. The squeaking is getting louder each day. And I'm one particularly sharp rock away from a blowout on the rugged streets of San Francisco. What I make from driving for Uber and Lyft, with the constantly diminishing rates, barely covers my bills, much less necessary maintenance on my car so I can keep driving for Uber and Lyft.

When the Wife found out Uber was charging me $200 for a piece of shit iPhone 4 (which goes for about $80 on eBay), she was livid. Absolutely forbade me from driving for Uber again. I swore up and down that I wasn't that stupid. But stuck in the car on The Embarcadero during a torrential downpour with Tight-Lipped Tina sulking in my passenger seat, I have to admit the thought crossed my mind.

After a grueling fifteen minutes, I'm $3.20 richer, but no closer to her destination. I notice a few taxis go by in the far right lane. I get behind a Yellow cab like a running back following a linesman towards a first down and hope for the best. I learned long ago to always follow cab drivers. If I'm on a street and there are no taxis, I know I'm on the wrong street.

Eventually other cars get hip to the possibility of escape and we continue crawling past Market. As soon as I can, I weave into the right turn lane and head down Mission. Fight my way onto Beale Street, trying not to get stuck in the middle of the intersection. In my infinite list of grievances with Bay Area drivers, the tendency to block intersections should be a crime punishable by public flogging in Union Square. And yet, here I am, my front end past the crosswalk as the light turns yellow and the car in front of me has nowhere to go. Not to be a hypocritical asshole, I drive straight and flip a bitch in the middle of the block. Crowd my way back to the corner. After four green lights, I finally make the turn. I get into the left lane so I can bypass the freeway traffic.

In between phone calls, tweets and Facebook updates, Tina keeps coughing and hacking. As I head down a glorified alley under the Bay Bridge, she starts making groaning sounds.

"Are you okay?" I ask.

"I haven't eaten today. I'm a little nauseous."

"Sorry. I'll try not to drive so fast." But what can I do? I cut through Bayside Village to Brannan. Then down a side street to Townsend. I take the turns easy, but all the other cars on the road are being aggressive. A dickhead in a BMW rides my ass. I have no choice but to fight to make it through the lights. I just want to get this girl out of my car!

When I finally reach her destination and she dashes out into the drizzle, I take a deep breath. End the ride. But Lyft's having server problems. The ride won't close out.

Fucking Lyft! I curse the app as I keep clicking the "wait" button until the command finally goes through. Certain I'll get a low rating from Tina, since I didn't have the Moses-like ability to part traffic, I rate her three stars. Go back into driver mode. Instantly, I get another request. 5th and Townsend. Postmates HQ, the delivery startup that used to be in a second floor walk-up on Valencia before moving to a slick new office space across from Caltrain. As bad as it is to be an Uber or Lyft driver, from what I've read, driving for Postmates is worse. There seems to be no end in sight to the exploitative business models of the emerging gig economy. Or suckers to participate in their mercenary schemes.

Tom is just as reticent as Tina. He sits up front too.

Kudos to Lyft for effectively brainwashing these kids into acting like they're really supposed to be friends with their drivers. But they're all just so… awkward. I wonder if they even have friends in the real world. Maybe if we were communicating through FaceTime it would be easier.

In my never-ending plight to neutralize awkward situations, I fancy myself a bit of a techie whisperer. I ease Tom into a conversation.

"My company has a deal with Lyft," he tells me, in response to my query about whether he also uses Uber. "We get a certain amount of free rides each week."

Lyft emailed me about this new program called Lyft for Work when it launched, in case I worked for a company that would benefit from the service. Oh sure… Like I would drive for Lyft if I had a real job to fall back on! But I guess in the so-called "sharing" economy, we're all supposed to be rubbing each other's backs. Only problem is, these days, I'm steady rubbing backs and there's nobody to rub mine.

Traffic through SoMa is as bad as it was on The Embarcadero. But the rain is letting up. I weave my way over to 7th Street. Cross Market and head through the Tenderloin. Tom lives in Nob Hill. Stopped at the light on Bush and Taylor, a block and a half from his destination, I suggest he might want to walk the rest of the way.

"That's alright," he mumbles

Whatever. Twenty-seven cents a minute is better than nothing, I guess.

I ask Tom about the pizza place on the corner. I've always wondered about Uncle Vito's. "It looks legit," I say. "Do you order from there?"

"No," he tells me. "They're not on Eat24 or Postmates."

"But the number's right there on the window. It says, 'For delivery call.' You should just put it in your phone."

"Yeah. I guess." He makes no effort to take his phone out.

"Man, that's the kind of place you don't even look up on Yelp first," I declare after a few minutes of silence.

Tom grunts. Between us, there is only a gear shifter and a center console. But the distance is wider than the San Francisco Bay.

Several green lights later, he finally says, "I think I'll walk the rest of the way."

"Might as well," I say with a slight chuckle. "I'm not going anywhere any time soon."

I end the ride. Fortunately, Lyft isn't having server issues this time. And hey, I scored 25 percent prime time on top of the regular fare. I give Tom five stars. Now I just have to hope he doesn't rate me low because of the added charge… or the traffic… or talking… or the weather… or for any of the other reasons Lyft passengers rate their drivers low.

I stay out of driver mode since I'm stuck in traffic. No point in trying to pick up a passenger until I can actually move.

At least the rain has let up.

For the next several green lights, parked in front of Uncle Vito's, I watch the pie maker toss dough and bang my fingers on the steering wheel along to the Cramps. Turn up the volume and hope there'll still be some prime time left once I get out of this traffic jam.

$7

PILTDOWNLAD

NO. 10.75

The third installment in the **Behind the Wheel** series is a ribald journey into the reality of driving a bonafide San Francisco taxicab. Gritty and raw, the view from a cab is not for the faint-hearted. From facilitating drug deals to abetting prostitution to just getting people home safely from the clubs, the job of a night cabbie isn't over until the sun comes up.

BEHIND THE WHEEL
FROM UBER/LYFT TO TAXI
3

The Unexpurgated I DRIVE S.F.
Collected columns from the *San Francisco Examiner*
expanded with new material

my other ride is a taxicab

©2016 Kelly Dessaint

First Printing, Sept 2016
Fifth Printing, March 2019

Cover by Irina Dessaint

Some portions of this zine were originally published in my weekly column for the *S.F. Examiner*, except for "Is This a Lyft or Do I Need To Pay You?" and parts of "It's A Cabbies Life for Me," which first appeared on Broke-Ass Stuart's Goddamn Website. The Late Night Larry stories were transcribed via iPhone during a weekly National barbecue. Irina helped with the graphics and cover manipulation.

The events in this zine take place between February 2015 and August 2016.

"Maxie the Taxi" was a comic strip that appeared regularly in the *New Deep City Press*, a magazine published by San Francisco cab drivers in the 70s and 80s.

BEHIND THE WHEEL 3

FROM UBER/LYFT TO TAXI

⊙ It's The Cabbie's Life for Me 187

⊙ The Road to Legitimacy 191

⊙ My First Taxi Shift 196

⊙ Taxi Driving as a Public Service 202

⊙ The Displacement Narrative 204

⊙ The Incurable Madness of Taxi Driving 210

⊙ Is This a Lyft or Do I Need to Pay You? 211

⊙ The Danger Dog Incident 213

⊙ Playlists, Profanity & Other Trade Secrets 216

⊙ On the Recitation of the Waybill 218

⊙ The Picky Couple 221

⊙ When Nature Calls, Business Picks Up 222

⊙ The View from a Taxi 225

⊙ Guilty of Driving a Cab 229

⊙ What's in a Passenger? 230

⊙ Adventures in Late Night Cabstands 236

⊙ Marching Backwards into the Future 238

⊙ Aiding and Abetting Passengers' Vices 248

⊙ Late Night Larry on Hope 251

⊙ The Patron Saint of Late Night Drunks 253

⊙ Cogs in the Wheels of Corruption 255

⊙ A Good Night Comes at a Price 257

⊙ Late Night Larry on Pukers 262

⊙ I Drive a Taxi So You Don't Have To 262

⊙ The Perils of Shopping on the Black Market 264

⊙ When We Talk About Uber/Lyft 266

⊙ A Hell Ride into the Peninsula 269

⊙ Late Night Larry on Orgasms 271

⊙ When the Driving's Over the Real Slog Begins 274

PILTDOWNLAD #10.75

TAXI DRIVER INSTITUTE

Teaching drivers from around the world the streets of San Francisco

Certificate of Completion

Kelly Dessaint

sequential # 8366 test # 10 license # 1482 expires 10,18

has completed twenty-eight hours of taxi driver training

including two hours of sensitivity training as required

by San Francisco Municipal Transportation Agency

on this 16 day of January 2015 AD

Ruach Graffis
Director
opeiu 3 -afl-cio-ab

IT'S THE CABBIE'S LIFE FOR ME!

I'm inbound on Post Street. Waiting for the light to change at Jones, I practice my double bass drumming on the steering wheel along to the Slayer CD blasting from the stereo in my taxicab.

It's rush hour. Up ahead, Union Square is a sea of brake lights.

There's something counterintuitive about driving into a traffic jam, but for a taxi driver, that's where the money is. After three months behind the wheel of a bona fide San Francisco cab, I've become Zen with downtown traffic. I embrace the challenge of gridlock. So when the light turns green, I charge headlong into the congestion.

At Taylor, I kill the tunes, roll down my window and listen for the acute whistles from hotel doormen that reverberate through the streets.

I cruise slowly past the J.W. Nothing. At Powell, I check the cabstand in front of the St. Francis. Too long. Glance towards the Sir Francis Drake, but the faux Yeoman Warder is minding his own business.

Across the street, an arm goes up. I zoom in to sweep him up before another taxi has a chance to snake my fare.

Businessman heading to the W. Hotel. Traffic is snarled as I creep towards Montgomery, but at least I'm getting paid to cross Market.

After dropping him off, I drive past the Moscone center. Another flag. This one back to Union Square. From there, I score a long fare to Monterey Heights.

Nice enough guy. Works in finance. Insists on taking 280, despite going so far out of the way.

Whatever. His dime.

We start chatting.

Eventually, he asks the sixty-four-thousand-dollar question: "So... why aren't you driving for Uber?"

I tell him I did the Uber/Lyft thing for ten months before switching to taxi.

He's surprised.

They always are.

"Shouldn't it be the other way around?" he asks.

Even though I get asked the same thing multiple times a night, I'm never sure how to respond...

Basically, there were more reasons not to drive for Uber and Lyft than to continue driving for Uber and Lyft.

For one, I wasn't making enough money after the two start-ups went to war for market dominance and began slashing prices. After ten months, my bank account was overdrawn, my credit cards were maxed out, I was riddled with self-loathing and, due to the insurance risks, I constantly worried I'd have to declare bankruptcy if I got into an accident.

My car was getting ragged out. The streets of San Francisco are ripped to shit, a minefield of potholes and steel plates from all construction going on across the city, not to mention general disrepair.

The backseat of my car was starting to look like I'd been transporting farm animals.

Then there was the insurance question...

One night, I was in Lyft mode, driving up De Haro in Potrero Hill to pick up a guy named Scott. As I climbed up the hill, a Mercedes coup rounded the corner on 19th and barreled straight at me. All I could see were headlights. I braced for the inevitable impact. Somehow, miraculously—no doubt due to German engineering—the driver of the Benz only came about two inches from sideswiping me.

In the wave of panic that followed, all I could think about was if she'd hit me and saw that Lyft placard in my window, she could have easily told her insurance company... and it's not much of a stretch to assume they would have used that as a loophole not to cover the damage. From there, I would have been at the mercy of Lyft's insurance, because my insurance company obviously wouldn't cover me since I was engaging in commercial activities. And even though it was a no fault accident, by using Lyft's insurance, I'd have to pay a $2,500 deductive.

Now, like most Uber/Lyft drivers, I was only using my car as a cut-rate taxicab because my finances are... Let's just say, precarious. I don't have $2,500 sitting around. But until I came up with the money, I wouldn't have a car to earn money.

Still... the most troubling part of driving for Uber and Lyft, though, was the realization I was subsidizing multi-million—or, in Uber's case, multi-billion—dollar companies. And for what? Empty promises and a sense of community?

What bullshit. I never felt like anything but an underpaid, untrained and unregulated taxi driver.

From the beginning, I was appalled by the self-entitled culture that spawned the phenomenon of "ridesharing" and the consequences on the livelihoods of cab drivers.

It wasn't easy participating in the destruction of a blue-collar industry. After all, I'm a descendent of coal miners, janitors, store clerks and army grunts. Being an Uber/Lyft driver was not in my nature. To be successful at it requires personality traits I'll never possess: the ability to cheat and scam. And a complete lack of conscience.

Since the only time you make decent money is during surge pricing, you have to take pride in ripping people off. The rest of the time, you're barely making minimum wage, so you must be somewhat stupid as well...

You're basically running your personal car into the ground and hoping to luck out with a ride that's more than five bucks.

Some drivers have figured out how to game the system and earn more money by referring drivers than actually driving themselves... but isn't that just a bizarre take on the pyramid scheme?

Despite Uber's political spin or Lyft's cheerful advertising campaign, using your personal car as a taxi is not sustainable. Each time I got behind the wheel of my Jetta and turned on the apps, I had to overlook the absurdity of what I was doing. It never ceased to amaze me that people would be so willing to ride in some random dude's car. But since my passengers acted as if the activity were perfectly normal, I went along with it...

Once I realized what I'd gotten myself into, I wanted to document the exploitative nature of this predatory business model. I wanted to expose the inherent risks associated with inadequate insurance, the lack of training and the vulnerability of not having anyone to contact in an emergency. I wanted to shed light on the reality of being a driver, what it was like dealing with the constant fare cuts, the enforced jingoism and the tyranny of an unfair rating system. I wanted to reveal the lies. All the dirty lies. I started a blog and published two zines about my experiences.

Naïvely, I thought reporting on these issues from the perspective of an actual driver would make a difference.

I was wrong.

Most people hold on to their faith in the corporate spirit even when it goes against their best interest. That's one of the things I've figured out from all this.

Oh, and that I really like driving the streets of San Francisco.

So I signed up for taxi school and went pro. Now I make more money, feel more relaxed and no longer have to worry about declaring bankruptcy if I get into an accident...

I don't tell my passenger any of this though... Now that I've been a real taxi driver for a few months, I try to deflect the Uber/Lyft question. I'm not proud to have driven for them as long as I did. In fact, I'm mostly ashamed of it.

So I say, "The way I figured it, people hate taxi drivers so much they must be doing something right."

I laugh. He doesn't join me. Instead, he tells me how much he prefers Uber. From the 101 interchange to the Monterey exit, he regales me with a litany of horror stories about taking taxis before Uber and Lyft came to town... How they wouldn't take people to the Richmond or Sunset districts... How the cabs smelled horrible... The drivers were rude... They wouldn't accept credit cards... And when you called dispatch, they never showed up.

I listen to his jeremiad patiently. It's all I can do. I've heard these claims repeatedly since I started driving a car for hire in San Francisco. As much as I want to apologize for the past transgressions of taxi drivers, I can't help but wonder why he's in a cab in the first place.

Oh, Uber must be surging.

"Honestly," he says at one point, "I don't take cabs because I don't want to deal with fucking cabbies. No offense."

I do take offense! I want to tell him. I actually enjoy being a cab driver. I feel more connected to San Francisco than I ever did with Uber and Lyft. And I admire the hell out of the veteran cab drivers, most of whom are longtime residents of the city.

And they have the best stories.

Becoming a cab driver was like joining a league of disgruntled gentlemen and surly ladies. The buccaneers of city streets. Taking people's money for getting them where they need to go. By whatever means necessary.

I want to this guy to fuck off for badmouthing my friends. I've met some amazing cab drivers since I started hanging around taxi yards and I don't want to just sit by as people besmirch my friends…

But I keep my mouth shut.

I drive.

Do my job…

After a while, though, the guy's vitriol gets to me. When I drop him off, I'm bummed beyond belief.

At least he gives me a decent tip. As I drive away, I turn the Slayer back on. Full blast. Take Portola down the hill. Should be plenty of fares in the Castro. Especially if Uber's still surging.

THE ROAD TO LEGITIMACY

I was talking about driving a taxi long before I ever went to cab school. In various blog posts detailing my experiences as an Uber/Lyft driver, I wrote about a quest for legitimacy.

On Twitter, I lambasted the predatory business models of the "sharing" economy and constantly tweeted my ambition to drive a real taxi. I joined a vast community of cab drivers and disgruntled Uber/Lyft drivers around the world who ranted about the companies online.

I got into fights with people on Facebook. I was often called a troll. I was blocked by many people and kicked out of several Uber and Lyft groups for talking shit. It never ceased to astonish me how loyal people can be towards companies that only want to screw their workers over.

After a while, it was too late to back down. Even though it was an intimidating prospect, I had to bite the bullet.

I'd read the list of requirements on the San Francisco Municipal Transit Authority website multiple times, but going through the intensive process was a daunting task. It's not easy becoming a cab driver in San Francisco. So I did what any self-respecting blogger would do: I tweeted about it.

Numerous taxi drivers were more than happy to offer advice.

In December of 2014, Thomas, a DeSoto driver, approached me on Twitter and answered all my stupid questions, like where I would park my car and what the deal was with the Flywheel app.

Then Mansur, a former cab driver I'd met at a protest outside Uber headquarters the previous October, introduced me to Jacob Black, who encouraged me to come to National/Veterans Cab Co. And since the first step to becoming a cab driver is going to taxi school, he gave me the number for the Taxi Driver Institute.

I called right away. When I told Ruach Graffis, the director of the Institute, that I'd been driving for Uber and Lyft and wanted to go legit, she said, "Don't worry, I'll make an honest cab driver out of you."

I bragged about knowing my way around the city. She gave me a pop quiz on the named streets of Noe Valley. I failed miserably.

The following Tuesday, I took BART to the Sixteenth Street Station. Since I'd made so little the previous week and over New Year's, I had to borrow the $120 I needed for cab school from my father-in-law.

The Taxi Driver Institute is located on the third floor of the Redstone Building, a historic landmark also known as the Labor Temple.

It was in the auditorium of the Labor Temple that San Francisco workers organized the General Strike of 1934.

In the lobby, I marveled at the murals depicting the accomplishments of the labor movement. As I walked through the hallways, I passed offices for local unions, social outreach organizations and publishers.

I couldn't believe a place like this still existed in San Francisco, where the on-demand economy first took hold. And where companies like Uber, Postmates and TaskRabbit practice free market capitalism under the guise of "disruption" and push workers' rights back to the 19th century.

In the Labor Temple, I found the legitimacy I was looking for.

The Taxi Driver Institute is in a small room filled with thousands of books and what might possibly be an exhaustive collection of taxi memorabilia. The feng shui is organized chaos.

Ruach sits at her cluttered desk in front of a conference table. The first thing she taught us was that "cabbie" is not an appropriate term for a taxi driver. Since the word is gender specific, a female taxi driver would then be a "cabette," which she finds insulting.

Over the next four days, Omar, the only other student that week, and I huddled together furiously taking notes while Ruach browbeat cab driving into our brains as if we were going into battle and our lives depended on what we learned in the next 28 hours of course work. Her lesson plan included numerous handouts, worksheets, checklists, multi-colored hi-liters, videos, maps and more than one tongue-lashing.

Omar's limited grasp of written English proved problematic at times, so I worked with him individually, both in class and outside.

To compensate me for my tutoring, he bought me lunch each day and cups of coffee. He told me of his time working in St. Petersburg and his family back in Oman.

Besides SFMTA taxi regulations and traffic laws, we covered ADA requirements and studied how to navigate the streets efficiently. There was even sensitivity training and instructions on safety and protecting ourselves as workers. In the afternoons, she quizzed us on that day's material. And each night, we left with homework.

On Friday, we had our final exam.

As I walked out of the Labor Temple with my certificate, I felt like I'd accomplished something way more significant than just filling out a form through an app. I'd passed Ruach's class! But this was only another step in the process of becoming a cab driver...

The next week, I got fingerprinted and waited in line at the DMV for a copy of my driving record. Finally, on Thursday, I attended a daylong class at the SFMTA that included lectures and Powerpoint presentations from San Francisco Paratransit, the SF Bike Coalition and Lighthouse for the Blind. Followed by a test, which was graded immediately.

That afternoon, I left the SFMTA building a bona fide San Francisco taxi driver.

Before I got on BART to head home to Oakland, I tweeted a picture of my temporary A-Card with an homage to Ai Wei-Wei: a shot of my hand, middle finger extended, in front of the Uber logo outside their headquarters on Market Street.

MY FIRST TAXI SHIFT

With varying bouts of anxiety and momentary bursts of excitement I drive to the National/Veterans Cab lot for my first shift behind the wheel of a real taxicab on Thursday.

A week has passed since receiving my temporary A-card from the SFMTA and now it's time to bite the bullet.

The day before, I'd met Jacob Black in the National office to meet the Russian manager, Alex, and get trained on the taximeter and other equipment in the cab. After that, I went to the DeSoto cab yard around the corner to sign up for Flywheel, the taxi-hailing app. Before issuing me a dedicated Android, I had to watch a bunch of instructional videos and take a test.

At the table, there was just an old-timer and myself. The process was pretty basic: an interactive program explained how to run the app, followed by some multiple-choice questions. I was blowing right through it while the old guy kept struggling with the process itself. At one point, he got up and asked the young kids behind laptops what SMS meant …

On Thursday, when I get to the National/Veterans yard, I meet up with Jacob Black in the office. He introduces me to Keith, an owner/operator who's agreed to let me work his cab for the weekend.

After sizing me up, Keith gives me the key and medallion to Veterans 1512 and tells me, "Put $80 in the glovebox after your shift. That's your gate for tonight. Tomorrow, the gate will be $100. Your shift ends at 3:30. Fill the cab up with gas and bring it back here." He shows me where to hide the key.

Since I'm working for an owner/operator, I don't have to deal with the dispatch window. Yet.

Pulling out of the lot, I try to remember everything I learned in Ruach's class and what to do with the cab. Despite Jacob's vote of confidence, my nerves are frayed. Much like when I started doing Lyft, except this time I'm in a Prius. So that's my first obstacle: figuring out how to drive this green, red and white tin can. Nothing about the vehicle's dash or the gear shifters makes sense. Everything is the opposite of a normal car. And why does it keep beeping? What am I doing wrong? Goddamnit.

It's like driving a pissed off computer on wheels.

Once I get my shit together, I head to the Mission, thinking I'd hit the Philz at Folsom, a pre-driving custom from my Uber/Lyft days. But I can't find a place to park on 24th, and worry about parking the cab on side streets. What if someone broke into it and stole the tablet displayed prominently on the dash and on the back of the passenger seat headrest? Is there a market for used taxi equipment?

While I'm about to circle back and try again, a man waves at me.

Oh shit! My first fare!

I stop. He walks over to my back door. I quickly check to make sure the door is unlocked.

He gets in and tells me an intersection I don't immediately recognize. "Where is that?" I ask.

"Bernal Heights."

"Oh, should I take Mission or Folsom?" I inquire, pleased with myself for knowing the best ways to approach Bernal.

"Folsom," he says. "I'll direct you the rest of the way."

I hit the meter and off we go, talking about how much the city has changed. He bought his house in the 80s but thinking about selling and moving out to Yolo County.

"You only live once," he quips.

When I pull up to his house, the meter amount is $9.55. He hands me a $20 bill and asks for five back. Jacob had told me to bring at least $40 in change, so I'm ready with the fiver.

"You know," I say as he opens the door. "I wasn't going to mention it, but this is my first ride as a taxi driver."

"I was your first fare?" He beams. "Well, it was my pleasure! I never would've known. You're going to do great cab driver!"

With my second vote of confidence that day, I shove the dub in my front pocket and set off to find more cash on the streets of San Francisco.

At first, I drive aimlessly. Unsure where to go. Still scared of SoMa and the Financial. Do what I did with Uber and Lyft: circle the Mission.

The Flywheel phone sits silently, clipped awkwardly to an air vent. My assumption in cab school that I'd be relying on the Flywheel app to get rides is proving to be a false one.

Normally, with Uber or Lyft, I'd have a ride within five or ten minutes of turning on the app. Not Flywheel though.

After driving around the Mission for half an hour without a request, I cruise into SoMa, inching towards the congestion of downtown.

As I'm driving down Folsom, a Flywheel order finally comes in for address on Howard. I take a left on an alley and pull up to the address. A girl comes out immediately.

"I'm in a hurry," she says. "I need to get to Serpentine. Do you know where that is?"

"Dogpatch, right?" I say. I'm almost certain it's on the corner of Twentieth and Third, since I'd taken people there multiple times with Uber and Lyft.

"If you say so," she responds, breathlessly strapping on the seatbelt. "I have no idea. I just need to meet people there in five minutes."

Not knowing any other way, I take Eighth to the turnaround. Then De Haro to 16th and down to Third.

Fortunately, she doesn't know her way around and accepts my route without question.

I deposit her right on the corner. She thanks me and walks down the block to the bar.

Driving away, I enter the metered amount into the Flywheel app. $12.80. She had entered an automatic 25% tip.

I'm almost halfway to my gate …

For the rest of the evening, I stay clear of the congested parts of the city. I still manage to get a few Flywheel requests and several street flags. I realize that it's pointless to patrol the places I used to take people in Uber and Lyft. Bars like Dear Mom, Blondie's and Zeitgeist. Not matter how many times I drive past, nobody wants in my cab.

My confidence begins to soar. As luck would have it, each ride goes off without a hitch. When I doubt my routes, I apply advice from a cab driver who visited Ruach's class, who suggested asking the passenger if they have a preference. Otherwise I just admit that it's my first night driving a cab. Everyone is kind and accommodating.

As business slows down around 10 p.m., I finally venture into the Union Square area. Explore North Beach. Then cruise Polk Street.

Around midnight, the lack of potential fares and the fatigue gets to me. I pull over on Polk near Jackson for a smoke. Contemplate my ability to last all the way until 3:30 a.m. This is my first 12-hour shift. With Lyft and Uber, the longest I'd worked was seven or eight hours in a day.

Check my phone for a late night coffeshop that's not Starbucks. Nothing. I flick the filter into the gutter and climb back into Veterans 1512.

As I'm heading south on Polk, a woman resembling a bag lady flags me at Sacramento.

It takes a while for her to get inside the cab.

"Jackson and Hyde, please," she says midway, in a British accent.

"My goodness. Are you even old enough to drive a taxi?"

"Uhm…" The question gives me a momentary brain freeze. I don't know how to respond, or how to negotiate her cross streets from our current location. I rack my brain to remember how to circumvent the one-ways of Russian Hill and get to Jackson. In the process, I fumble with the gear shifter, forgetting that, in a Prius, you push instead of pull, and the car jerks forward.

I gasp.

"What's going on?" the woman snaps.

"Sorry," I mumble, struggling with the shifter. "Minor technical difficulty." I laugh.

"Do you even know what you're doing?" she asks sharply.

"I uhmm…"

"You don't, do you?" Her tone is all disappointed British schoolmarm.

For half a millisecond I try to conjure up an appropriate defense, but quickly admit defeat. "No, ma'am," I reply.

"Just go down to California and take a right on Larkin."

"Yes, ma'am."

When I pull up to her building, I realize I've forgotten to turn on the meter. "Don't worry about the fare," I say, continuing to apologize profusely.

"Here." She hands me a five-dollar bill. "It's usually a five dollar ride."

"Thanks."

While removing her possessions from the back seat, she resumes the chiding. "You better get your act together, young man, if you're going to make it as a cabbie."

"Yes, ma'am."

Before closing the back door, she gives me a final look of disapproval. I drive away, grateful she didn't rap me across the knuckles ...

Around 3:30 a.m., I pull into the Arco at 14th and Mission. When the pump stops at $7.23, I try to squeeze more gas into the tank.

In the bay next to me, another cab driver is gassing up.

"Is this normal?" I ask. "Seven bucks?"

He shrugs. "Sometimes it's eight dollars."

Maybe a Prius isn't such a stupid car after all...

Back at the National yard, I put my gate fee in the envelope Keith left for me in the glove box and count the cash I have left. Minus my initial $40 in change and factoring in my Square and Flywheel payments, I'm ahead $70.

Not bad, I think. Especially since Jacob had told me not to feel bad if I only broke even, seeing as how it was my first night in a cab. But I proved that theory wrong.

Now to make it through my next shift...

TAXI DRIVING AS A PUBLIC SERVICE

The National/Veterans Cab Co. is essentially a junkyard in the Bayview. A methhead named Patrick lives in the alley. When he's not showering in the car wash, he smashes windshields and knocks over garbage cans.

Every day, I wait outside the office window with the other night drivers until cabs become available. We talk taxi and mingle with the day drivers who report on traffic conditions and activity at the airport.

When Aziz finally calls my name, he throws a medallion and key into the drawer. I exchange them for a fiver.

More than ready to hit the streets, I quickly vacuum and wash the latest clunker. I race out of the yard and head over Potrero Hill to Caltrain. Before the 5:05 train pulls into the station, I get my accouterments in order, log in to the Flywheel phone and load a Motörhead CD into the stereo.

My first ride has multiple stops. All the while, the guy's telling me he'll tip me big. On an $18 fare, he gives me $20.

Whatever. I head down Market. A hand goes up but a Yellow Cab jams in front of me and snakes the fare.

Undeterred, I continue on Market. At Seventh, I'm waiting for the light when an elderly woman approaches my cab. She opens the front door and, despite my protests to get in the back, takes the passenger seat.

The light turns green. A bus is right behind me.

"Where to?" I ask impatiently.

She looks me in the face and says, "Momomomomomomomo."

I glance in my rearview, surprised the bus driver hasn't starting honking yet. They're usually unforgiving.

I swallow the gob of panic rising in my throat and ask again, "Where?"

"Momomomomomomomo." There's a slight inflection in her chant as she motions to the left. "Momomomomomomomo."

"The Tenderloin?"

She shakes her head. "Momomomomomomomo."

Since I can't turn left off Market, I head down Sixth. My brain is bouncing around my skull slapping itself in desperation. Think! Think! Think! I try to remember what I learned in taxi school about transporting passengers with special needs. But the ADA videos we watched didn't cover situations like these.

As much as I believe in taxicabs as a public utility, sometimes I have to remind myself that, unlike my previous Uber/Lyft experience, I drive all of San Francisco now. Not just the people with smart phones who don't mind having their personal details catalogued. I'm a taxi driver. This is the job I chose.

I look at the woman. She's wearing grandma clothes. Her hair is styled. She reminds me of my mother. At least before the Alzheimer's got so bad they had to take her away.

At Mission, she directs me to the right. At Ninth, she has me take another right. It seems we're starting to communicate. I still assume we're heading to the Tenderloin, but she indicates the lane that goes onto Hayes. So, Van Ness?

Stuck in traffic, I watch as she calmly digs into her purse and pulls out a pair of glasses, wipes the lenses and replaces the ones she's wearing. Even her purse is like my mother's, jammed full of papers and mementos.

We cross Market and she hands me a $20 bill. I realize I haven't turned the meter on. I hold the money as I get in the middle lane on Van Ness. A few blocks later, she signals to the left.

"Ellis?" I ask.

"Momomomomomomomo."

After the turn, she emphatically has me pull over. I give her $10 change. She walks back to Van Ness.

At this point, I'm overwhelmed with emotion. I can't stop thinking about my mother and how, in less than a decade, the Alzheimer's took over and she forgot how to talk and then how to eat. We were all so helpless.

It was sad as hell.

I turn right on Franklin. At the light on O'Farrell, I see the woman walking up Van Ness.

I take off, heading towards Union Square. But I can't keep going. I have to know she'll be okay. I circle back around on Geary.

As I wait for the light at Van Ness, I see the assisted living facility next to Tommy's.

Everything comes into focus. I freaked out for nothing! She knew where she was going all along!

I laugh away the tension and wipe my eyes. It's 6:15. I've had the cab for over an hour. I'm nowhere close to making my gate. When the light turns green, I come out of the pocket like a bullet and race into the belly of the beast.

THE DISPLACEMENT NARRATIVE

San Francisco is like a drug. When it gets inside you, each moment is a revelation. Until things get ugly.

On Friday and Saturday nights, after the bars have dumped their cock-eyed patrons onto the sidewalks and the feeding frenzy for rides is over, I look for a good cabstand. I used to work the Gold Club, a strip club on

Howard Street. I'd wait in line until it was my turn to drive some businessman to his hotel room, or some poor sod home to his girlfriend/wife as he freaks out about smelling like a stripper.

"Their perfume is like an living entity, once it attaches itself to you, it never goes away."

"Just tell her you took a cab," I say. "Everybody knows taxis stink."

Many a time, though, I end of with the strippers themselves... tragic cases of girls trying to milk desperate men for whatever they can get, whether it's a car or tuition at SFSU. Several times I get girls trying to hook up with a drunk customer for a date outside the club, which is apparently against the rules and usually involves multiple phone calls while I'm pulled over on the side of some street in SoMa until they seal the deal. And then, when I drop them off, they only pay the meter amount. Sans tip.

I learned fast. Strippers are not tippers.

Then I discovered the DJ venues.

Unlike the guys who frequent high-end strip joints and reek of alcohol and desperation, the passengers I pick up from places like 1015 Folsom and Mighty climb into my backseat with bottled waters and cat-that-ate-the-canary grins.

Occasionally, they're chatty. It's not always easy, though, having a conversation with somebody in the grips of a chemical high.

One Saturday night, double-parked outside Public Works in the ad hoc cabstand, my back door opens. A couple in their late thirties gets in.

"Seventh and Mission."

It's been a busy weekend for tourists and I instinctively ask if they're going to one of the motels there.

"No, my condo," the guy says.

The woman laughs. "'My condo...' You sound like a douchebag."

"Hey, I'm too high for semantics." He asks if I'm cool making two stops. They're going to her apartment after picking something up at his place. Which is actually on Natoma. He tries to give me directions.

"Don't worry. I got you." I take a right on Eighth and a left into the one-way alley.

"See, he's a real taxi driver," the woman says.

While he runs inside, she asks me how long I've been driving a cab.

"Almost a year." I don't mention that I did Uber and Lyft for most of that time. I'm not in the mood for another one of those discussions.

"Where do you live?" she asks.

"Oakland."

"Oh. That's too bad. It seems like everyone is getting priced out of San Francisco these days." She tells me about a friend who had to move to Oakland recently. "Now I never see her anymore!"

She continues to rant about displacement and gentrification until the guy returns. Then it's on to the next stop.

"The Fox Plaza."

I ask for the cross streets. They direct me up Seventh to Market and then onto Hayes.

When I see the high-rise apartment building on the left, I say, "Oh, I know that place." I'd picked up and dropped off there multiple times during my Uber/Lyft days. Which is why I don't know the name of the building. Just the pinned location in the app.

"You lie," the woman seems to whisper.

"No, really." I laugh, thinking she's messing with me.

"You're lying."

I realize she's not whispering. She's seething.

Confused, I pull up to the front door. The fare is $9.55. She hands me a twenty.

"Give me back ten," she says snidely. "You know, I would have given you a fat tip, but I don't reward dishonesty."

"What are you talking about?" I ask, dumbfounded.

"You're a liar," she snaps at me while getting out of the cab. "You said you were from here. That's not cool, man."

As I cruise down Tenth Street, I try to process what just happened. I never said I was from San Francisco. In her drug-addled mind, she assumed I'd been priced out of the city because I live in Oakland.

Sure, before Irina and I moved to Temescal a year and a half ago from Los Angeles we looked for an apartment in San Francisco first. But of course we couldn't afford anything. So while we may not have BEEN priced out, we definitely ARE priced out. Is there a difference?

Yes. There is.

I can hardly blame the woman for getting angry. Even before the latest housing crisis, assuming the role of a native San Franciscan was tantamount to criminal activity. Now that the stakes are higher, it's an outright sin.

At Howard, I wonder how many cabs are in the EndUp stand… But it's late. And the woman's scorn still burns. My head is dizzy and full of regret.

I hit 101 and drive back to the yard. I've had enough San Francisco for one night.

"Must be nice, though, to forget everything. Personal and financial problems, the constant tragedies in the world and the possibility of a future overrun with technology straight out of a dystopian movie."

Everybody must get stoned

O n Thursday night, after dropping off in Bernal Heights, I circle through the Mission looking for signs of life. I cruise past the Alamo Drafthouse as a movie lets out. I pull over and watch the crowd dissipate until I'm single and lonely. Then, I investigate Valencia Street. For once, I'm the only taxi around with an illuminated toplight. But it doesn't seem to matter.

I head to SoMa.

At 14th Street, a guy flags me. He's older, bespectacled, dressed in jeans and a V-neck sweater. Has the air of a successful middle manager.

"Where ya heading?" I ask.

"Can you take me to ..." He trails off and rests his forehead in his hand. Seems to fall asleep.

"Take you where?"

He looks up. "Yeah, I need to go to ..." Again, he leans forward like "The Thinker."

Goddamn it. Not again. I trust him from his contemplation. "Are you OK?"

"It's been a rough night." He chuckles.

"You going home?"

"Yeah."

"Can you at least tell me which neighborhood you live in?"

"It's ... uh, you know ... it's ... you know!"

"No. I don't!" I begin to list neighborhoods in The City.

"It's near Coit Tower," he says, finally.

OK. I start driving toward North Beach.

"So ... what kind of drugs did you take?" I inquire.

"No drugs. Just weed."

"Just weed?" I ask, like a dubious parent.

I DRIVE S.F.

"Strong weed!" He laughs and then goes quiet.

As I head down Mission Street, I think about the possibility of getting so high on marijuana I forgot where I lived ...

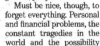

kelly DESSAINT

It hardly seems probable, although there was that one time in college when I smoked a joint with a co-worker and ended up in bed, swaddled in my duvet, rocking back and forth and chanting, "I'm good enough, I'm smart enough and doggone it, people like me."

Must be nice, though, to forget everything. Personal and financial problems, the constant tragedies in the world and the possibility of a future overrun with technology straight out of a dystopian movie.

But it seems impossible to escape, what with Facebook and Twitter. My phone is like a needle I use to mainline the distorted fire and brimstone of the 24-hour news cycle into my brain — a speedball of conflicting narratives — until I can't turn away from the strobe light of information

I'd love to forget all that. Even for just 10 minutes ...

Halfway up Kearney, the guy in back leans forward.

"OK, I know where I am now," he says.

I realize I've been holding my breath and sigh with relief.

After we cross Broadway, he directs me into the Bank of America parking lot on Green.

"What are we doing here?" I ask.

"We're going to smoke this joint."

"No, we're not!" I state, adamantly.

"Why not?

"Cause I'm driving! What's wrong with you?"

"C'mon. Let's get high." He hands me a conical plastic container with a joint inside. The label reads "Coated J."

"There's no way I'm smoking this."

"Huh?" He looks at me confused.

"You can't even remember where you live, and I have to drive a taxi!"

"But we have to!"

"No, we don't," I say. "I'm taking you home, and you're going to pay me."

"Alright. How much do I owe you?"

The meter reads $14.50.

"OK. I'll be back." He opens the back door.

"Wait a minute!"

"It's fine. I won't screw you over. Here." He gives me his phone and walks toward the alley at the end of the parking lot.

"Where are you going?"

"I'll be right back." He disappears into a random door that could easily be a utility closet.

As I sit there, I'm not sure how worried I should be. I have his phone, so he has to come back, right? It's an iPhone 7. The SIM card is missing. That's not a good sign. Nice case, though.

I hold the joint up to the light. It's covered in crystals and what I assume is some kind of wax or tar. No wonder he's stoned out of his gourd.

Five minutes go by. Just as I'm about to investigate the door he ran into, the guy returns, all smiles. Walks up to my window and hands me a credit card.

"You going to be OK?" I ask, handing over his stuff.

"Sure!" He holds up the joint like the Olympic torch, giggles and runs off into the night.

Kelly Dessaint is a San Francisco taxi driver. Write to Kelly at piltdownlad@gmail.com or visit his blog at www.idrivesf.com.

THE INCURABLE MADNESS OF TAXI DRIVING

In my rickety National taxicab, I own the streets of San Francisco. I take my turns with a vengeance. I converge on Union Square at full tilt. Like all cab drivers, I follow the rules of the road that were lain down by the cab drivers who preceded us.

I'm a Fusion driver. Besides having the extra power when I need to beat the lights or just carve the streets when there's nothing else to do but form figure eights around the clubs and bars, the Ford Fusion is better suited to my 6'2" frame than the Camry or Prius.

National 182 is my preferred cab. There's something about the black leatherette backseat with its worn-in mitt quality, the purple lights along the floorboard, the superb sound system and the ability to adjust my seat into countless positions to alleviate potential leg cramps.

I've happily greased palms to make sure the keys and tin medallion for 182 slid through the drawer when I walk up to the window.

This week, however, 182 is on a spare. So I'm back in rotation, vying for the best available jalopy on the National/Veterans lot.

On Thursday, I get Veteran's 233, a Camry with suspension problems like most cabs in the fleet, but still better than the cramped Prius.

I end up with National 1100 the next day. A Fusion. When I turn the wheels, though, it's obvious that, besides the usual mechanical issues, the CV joints are shot.

As I wait for an Uber driver to clean his Towncar in the car wash, I make sure the input jack works. With all the racket this cab is going to make, I'll need to cloak the clamorous squeaking and clanking with music.

Wait.

Why is an Uber driver washing his Towncar in our lot?

Not to be detained from going to work by a scofflaw, I pull into what little space is left. The guy is cordial enough about sharing the equipment, but I trip over the hose as he rinses off his car, adding injury to the onerous insult of a former cab driver exploiting the facilities we pay for with our exorbitantly high gates.

You know, sometimes I wonder why I remain loyal to National and don't just walk down Upton Alley and become a Luxor man. Numerous cab drivers have asked me this very question. But the reason why I stay at National and why I drive a cab in the first place are one and the same. And honestly, I don't really know the answer.

Could it be that, as a kid of the 80s, I was more impressed by Mr. T. in *D.C. Cab* than De Niro in *Taxi Driver*? After all, National/Veterans is a perfect example of a cab company teetering on the brink of collapse, even though all the cabs in the yard go out each night and they're remodeling the stink hole that was the restroom.

Perhaps I'm a masochist, as Ethan once suggested. Or does it go deeper, to what Juneaux calls the "unique shade of exclusivity," the mysterious quality surrounding cab driving that draws those who have left the fold to return and try to validate their new career move by maintaining a connection to the legitimacy of the yard?

The best cab drivers are misfits. Rebels. Lunatics. Who else would do a job that requires you to sit behind the wheel for ten to 12 hours at a time, any number of days in a row, navigating the treacherous streets of San Francisco in hopes of getting enough decent rides or tips to make a profit? And since sleep deprivation seems to be an integral element, I can't help but think that if I got enough rest, I just might realize how absurd this entire venture is.

Taxi driving is an addiction. For which there are no meetings, just a barbeque on Sunday mornings, where I can air my grievances until the light fills the sky and I'm overwhelmed by the camaraderie and wonder that comes with the job.

I guess that's why I stay at National. For all the irritations and hassles I face, at least I'm not alone. And when I'm behind the wheel of a Fusion, no matter how rickety it may be, I'm part of something bigger than just driving a car for hire. I'm a San Francisco taxi driver. And for that, there seems to be no cure.

IS THIS A LYFT OF DO I HAVE TO PAY YOU?

It's Saturday night. I'm cruising through Hayes Valley, keeping a watchful eye for street hails outside the Jazz Center. On Franklin, a hand goes up, though somewhat feebly. I pull over anyway. A young guy approaches my window.

"Can you take me to Safeway?"

I look in my rearview at traffic approaching. "Of course! Get in!" I take off right before a wave of cars pile up behind me. "Which Safeway you want?"

"The one in the Marina. Do you need the address?"

"No."

I head up and over the hills, fighting to catch the timed lights. As I descend into Cow Hollow, I get in the right lane to bypass Lombard traffic.

Take a left at Bay. Past Fort Mason to Laguna. Pull into the Safeway parking lot and deposit the guy at the front door like a rock star. He thanks me and gets out of the cab.

"Hey! Don't forget to pay me!" I shout.

"Oh, sorry." He chuckles. "I'm just so used to Uber and Lyft…"

I laugh along good-naturedly. This happens all the time. Even though I'm driving a bright yellow cab with green checkers on the side. Even though there is a top light that boldly states "TAXI." Even though numbers and insignias are painted on the doors. Even though the windows have credit card stickers and permits. Even though "SAN FRANCISCO TAXICAB" is written on the side and trunk. And even though there is a taximeter on the dash, a tablet on the headrest of the passenger seat and plaques on the inside of the doors, I go through this farce multiple times a night.

I make an off-handed comment to the latest case in point that money still needs to exchange hands sometimes…

"That's why these apps are so great," the guy tells me earnestly. "They store my payment information. I request a car through my phone and—"

"I know all about them," I cut him off. Thinking, If Uber and Lyft are so great, why the fuck are you in a taxi? Then it hits me… Uber must be surging and Lyft is no doubt in prime time. When multipliers hit 1.9 or 200 percent, all these loyal rideshare users are suddenly clamoring to get in cabs, where the price is always the same, regardless of demand. (Although during rush hour when everybody wants in my cab, sometimes I think about auctioning off the seats to the highest bidder. But that would be illegal, right?)

"Fare-weather" passengers are a crapshoot. There are those who seem unsure how to behave in a taxi. Like this guy. While others tell me straight up Uber is surging 4.6x and that's the only reason they're slumming it in a cab. Some just act like they're in a rideshare and I have PTSD flashbacks to the ten months I drove for Uber and Lyft before switching to taxi.

As I run the guy's card through the Square on my iPhone and hand it back, he apologizes again.

"Don't worry about it," I tell him. "Happens all the time."

"Maybe you should consider driving for Uber then." He laughs.

I'm not sure how to respond. I consider mentioning that cabs have apps too. Flywheel works just like Uber, expect you get a real taxi driver who's fully insured and licensed. But instead, I mumble something about not wanting to be part of the problem anymore…

Whatever. It's getting late. I'm on my fourth 12-hour shift in a row. And now I'm in the Marina. During surge.

Unless I bug out, I'll end up on Union, getting flagged by seven bros who want to ride in my cab all at once ("we'll tip you") or a pack of girls heading to the Mission, commandeering my stereo and screaming at each other the whole way down Gough.

On occasions like these, I remember what Late Night Larry once told me: "You're a night cabbie! It's your job to make sure people have fun."

As I pull out of the parking lot and head down Laguna to Chestnut, I groan and join the party.

THE DANGER DOG INCIDENT

Last call on Polk Stret is a comple shitshow. As the bars let out, this kid flags me around Pine. Gets in with a danger dog. Now, I absolutely detest the smell of these noxious concoctions they make on all the street corners around bars and clubs: hot dogs wrapped in bacons and served with onions and jalapeños. But he's going to Glen Park – a $25 ride. So I let it slide.

As I race to the freeway on Hyde, he slurps down the hotdog like a porno chick sucking a cock. I roll down my window to relieve some of the stench and create an auditory distraction.

On I-280, he passes out. Cool. Makes for a better ride.

When I pull up to his house and try to wake him up, he doesn't stir.

"Hey man, we're at your place. You need to wake up."

"No," he says, like I'm his mommy trying to get him up for school in the morning.

"Hey! Wake up!" I turn the overhead light on. I shake his leg and try to get him conscious.

Eventually he sits up and tries to open the door.

"Don't forget to pay me," I remind him.

"You do it through the app."

"What app?"

"The Uber app."

"Man, I don't have anything to do with Uber. This is a taxi."

"You can still do it."

"Uhm, no. You need to pay me."

He reaches into his pocket and pulls out a wrinkled dollar bill and some coins.

"The fare is $24.55," I say. "If you don't have cash, I can run your card."

In his drunken state, he seems to be trying to process what's going on. "Why can't you do it through the app?"

"Man, there is no app. You hailed me on the street."

He opens the door.

"Hey!"

I put the taxi in park and follow him around to the other side. He continues to insist on using the app.

"C'mon, man," I finally say. "I'm really tired. It's late. Just pay me so we can get this over with."

He still refuses. His disdain is palpable.

I try to cajole him into giving me his card. I know he's drunk, but he's taking his attitude of entitlement and disrespect to a level of extreme belligerence.

I get it. This guy thinks he climbed in an Uber or a Lyft and can't grasp the fact that it turned out to be a taxi. And I'm sure he thinks taxi drivers are lowlifes. Beneath his stature as an overpaid grunt at some startup. But it's 2:30 in the morning. I'm tired from four 12-hour shifts in a row. I just want to get paid and get this ride over with.

In taxi school, we covered the prospect of non-paying customers. I also have the numbers for all the local police precincts preset in my phone. I scroll through for the Ingleside station, figuring that's the closest one. I show him that I'm going to call the cops if he doesn't pay me. After all, I'm in front of his house. I have his address.

But instead of getting scared, he starts insulting me, making fun of my long hair and glasses.

"What is this, second grade?" I ask him. I want so badly to slap this kid upside his head, Tell him, If I make this call, it's not going to be Travis Kalanick on the other end. It's going to be a wake up call, you smug little prick. You're committing a crime by jamming me up. But I keep my cool. I show him my phone with the card reader sticking out the end.

"Just slide your card, man."

He laughs. "Look at your hand, it's shaking. You need to control your blood pressure. You're going to have a heart attack!"

I look at my hand. It is shaking. But not because of my blood pressure. I'm pissed and I'm trying to control my anger. It's not a seamless process.

At this point, his disdain for me is radiating out of every drunken pore. "Let me see your phone."

I show him my iPhone. "You know what this is, so let's run your card."

"No, I want to run it myself."

"Whatever." I hand him the phone. I just want to get paid and get out of here.

He runs his card and hits the "no tip" option.

"Of course you'd stiff me on the tip."

"Why would I tip you? Your customer service is awful."

"Yeah, well," I take my phone back. "You're a lousy customer."

As he walks to his house, he shouts more insults.

Now that I've been paid, I ignore his childish antics and get in the cab. My hands are still shaking though. I'm fucking pissed. I wish I could have retaliated, run him over his my cab or something. His entitled smugness reminds me of everything I hated about driving for Uber and Lyft. The way these drunk assholes would lord the rating system over my head and demand the entire world, expect royal treatment, all at a cut rate price. It was hardly worth it, but they knew we were bound to serve them, regardless, because of that rating…

There was nothing worse than feeling like somebody could control you or get you fired by tapping a screen on their phone. It was degrading.

As I head down the hill to I-280, I'm grateful I switched to driving a taxi. At least I don't have to worry about ratings anymore. I contemplate heading back into the city, but there's no way I could deal with another passenger after that guy.

Back at the yard, I clean out the cab. I notice the guy has smeared grease all over the seat and door handle. On the floorboard is a half-chewed piece of hot dog. I get some paper towels and clean the mess, thinking, At least now that I'm a taxi driver, I only have to deal with these douchebags when Uber surges...

PLAYLISTS, PROFANITY AND OTHER TRICKS OF THE TRADE

Tonight I'm all alone in my cab. Although I may not be the only one prowling the streets of San Francisco playing the Modern Lovers, if I don't get a fare soon, I just might go insane.

It's still early but I'm a little cranky from waking up at nine in the morning to a cacophony of power tools drilling into concrete and slicing through wood. Coming off my second 12-hour shift in a row, I was tired as hell, but there was no way to sleep through the noise.

In the two years I've been in this apartment, I've suffered one construction project after another. But that's the price you pay for living in an "up-and-coming" neighborhood.

I began my shift that afternoon by dialing in a Pandora station based on a playlist of garage and noise rock bands. A proud Luddite, I only recently discovered streaming music through my iPhone. I started with the free service, but once the Lyft ads became overbearing, I upgraded.

As I troll the Embarcadero for a fare, "Astral Plane" segues nicely into Thee Oh Sees.

I don't get a flag until I'm on Jefferson. Two guys going to the Best Western Americana. About two-thirds into the ride, one of the guys asks me in a German accent why we don't have partitions like New York cabs.

"Cause we're fucking friendly!" I shout.

My feeble sarcasm doesn't translate well and we spend the next several blocks in awkward silence as the Wooden Shjips drone on in the background.

So much for taking Late Night Larry's advice.

Last week, at the National barbeque, Larry was telling me how to break the ice with passengers.

"I ask every person who gets in my cab, 'How the fuck are you?' Unless they're the sophisticated type. Then it's, 'How the hell are you?'"

I was dubious about using profanity with my passengers, but several other drivers nodded their heads in agreement.

Even though I'm constantly soliciting tricks of the trade from experienced cab drivers—like creating a soundtrack for the cab—as I head up Seventh Street to see if the Orpheum is breaking, I wonder if they were just pulling my leg this time.

Of course, it's easy for Larry to pull off a faux-surly attitude with his passengers. He already comes across like a college football coach. Before driving a cab, he was the house dick at the St. Francis. Before that, an MP homicide detective in Vietnam. At some point he was involved in banking.

It's difficult to keep track of Larry's myriad adventures and his long history, which began in San Francisco during the Gold Rush, when his family moved to California from St. Louis to start a riverboat company on the American River.

Like most native San Franciscans, nothing shocks Larry. When he tells a story, whether it's about driving a cab or solving a murder, he punctuates the most gruesome aspects with sadistic laughter.

Or the night he had two pukers and never seemed happier.

"Two!" he shouts gleefully. "In one night! What are the odds? I made an extra $200.00!"

"Yeah, but the puke…" I point out.

"Ah, I'm not worried about a little vomit," he says, brushing away the insignificant detail with a wave of his arm.

At the Orpheum, I get a short ride to the Hilton, where I pick up a couple going to Ashbury Heights. Then a flag on Divisadero to the Hotel Kabuki.

I cruise down O'Farrell just as the Shannon and the Clams show at the Great American is breaking. With King Kahn and the Shrines blasting, I pull behind a Yellow cab and wait for a like-minded fare.

After the initial wave has dissipated, I watch the remaining concert-goers stand around holding their phones and looking up and down the street for their Ubers and Lyfts. Somebody gets into the Yellow cab in front of me, but I sit empty until it's just the roadies and me.

I give up and turn left onto Larkin. Outside New Century, I immediately get flagged. A guy climbs into my backseat.

Before he can tell me where he's going, I turn around and ask him, "How the fuck are you doing tonight?"

ON THE RECITATION OF THE WAYBILL

The National barbeque is a cross between a hobo cookout and a bunch of pirates carousing after a night of pillaging and plundering. It takes place on Sunday mornings in a junkyard, among the remains of disemboweled taxicabs and assorted automobile parts rusting outside the front office.

The only indication the area is a driver lounge is the Coke machine and couch, which has become loudmouth Toler's bed ever since his wife allegedly kicked him out of the house. During the festivities, he snores like a freight train. "Shut the fuck up, Toler!" is a common, albeit futile, refrain. As Juneaux, who's an expert at summing things up, once put it: "That's the sleep of a man with a clear conscience."

Daniel is the chef. He handles the grilling and arranges the hors d'oeuvres and condiments on a lopsided table he fixed by shoving an old tire under the shorter leg.

With a belly full of snark, Chucky is the master of ceremonies. He brings the cake. It was Chucky who started calling me a green pea until he decided I was no longer one. Now he just reminds me that I used to be a green pea.

Speaking of vegetables, Colin always shows up with meatless victuals and a six-pack from a local microbrewery. A wonk on all things taxi, it's

Not all mistaken forays into the sex positive climate of San Francisco have happy endings.

PY SPANKSGIV
POWEREXCHANGE.COM

220

From the wrong sex club to the right sex club

I'm cruising down Folsom Street on a quiet Thursday night at about midnight. An arm goes up in front of Powerhouse. I pull over. A man with a strong accent gets in the back of my taxi.

"Can you take me here?" He shows me his phone with the Google details for the Power Exchange on the screen.

As I head up 7th Street, I ask nonchalantly, "Not the crowd you're looking for back there, huh?"

"Too many problems!" he exclaims. "I'm looking for women."

"Well, you're going to the right place now."

Racing through the littered streets of the Tenderloin, I can't help but wonder how this guy ended up at a gay cruising bar instead of the hetero sex club he was looking for. Poor communication with a cab driver? A mix up in a Google search?

Whatever. These things happen. A few months back, I had a similar situation, albeit in reverse, while driving past the Power Exchange ...

A guy flags me down and immediately tells me he's a tourist and has ended up at the wrong place.

"The doorman told me I should check out Blow Buddies," he says. "Do you know where that is?"

Of course. I'm quite familiar with the place, I tell him. But instead of assuming that, as a night cabbie, I know where all the sex clubs are in San Francisco — gay and straight — he thinks I'm a regular and grills me on the details.

"It's all gay, right? Is it OK to just watch? Do I have to take off all my

I DRIVE S.F.

clothes? Are there condoms available? Showers?"

"All I know is that, once you're inside, they'll explain everything."

When I pull up to Blow Buddies, which is a shuttered storefront on a dark street, my misguided fare is understandably nervous. I assure him they're open and that I'll wait to make sure. As he enters, he turns to flash me a Cheshire grin and then recedes into the flaming red light.

Not all mistaken forays into the sex positive climate of San Francisco have happy endings though ...

Two or three weeks ago, I'm heading back to the National yard, about to hit the Chevron on Bayshore, when a tall man runs toward my cab, flailing his hands in the air.

First thing I notice are his pink shorts, white shirt and topsiders. Did he just fall out of a J. Crew catalogue into the industrial part of the Bayview?

I stop. More out of curiosity than anything.

"I need to get to the Westin," he gasps. "Don't worry, I have money."

"Union Square?"

"No, in Milanbay, I think."

"What?"

"Hold on, I have a card." He reads off the address for the Westin by the airport.

As I circle back to the freeway, I ask, "Why are you wandering around the Bayview?"

"It's a long story."

kelly DESSAINT

"We got a little time before we reach your hotel," I point out.

"Well ... I'm only here for one night on business. So I figured I'd head into San Fran, get something to eat and have a couple drinks. My cab driver recommended Polk Street. After getting a decent steak, I walked down to Jackalope. I was smoking outside and this hot chick approached me. She invited me to a bar across the street. A place called Divas. Everything was going great. We were totally hitting it off. Then she wanted to go back to her place. Awesome. We get in her car and start driving. At a red light, I lean in and ..." He pauses. "That's when I figured out something wasn't right."

His eyes are full of despair as they meet mine in the rearview, and I quickly stifle my laughter.

"I'm from Detroit, man! I was in the Marines!"

"What did you do after that?" I'm almost afraid to ask.

"I jumped out of her car! Just started walking. I would've walked all the way back to the hotel. I don't give a fuck. I was a Marine!"

I'm inclined to tell him it's not his fault he didn't know Divas was a transgender bar, but would it even matter at this point?

"I just wanted to have a little fun in San Fran ..."

Slowly, his voice fades, and I leave him to his thoughts. He's got a long night ahead of him, and a long flight back to Detroit, which might be enough time to sort out all these new emotions.

Kelly Dessaint is a San Francisco taxi driver. Write to Kelly at piltdownlad@gmail.com or visit his blog at www.idrivesf.com.

hard to keep up with the boundless information he spews, almost reluctantly, in a rapid-fire slur.

Once Mary has fed the numerous cats who live in the yard and who seem to recognize her cab as soon as she pulls into the lot (it is, after all, the cleanest cab in the fleet), she joins the party.

As his soubriquet implies, Late Night Larry usually arrives last. A raconteur of the highest degree, whenever we need to know what it's really all about, Larry is there to tell us. Though we'll also happily settle for a ribald tale from one of his past lives.

Throughout the night, people come and go, including former Veterans and Arrow drivers like Marty, Austin, Ben ("I got nothing to live for!") Valis and Trevor Fucker. Mingling in the crowd is Other Larry (AKA, Early Morning Larry), Mathias ("a feast of rats upon you"), Steven, Willie, Byron and Glover, the only taxi driver who gets a pass for switching to Uber because he's probably driven a cab longer than anyone else and justifies his betrayal with, "It's all about the money, baby!"

Occasionally, we are graced with the presence of TJ, an erstwhile cab driver and one-time medallion holder, who went nuts and now calls a broken down Towncar in Upton alley home. Wasted on cheap booze and his homemade hashish, he can be downright rude at times. But Jesse, the night cashier and the sweetest man you'd never want to mess with, keeps him in check.

In the midst of our revelry, day drivers cycle through the office. Some look at the ceremony dubiously, through bleary eyes, while others happily grab a plate of food before starting their shifts.

Standing around in small groups, we get into heated discussions about geography and chronicle noteworthy rides, what's known as the recitation of the waybill.

Everyone gets a chance to purge the details of that week's trips—the good, the bad and the ugly—even if you have to raise your voice to get center stage.

It's not the bizarre rides, though, or even the most profitable rides that impress cab drivers who've seen it all… It's the rides that turn into tours, where we get to show off the city and bask in its grandeur with out-of-towners, like true ambassadors/historians.

"Did you show them the mansions on the Gold Coast?"

"Did you tell them about Alma Spreckels?"

In between the breakdown of rides, there are biographies of legendary cabbies, tales of the "good ole days" and speculations on the future of cab driving.

Sometimes it seems the history of San Francisco's taxi industry is the history of San Francisco itself.

Slowly, as the fire dwindles, people disappear into the darkness and those who remain huddle to stay warm, until the sky brightens and the hardliners begin to arrange rides home, an easy task in a cab yard.

If no one is heading to the East Bay, I get dropped off downtown.

Waiting for the first Pittsburgh/Bay Point train at 8:15, I roam Market Street, empty but for the few remaining street people who call out from the shadows, "Good morning," knowing I'm a working stiff, not some mark.

That's when the madness of driving a cab dissipates. And for a few moments, before I descend into the BART station, the city feels like... home, maybe.

"THE PICKY COUPLE" BY LARE NIGHT LARRY

So I'm coming down O'Farrell and I get flagged by this couple. They're young, good looking... From the early conversation I realize they're husband and wife.

The guy says to me, "You look like the kind of cab driver we've been looking for."

I say, "Yeah?"

He says, "Yeah."

"So what do you have in mind?" I ask.

"We're looking for a hooker. But we're picky."

"Well, let's go have a look around."

We drove around for 45 minutes looking for a black girl with some white in her. Because they really were picky. Eventually, they found someone they liked.

At this point, the meter is at $45.

He hands me a fifty and says, "Now, if you don't mind. We'd like to fuck her in your cab."

"I don't have any rules in this cab," I tell him. "So let's go."

He hands me a hundred dollars.

I drive them to the back of St. Mary's Cathedral.

At first, the hooker protests. "I ain't gonna fuck behind no church!"

Just my luck, a hooker with scruples. But in the end, she agrees to go along with it.

I tell them, "Look, I'm going to take a walk around the block and smoke a joint. You guys have some fun."

This was back in the days of the Crown Vics, which were spacious and easy to clean. So I wasn't worried about any messes. Everything was plastic and you could just hose the backseat down afterwards. I'd just made $150, so what did I care?

Anyway, I stroll around the block slowly, giving them plenty of time to do their thing. And when I got back... what a sight to behold! Three of the four doors were wide open. The hooker is spread eagle on the back seat while the wife is going down on her and the guy's standing a few feet away, naked except for his socks, jacking off.

I take one look at this scene and say to myself, I need to go around the block again.

As I walk away, I light another joint and wonder, how am I going to explain this to the police?

WHEN NATURE CALLS, BUSINESS PICKS UP

The city is moving. Or so it seems. For once, it feels like the good old days. At least based on the stories I've heard from the veteran cab drivers who, before Uber and Lyft, used to make enough money to pay mortgages and college tuitions. But tonight, it only feels busy because I need to take a leak.

I've been driving nonstop for three hours. I'm just looking for a hotel cabstand with a vacancy so I can use the restroom and smoke a cigarette. Each time I get close to one, though, I get hailed.

It never fails. When I don't want a fare, everybody wants in my cab. But these are tough times. You don't turn down rides. Otherwise, according to cab karma, you'll end up driving empty for the next two hours.

I'm hoping to make it to the Intercontinental on Howard Street. Their lobby restroom is sublime. And while it's not as fancy as the one at the Fairmont or the Ritz Carlton, it's good enough for my needs.

VIP access to the facilities at high-class hotels where visiting dignitaries stay when they're in the city is one of the advantages of having a taxi badge pinned to my shirt. The doormen just wave me through like I'm on official business.

Back when I was driving for Uber, after Whole Foods closed, I had to rely on the space toilets, AKA, the "self-cleaning" public bathrooms around town. There is nothing even remotely pleasant about the experience. If a junkie isn't passed out in the doorway, the toilets are out of order, or, when the door slides open, a nefarious odor greets you like a punch in the face. It's no wonder homeless people use the streets instead.

After dropping off at Hyde and Sutter, I head towards the Hilton Union Square, another convenient place to take a pit stop. I like to smoke on Taylor Street, with the bums, where the hookers and the bridge-and-tunnel girls dressed like hootchie-mommas share the same turf. After several months, I've figured out how to tell the difference between the two: the half-naked club-goers walk as fast as their six-inch stilettos will carry them while the ladies of the night slink down the sidewalk like cats on the prowl.

I race down Post and turn onto Mason. I'm waiting for the light at Geary when a girl with what looks like a bed sheet wrapped around her shoulders flags me. I give her a quick ocular patdown. At first I think she might be homeless. But who am I to judge?

She plops down in the backseat.

"Can you take me to Polk Street?"

I hit the meter. I've only gone about a block when she leans forward between the front seats and asks if I want "a little sexy time."

"No, I'm fine." I glance in the rearview. She doesn't look like your typical Union Square streetwalker. Based on my field guide to San Francisco prostitutes, the girls who work Union Square are usually dolled up. This one… she's not much of a looker. Super skanky. And not in a good way.

"Well, just let me out here then."

"I'll take you to Polk if that's where you want to go," I tell her, trying

Juneaux's cab is always spotless. He focuses on customer service and has an uncanny ability to twist fortune in his favor.

COURTESY TREVOR JOHNSON

The Luck of Juneaux

I f it wasn't for bad luck, I wouldn't have no luck at all. Or so it seems, when you've got them taxicab driving blues ...

For the past several months, I've been without a regular cab. My beloved 182 is long gone. And 1462, the cab they had me on afterward, is out on a long-term lease. So I've been back at the window playing taxicab roulette.

One afternoon, while washing the latest clunker, Abdul walks past and tells me I'm wasting my time.

"How so?" I ask.

"The inside of a taxi is supposed to make the passenger feel at home, but the outside should be a middle finger to everyone else."

I laugh, but keep scrubbing the freeway grime off the side panels. Maybe in the old days, that was the case, but not in this current market. Times have changed.

Take Juneaux, for example. He's the most fastidious taxi driver I know. His cab is always spotless, inside and out. He focuses on superior customer service and, in the process, has an uncanny ability to twist fortune in his favor.

I call it "The Luck of Juneaux."

A few weeks ago, I wake up to a salvo of texts that began at midnight.

"I'm so fucked," Juneaux writes. "I accidentally overslept and now I only have six hours to make my nut. I'm going to end up hanging a gate."

After several texts describing the hopelessness of the situation, his tone changes drastically.

"Dude! You'll never believe what just happened ..."

Around 3 a.m., he picks up a guy

who's lost his Lexus somewhere in SoMa and has Juneaux drive him around while he clicks his key remote. An hour later, the meter is at $34.75, and the guy realizes it's a lost cause.

"So, he asks me, 'Can you drive me home?' Sure. Where's home? 'Half Moon Bay.'"

His good fortune doesn't stop there. Back in The City, he gets a timed SFO through Flywheel.

His final text reads: "After gate, gas and tip, I'm $146 in the black. Not bad for starting my shift six hours late."

While Juneaux is dubious of its veracity, I have complete faith in The Luck. So much so, I'm convinced it's even transferable ...

Two weeks ago, my new regular cab was finally ready. Veterans 233 is a Fusion, like 182, but much newer, with a sunroof, leather seats ... all the bells and whistles.

On my first night in the new cab, I run into Juneaux outside Public Works around 3:30 a.m. While smoking cigarettes, we check out the various features of 233. He points at the faded USC sticker on the back window.

"That's got to go."

While he grabs his Swiss Army, I pull out my Mercator, and we go to work on the aged sticker. Then, we scrub the remnants with the alcohol wipes Juneaux uses to keep his cab clean.

Once we realize there are no more rides coming out of the DJ club, we bail. I contemplate going home, but

kelly DESSAINT

it's been a crappy night. I need a good ride. Or a few decent rides. I head to SoMa, hoping for something big in the small hours ...

Following an investigation of an after hours club, I'm outbound on Harrison when a guy waves his phone at me. I make a half-assed attempt to pull over to the right and roll down the passenger window.

"You need a cab?"

A few feet away, an Uber/Lyft car without a license plate is stopped in the middle of the street, hazards flashing. The driver's door is open and a woman is leaning out yelling at the guy. I can't make out what she's saying, but it's obvious they're having an argument.

"I'm just going to be a rich asshole then and take a taxi," he shouts at her.

"Don't get in that taxi!" the woman yells.

It's hard to tell what's going on, but as he approaches my cab, he taps his phone, like he's cancelling a ride.

In the backseat, he says, "I need to go really far. Are you OK with that?"

"Sure." Gulp. "Where to?"

"The Juniper Hotel in Cupertino."

I jump on the freeway before he can change his mind. As I approach the hospital curve, I ask if he wants some tunes, but he just thanks me and apologizes for the long ride.

"No problem," I say, glancing at the taximeter, clicking 55 cents higher each minute and every 1/5 of a mile. "At this time of night, we'll be there in 40 minutes. Less, if we're lucky."

Kelly Dessaint is a San Francisco taxi driver. His zine, "Behind the Wheel," is available at bookstores throughout The City. Write to Kelly at piltdownlad@gmail.com or visit his blog at www.idrivesf.com.

A7

to be courteous. "And I won't charge."

Mr. Benevolence, that's me.

"Okay. Take me to Polk then."

I try to make small talk. "Must be hard to make a buck out on the streets these days…"

But she's not interested in honoring the simpatico tradition between cab drivers and hookers. "You sure you don't want a date?"

"Nah, I'm cool." Even if I did want a blowjob, she isn't my type.

"Can I have a cigarette then?"

"I only have one left." And I was planning to smoke it when I finally took my break.

"Ah, c'mon."

Reluctantly, I hand her what's left of my pack. Mr. Sucker, if we're being honest.

As I approach Polk Street, I pull into the bus stop.

"No, drop me off at the corner. Proper."

Oh sure. Under the gaze of the working girls across the street, she emerges from the back of my taxicab like Grace Kelly hitting the red carpet, wraps the dingy sheet around her shoulders with panache and sashays down the street.

What she lacks in class she makes up in moxie. Bravo.

I turn onto O'Farrell and head back to the Hilton, hoping the tour buses haven't taken over the cabstand again. Now I really have to use the restroom.

THE VIEW FROM A TAXI

Coming back to the city on 280 after an airport run, I take the Sixth Street exit, which offers one of the best money shots of San Francisco. As I head down Brannan to check out the cabstand at Caltrain, I start to think about the first time I saw this jagged city spread out across the sky like a stately pleasure-dome. Hey, it's easy to feel nostalgic after making fifty bucks on one ride.

During a road trip in 1991, while going to college in Alabama, I investigated all the major cities west of the Mississippi. None captured my imagination like San Francisco.

Two years later, I stepped off the Greyhound with no money and even less experience. Just an English degree and a backpack filled with all my worldly possessions.

My horoscope that day offered one word of advice: surrender.

For the next eight months, I stayed at the Green Tortoise hostel rent free. I did light housekeeping in exchange for a bunk. Too broke to afford Muni, unless I found a discarded transfer, I spent my days wandering the neighborhoods of the city.

When I wasn't mingling with the Beat ghosts in North Beach, I lingered in the psychedelic revival of Haight Street. Some days I'd sit on top of Russian Hill and watch the light change. I killed time at Buena Vista Park or the Panhandle until the fog rolled in. I wasn't even reading anymore. I just sat there, thinking. I was 23. My entire future was ahead of me, but I was confused and hurt. I had just lost the first woman I'd ever loved and trusted. I was devastated. I felt betrayed.

The only consolation was San Francisco. No matter how bad things got, each morning I woke up and the city was always outside waiting for me. The air itself was a comforting embrace.

Eventually, the Green Tortoise manager threw me out for selling pot to the foreign backpackers. That night, I rode the 38 bus from downtown to the beach until dawn. I didn't know what else to do. Since the Grateful Dead were playing the Oakland Coliseum over the weekend, I figured I could hitch a ride home to LA with one of the Deadheads on tour. Penniless, I jumped the BART turnstiles. For three nights, before we left town, I slept in some guy's van with his dogs in the parking lot of the airport Holiday Inn.

Over the next two decades, I came back to San Francisco every chance I could, hoping to make an inroad. I got close during the Dot Com bust. And shortly after we got married, Irina and I considered an apartment in Noe Valley for $1125 a month. But then she got promoted at work. They offered her the kind of money you don't turn down at the height of a recession. When she was laid off in 2012, though, we immediately started looking for a place in San Francisco.

We got as close as Temescal. While Oakland offers a sense of stability, driving a taxi keeps me connected to the city. That's why I don't play the "airport game." I'm a city driver. I can't stop exploring. As much as things have changed here, an exhilarating madness continues to permeate the streets. And everywhere you look, there's shameful poverty.

San Francisco is no place to stumble, much less fall. Like so many other Bay Area residents, new and old, Irina and I had been barely scraping by. Even though I started making decent money once I got in a cab, there are always unexpected twists. I can't shake the feeling I'm just one misstep from ending up in some guy's van again.

Sometimes it seems living in a boomtown is the same as being in love. It probably won't last forever and you're going to miss her like hell when she's gone. But what can you do except admire the view while you can…

GUILTY OF DRIVING A CAB

Driving a taxicab in San Francisco is like wearing a target around your neck. It's always open season on taxis. On good days, the contempt most people have towards the taxi industry misses its mark. But on the bad days, it's a shot straight to the heart.

In the four months I've been driving a cab, I've been disrespected as a matter of course. As if I'm asking people to sacrifice their first-born to let me change lanes in front of them. Nobody cuts me any slack. During rush hour, I have to fight for each one-fifth of a mile to get passengers where they're going.

I've been honked at so many times, it doesn't even faze me anymore. The sound of car horns is like the chirping of birds, or wind rustling leaves on a tree.

Last Saturday night, I was driving up Kearney and a guy in an Uber SUV spit on my cab. The tourists in my backseat were horrified.

"Oh, just part of driving a taxi in San Francisco," I joked.

A month ago, while picking up a fare on King Street, some joker knocked my side mirror off and drove away. I spent two hours at the police station filing a report. "Won't be the last time," the officer doing the paperwork told me nonchalantly.

This week I paid the city of San Francisco $110 for "obstructing traffic" in front of a strip club at 1:30 a.m. The SFMTA mailed the citation to my cab company. Claimed I was a "drive away." Of course I drove away. I'm a taxi driver. That's what I do. I drive, I stop, I pick up passengers and then I drive away.

From City Hall to fresh-faced transplants, everyone hates taxis. And yet, I can't help but wonder, whatever happened to the mythology of cab driving?

My earliest memory is being in a taxi. The family station wagon was in the shop. I remember sitting in the backseat with my mother. The driver was listening to news radio. Something about President Ford.

As a child of the 70s, glued to the TV set, I never missed an episode of *Taxi*. I couldn't wait to see what shenanigans Latka and Iggy would get into. I'd laugh as Louie berated all the drivers who hung around the garage solving each other's problems. In *Taxi Driver*, there was Travis Bickle, the loner moving through the streets of New York like a reluctant servant to the night and all its proclivities. Even *D.C. Cab* portrayed a struggling taxi company as the ultimate underdog, with Mr. T. the baddest cab driver who ever lived.

As fascinating as cabs were to me growing up, I didn't use them much until I moved to New Orleans, where most of the drivers doubled as tour guides, concierges of vice or therapists. I've sighed more than once in the back of a New Orleans cab and had the driver say, "Lay it on me, baby."

I never thought I'd drive a taxi myself. In my illustrious career as an overeducated slacker, I've worked as a cook, painter, flea market vendor, book dealer and personal assistant. Taxi driving isn't much of a stretch.

San Franciscans love to complain about transportation. And the only thing worse than the Muni and BART are taxis.

I thought it would be different for me. Despite the muddied reputation I'd inherited. I want to be a great taxi driver. But it doesn't matter who's behind the wheel. In this city, a color scheme and a top light will always be targets for disdain.

WHAT'S IN A PASSENGER?

Not much is happening. Just a boring Thursday night. I pull up to the Cat Club and shoot the shit with Chucky, Liz and John, the stalwarts of the ad hoc cabstand there, until I'm on deck.

As I watch the throng of smokers for a potential fare, I get a Flywheel request for 1190 Folsom: the address of the Cat Club.

Bingo.

A few minutes later, two women approach my cab.

"This is for Gina, right?" one asks me. I nod and she opens the back door, helps the other inside and says, "Make sure she gets home safe."

I turn around. Gina looks a little rough around the edges.

"Where to?" I ask.

She mumbles something about Battery and Jackson.

As I head towards the Financial, Gina starts to whimper slightly.

"Are you okay?" I ask.

"Sure. I mean… Not really."

"You wanna talk about it?"

She garbles something. Goes silent.

The worst cab driver in San Francisco might be on to something the rest of us are missing.

COURTESY PHOTO

The worst cab driver in San Francisco

The worst cab driver in San Francisco doesn't work the DJ clubs, doesn't troll the bars in the Mission and avoids Polk Street like the plague. He doesn't play the airport or cabstand at hotels. Most of the time, he sits in front of the Power Exchange or Divas waiting for a call from a regular rider.

The worst cab driver in San Francisco has said, given the option, he'd prefer to exclusively deal with transgender passengers.

"They're the only normal people around anymore." He doesn't mind the patrons of sex clubs, because they don't expect more than a ride. But he never asks questions. He'd rather not know what goes on inside those establishments.

The worst cab driver in San Francisco doesn't collect kickbacks when he drops off at massage parlors or strip clubs. He just moves on to the next fare. "Why would I expect to get paid to take somebody one place and not another?"

The worst cab driver in San Francisco doesn't make much money, even though he works every day. He hasn't missed a shift in more than a year, but he only does splits, showing up at the yard around 10 p.m. Sometimes he doesn't hit the streets until midnight. There are nights when he barely covers his gate and gas, and nights when he's lucky to go home with $15 in his pocket.

The worst cab driver in San Francisco usually drives the shittiest cabs

kelly DESSAINT

in the fleet. By showing up late, his options are limited to whatever's available, and that's almost always a clunker or a spare. But he's all right with it ...

The worst cab driver in San Francisco isn't picky. He never complains. And if he does express displeasure, he quickly blames himself. He knows he's the worst cab driver in San Francisco and isn't afraid to accept that distinguished role. After all, someone has to be the worst.

The worst cab driver in San Francisco focuses on developing relationships with regular clients and providing safe transport. Once, a woman he'd just dropped off at her apartment returned to his cab and asked why he hadn't driven away yet. "I'm waiting for you to get inside," he told her. "Why?" she wanted to know. "Because it's my job."

The worst cab driver in San Francisco may be odd, but he is so trustworthy his regular customers have asked him to housesit while they're out of town.

The worst cab driver in San Francisco will stop and help out any driver in distress, cab or otherwise. It's not like he has anything to lose by taking the time to jumpstart a stalled vehicle or push it out of the flow of traffic. And if they offer him a tip, he adamantly turns it down.

The worst cab driver in San Francisco once left his cab running outside his apartment while he ran up to use the bathroom. In the few minutes he was gone, someone snatched his pack of cigarettes from the console, the key from the ignition and the medallion off the dash. Figuring the thief would ditch the medallion once he realized it was just a worthless piece of tin, he spent the next morning wandering around the neighborhood looking for it to avoid the fine for getting a replacement. When his search proved futile, he went to the police station to file a report and there was the medallion, sitting right on the officer's desk. How it got there, no one knew. The key and his cigarettes, however, were never recovered.

The worst cab driver in San Francisco doesn't charge meter and a half for rides 15 miles outside The City. He's just happy to get what's on the meter. And besides, he points out, during the hours he works, traffic isn't an issue.

The worst cab driver in San Francisco always makes sure to stretch before and after each shift. "I may look silly doing this," he says while doing crunches on an abandoned bucket seat in the yard with a cigarette hanging out of his mouth. "But my back feels amazing."

The worst cab driver in San Francisco, whenever I tell him he might be on to something the rest of us are missing, always says, "Nah, man ... I don't know shit."

Kelly Dessaint is a San Francisco taxi driver. Write to him at piltdownlad@gmail.com or visit his blog at www.idrivesf.com.

Guess not.

At each red light, I watch her in the rearview gradually keel over onto the backseat. She seems to be sleeping, even though her eyes are half open.

Nothing about her condition indicates she's consumed enough alcohol to be this wasted. I'm no doctor, but I can only assume she's been roofied.

It's alarming how many women I encounter who unknowingly have their drinks spiked in bars. No place is immune. Not even the Cat Club, which usually has a very sophisticated clientele.

Recently, I had a long conversation with a bartender who told me that in the ten years she's been in San Francisco, she's been roofied three times. Once she woke up in a strange bed, in a strange apartment, with no clue how she got there. Turned out a guy found her the night before raving like a lunatic on the median at Van Ness and Union. Since she'd lost her purse and couldn't remember her address, he took her home, gave up his bed and slept in the office chair at his desk.

That was a fortunate turn of events.

Unlike two years ago when Irina met a friend at Kingfish in Temescal for a couple drinks. After a while, Irina felt sick, went to the bathroom, threw up and walked back to our apartment four blocks away. I came home later that night and she was still asleep. Her friend, however, woke up in the emergency room.

Sadly, I've dealt with so many drugged women in my taxi I've become adept at dealing with the nerve-racking process of getting them out of my backseat and into their homes.

Every time, though, I'm still paralyzed with fear that something I do may seem or come across inappropriate.

With so many news reports about Uber drivers sexually assaulting passengers, it's terrifying to be in these situations. Because I can see how easily temptation arises while transporting extremely young girls, especially when they pass out in the backseat of your car in their tiny skirts, with their legs open, or their tops in disarray…

For a man with little to no willpower, or possessed with an uncontrollable momentary urge, these types of opportunities would be hard to resist.

Whenever girls pass out in my backseat of my cab in a short skirt, I don't look between their legs. Not just because I'm trying to be a gentleman, or that I'm trying to resist temptation. No, I'm respecting a woman's body and her right to privacy, even in – *especially* in – a weakened state.

I keep my eyes up. I turn the lights on and roust them from their slumber. If they come to and are cognizant enough, I make sure they know my eyes are in the rearview mirror, where I can only see their faces. Or at the least, if they're completely oblivious, I know in my mind that I've done all I can do to protect them when they're helpless.

As a taxi driver, it's my job to get people home safe and sound. And that's what I do. With as much dignity as possible...

When I arrive at Gina's building, I wake her up and ask if she needs help. Once she gives me permission, I open the back door and extend my arm. She stands up and wobbles, but I hold her steady.

As she gains her balance, she swings around and tries to embrace me, giggling. I sidestep her advance and grab the strap of her shoulder bag from behind. Slowly, I guide her towards the building like a marionette. Along the way, she gets more playful and tries to impede the operation.

"Let's focus, okay?" I tell her sternly. "You need to get home."

When we get to the front door, I ask if she has her keys.

"Right here!" She pulls them out joyfully.

I open the door for her, but there's no way I'm crossing the threshold. "Can you make it to the elevator?"

"I'll be fine!" she insists, though not very convincingly.

"You're a pro!" I psych her up to make the final stretch into her apartment. "You got this!"

"I'm a pro!"

"Yeah!"

As she's about to enter the lobby, she turns around and demands a kiss. Just then, someone emerges from the elevator and I'm able to redirect her advance.

"Quick! Get on the elevator before the doors close!"

Gina careens back inside but doesn't reach the elevator in time. While she staggers back towards me, laughing hysterically, the girl who got off the elevator stands nearby staring into her phone.

"No! No!" I shout. "Press the button again!"

Gina follows my instructions and, when the doors open, she goes inside. As I wait for them to close, she opens them at the last moment to play peek-a-boo.

"That's not being pro!" I yell.

Finally, the doors close and I take off.

Back in my cab, I head to the yard. I've had enough excitement for a boring Thursday night.

ADVENTURES IN LATE NIGHT CABSTANDS

I work the night. Whether I ride to San Francisco in style with Colin in his Benz or drag my weary bones down Telegraph Ave to the MacArthur BART, I leave my apartment each afternoon when the sun is on the wane and rarely get back home to Oakland until the sun is rising the next day.

On the streets, I exchange knowing glances with drivers from all the cab companies. After six months, I can usually predict what another taxi driver will do, because we're part of the same hive mind.

After all, who drives the streets of San Francisco more than cab drivers? Who else knows the shortcuts and the fastest way to get from any point A to any point B? We've been trained and licensed by the city to transport its citizens and visitors across the entire Bay Area. That's our job. We move people around.

I watch other cabs constantly. Even in my Uber/Lyft days, if I was on a street and there were no taxicabs, I knew I was on the wrong street. Still, to this day, I try to learn from the maneuvers of other cab drivers. I pay particular attention to top lights in relation to mine. If I'm driving northwest on Columbus and most of the cabs going southeast have their lights off, I figure I'm heading in the right direction.

In cabstands, we compare notes. Throughout the night, a group of drivers use GroupMe to stay informed about when events are breaking and where to find "needs." Or, at the very least, "possibles."

While driving, I listen to the action on the dispatch radio. Ben is my Jon Miller when there's no Giants game. On the nights Artur is calling out rides, I hope a little drama between drivers makes it on the air.

From rush hour to the small hours, I feel the pulse of the city, constantly moving until the belly to the bar slump, when business dies down long enough to take a prolonged break.

On Friday night, I'm smoking on Valencia when I run into Jimmy Flowers, the Haight Street Gardener. We chat about his recent memorial plot to Jim Morrison and the struggle to maintain one's convictions in today's San Francisco, whether you're fighting off tech workers or the Russian mafia.

After 2 a.m., I head to the ad hoc cabstand at Public Works, seven cabs deep. Trevor, the street ninja, is in front of me, sitting on the roof of his Desoto/Flywheel Escape, house music thumping from the stereo. I get out to stretch my legs and watch the Phonies on the sidewalk gyrate to the beat and then dance towards the cluster of four-door sedans blocking the flow of traffic on Mission.

"Are you my Uber?"

"No, I'm Lyft."

Like most weekend nights, it's about four Uber/Lyft pick-ups to each taxi ride. So what else is there to do but have a little party with a contingent of the SF Hackers?

Thomas pulls in behind me. A few minutes later, Irina Borisovna shows up. And what would an ad hoc cabstand outside a DJ club be without Mary, one of the best landsharks on the road?

Standing outside our cabs, we joke and talk shop as an endless stream of Uber/Lyfts, trusting GPS more than what's before their very eyes, charge recklessly into Erie Street, a dead end alley that serves as a smoking area for the club.

A group of guys who live in the apartment building across the street hang out on their stoop drinking beer and cracking up each time one of the grossly untrained drivers realize they're about to slaughter a crowd of zonked out clubgoers, slam on their brakes and slowly reverse back into traffic, creating more congestion.

Once I'm finally on the throne, a couple climbs into my backseat.

"Follow that Uber!" the girl directs me.

I turn around and calmly say, "One, I don't follow Ubers. Two, where are you going?"

She rattles off the address of a familiar after hours club. I assure her I can get her there effortlessly.

"But my friend in that Uber has the code."

"You can't just meet her there?" I ask.

"Please," she implores me. "We can't get in without the code!"

Knowing this to be true, I reluctantly get behind the beat-up Astrovan. When the light at Division turns green, the driver takes a right.

"Where is he going?" I wonder aloud. "Why's he getting on the freeway?"

"Are you sure that's the right Uber?" The guy with her seems to be taking my side.

"Yes! I'm positive."

As we careen down the Central Freeway onto the 80, I complain bitterly about how far out of the way we're going. "Are they headed to Oakland?"

At the very last second, the van swerves across two lanes and takes the last San Francisco exit.

Once we finally make it to Third, he drives at a snail's pace. I have to pull over a few times and wait for him to catch up.

When we finally reach our destination, the meter reads $15.05. With a tip, I make $18 on what should have been a ten-dollar ride.

As I race through the empty streets, I rethink my policy on following Ubers. I've always prided myself on using the most efficient, fastest routes to save my passengers money and time, but perhaps I could be making bank by just following the path laid out by a computer.

Maybe I should have listened to Late Night Larry when he told me, "The customer is always right! Especially when they're wrong."

Back at Public Works, the line is longer. I pull in behind Trevor, get out to stretch my legs and make fun of the clueless Uber/Lyft drivers until I'm on the throne again, ready to head out into the night one more time.

MARCHING BACKWARDS INTO THE FUTURE

When I agreed to be on a drivers panel at the Next:Economy forum, I wasn't exactly sure what I was getting myself into. I knew there would be three of us on the hot seat: a cab driver turned Lyft driver, a fulltime Uber driver and me, the Uber/Lyft driver who became a "cabbie."

Since making it clear to the moderator during our preliminary interview that I was no fan of the on-demand economy, I figured my role was to be the lone naysayer, or to provide some requisite objectivity. Other speakers at the conference included the CEOs of Kickstarter, GE and

Lyft, as well as David Plouffe, Uber's Chief Adviser.

On Thursday morning, I woke up hungover with a mysterious gash in my forehead. After a quick shower, I put on a grey suit, a black shirt and my Florsheims. If I'm going to be a dancing monkey, I should at least wear a shiny red hat.

While on BART, I received word from my friend Maya that her husband had lost his battle with cancer. Even though I knew he'd been fighting the disease for a while, news of his passing hit me hard.

Bill Doyle, who used the nom de guerre Guss Dolan in his activism on the web, was a hero of mine. A major advocate for progressive politics in the city, he railed against the negative changes he saw happening around him as tech money displaced his friends and the new Silicon Valley workers took over neighborhood after neighborhood and threatened his own ability to remain in the city he loved. He spoke at public hearings about the impact of Google buses and rabidly opposed Airbnb and the rest of the so-called "sharing economy."

I admired his tenacity and ferocious wit. When I started challenging Uber and Lyft, Bill's encouragement meant the most to me. So while my train barreled through the Transbay Tube, I kept thinking, San Francisco lost a true citizen today.

At the Montgomery station, I climbed the escalator and walked right into the majestic Palace hotel, where the conference was being held. In the green room, I met Eric Barajas, the Uber driver, who, it turned out, organized the protest at Uber HQ in October and is just as disgruntled as I was last year, stuck in a vicious cycle with Uber, barely making enough to survive, but never enough to move on to something better.

While we waited backstage, I watched the CEO of TaskRabbit on the monitor. She seemed to be selling her company to the audience, which I thought was odd. During the Q&A, a woman asked if "Taskers" were being adequately protected from their clients.

Huh?

Who cares about workers these days?

When it was time for our panel, I walked through the curtain into the glare of stage lights. The next twenty minutes were a blur. I just imagined what Bill would say if he'd had the opportunity to voice his dissent at an event like this.

I ragged on all the proponents of the gig economy. Surprisingly, I got laughs. Both Eric and I trashed Uber. At one point, much to the audience's delight, I got into a heated argument with Jon Kessler, the third driver, who saw the writing on the wall a year ago and leased a car to do Lyft after six years of taxi driving.

Eventually, we were ushered off stage and released into a crowded room of networkers who congratulated us on our lively panel, some comparing it to *The Jerry Springer Show*.

After talking to several dozen attendees, who paid $3,500 to be there, I realized the conference wasn't a celebration of the on-demand economy. It was more of an examination of how these advances in technology will impact labor and shape the future of work. Most people I talked to were affiliated with labor organizations or non-profits. I even ran into Steven Hill, whose latest book *Raw Deal: How the Uber Economy and Runaway Capitalism are Screwing American Workers* rips these on-demand companies a new asshole.

Still, tech was in the air. The CEOs were there to pitch their disruptive technologies and most of what they said was obvious doublespeak. If the future of work means the end of professionalism and less need for workers, what do we do with all these people being born each day? Isn't this what Marshall McLuhan meant when he wrote about how we're driving into the future using only our rear view mirror?

Throughout the afternoon, I took advantage of the open bar, sampled the free food and marveled at the vaulted ceilings, ornate fixtures and chandeliers. The combined experience was Orwellian and surreal.

After the conventioneers went to lunch, I wandered down Market

Street with Eric and Nikko to get Chinese food by the pound at Lee's. Nikko is a filmmaker whom I met at an Uber protest the previous year. He was at the convention as Eric's guest.

Over chow mein and fried rice, we talked about feeling out of place at the convention. As much as these people seemed to like us because of our performance, there was something off-putting about their acknowledgment. It was obvious they weren't around real workers much, despite claiming to fight for the rights of workers.

Then we discussed David Plouffe's segment the next day and how great it would be to confront him during the Q&A session that would follow. On video.

Hahaha. We all laughed. That would be awesome!

But wait! Don't we have badges for the entire convention? They told us we could come back the next day.

The more we talked about it the more we realized this opportunity was too good to pass up. A plan began to form quickly. We went back to the Palace and, in the extravagant lobby, hatched the plan.

After spitballing a bunch of ideas, we concluded that Eric should do the talking. He should just get up and speak his mind. No script. The confrontation would have more of an impact if Eric questioned Uber's claims of helping working people when working people like himself weren't able to survive driving for Uber.

Eric was the real deal. He came off as a genuine hard-working parent effortlessly, because that's who he is. Eric lives in Fairfield. Sometimes, he gets so tired, instead of driving home, he sleeps in his car. When he wakes up, he starts driving again. He doesn't see his wife or his kids as much as he'd like because he's too busy trying to fulfill the promise of this "flexible job" to be able to tuck his kids in at night.

The next morning, I headed into the city. Nikko and Eric were already there, ready to go. After watching a few presentations, including the CEO of Microsoft talk about "augmented workers," it was time for Plouffe to hit the stage.

There was something surreal about seeing his smug face in person, as he bragged about how Uber changes peoples' lives for the better, how they're helping the middle class earn extra money, how the flexibility of driving for Uber is great for people with regular jobs so they can tuck their kids in at night… I resisted the urge to shout rebuttals.

"We've onboarded thousands of drivers," he said proudly. "And in the process helped the environment by taking cars off the road."

I wanted to scream, You can't add thousands of cars TO the road while taking thousands OFF the road at the same time! It's one or the other!

He spoke at length about the independent contractor business model, pointing out that they aren't the first to use it. And that based on their "research" drivers prefer flexibility over a set schedule.

When asked about disrupting the taxi industry, he said, "That's not something they even think about."

When Tim O'Reilly, the moderator, brought up our panel from the previous day, Plouffe evaded the question. He was there to sell an idea and anything that contradicted his narrative was irrelevant. Plouffe is a compelling speaker. His carefully crafted presentation was proof that if you tell a lie long enough and tell it well enough, people will believe it, no matter how much evidence there is to the contrary.

When it came time for the Q&A, Eric got up quickly to be the first in line to ask a question.

"I just wanted to ask how it's possible Uber is helping the economy when I'm working full time, eleven hour days, six days a week, and I am barely making minimum wage. After all the expenses are factored in, I don't know whether to pay my phone bill or my PG&E bill."

Plouffe, slightly taken aback, suggested that he get together with Uber and talk about options...

Eric expressed concern that he would be deactivated for speaking out.

But Plouffe assured him he wouldn't be deactivated for speaking his mind, pointing out that the rating system was only used to determine driver quality. Not for retaliation.

After Plouffe left the stage, everyone wanted a piece of Eric. Champions of workers' rights and labor reformers wanted him to join their cause. One woman wanted him to speak at a Wal-Mart workers' rally later in the month.

I faded into the background. Eric is a compelling figure: the perfect example of a hard working family man just trying to survive in the world.

After that, we had lunch in the ballroom. They put out quite a spread. We started off with a Caesar salad, followed by salmon with a tasty lemon and butter sauce, white rice, two asparagus spears and some kind of couscous concoction. For desert, a chocolate tart and a cup of coffee.

Once I'd finished eating, I said what I wish I'd said on stage, but even though I spoke loudly, only the people at our table could hear me:

"A friend of mine died from cancer yesterday. For two days I've been listening to presenters tout this new technology that will outsource work to machines and amateurs and all I can think is, find a cure for cancer and then I'll be fucking impressed."

With that, I wiped my mouth on the fancy cloth napkin, stood up, walked out of the Palace hotel and took BART back to Oakland.

The next day, Nikko called to tell me that Eric was kicked off the Uber platform. He was able to log in to the app, but he wasn't receiving ride requests. He drove around the city for three hours without a single ride.

Unbelievable. Despite Plouffe's claims on stage, in front of thousands of people, Uber retaliated. Even though several news sites, *Business Insider*, *Fortune* and the *San Francisco Chronicle*, had all written stories about the confrontation, they went ahead and cut him off.

I immediately phoned Eric. He told me that some high level official at Uber was leaving him messages. They wanted him to come to Uber headquarters and "discuss his situation."

Eric didn't trust them and didn't want to go alone. He never returned their calls. He told Tim O'Reilly, the founder of the convention, about what happened and Tim offered to go to the Uber offices with him.

Late that night, Eric went over to Nikko's apartment. Nikko is also an active Uber driver and they opened their apps next to each other on video. While Nikko's phone received request after request, Eric's phone sat idle.

With undisputable proof, the next day, I emailed Joe Fitzgerald at the *Examiner*. He got in touch with Eric.

Joe contacted Uber. They made some bullshit excuse about a problem with his account, but it was obvious what happened. They'd blocked his access to the app for publically calling them out.

After Joe's story hit the internet, Eric started received ride requests again. As if nothing had ever happened.

Pretty fucked up, right?

Well… just like every other negative story about Uber, as soon as the news cycle revolved, everyone moved on to the next routine atrocity…

Still, Eric, Nikko and I all felt a tinge of pride. Even though we weren't able to hurt Uber's image much, at least we blackened their eye a little.

HOW I MADE $500 ARGUING WITH SOMEONE ON THE INTERNET

A few weeks after the Next:Economy convention, Lauren Smiley suggested an online showdown through Medium.com between Jon and myself. Due to our Phil Donahue stage chemisty, the editors there figured it would made for good content. Enough to offer us both $500.

Dubbed "The Lyft vs Taxi Thunderdome," things got heated at times, but in the end, Jon and I got to hang out at a startup in the Flood Building, eat their catered lunches, drink some aged scotch and laugh at the absurdity of it…

all the way
to the
bank.

"They're searching for something underneath the seat. The girl tries to make an excuse, but I know it's either a bindle or a rock."

COURTESY PHOTO

Crackheads are people, too

Bill Graham is breaking. As M83 fans pour out of the auditorium past the metal barricades into the steady rain that hasn't let up all evening, I wait in the intersection of Grove and Polk for a fare. But there are no takers. I swing around to the Larkin side and strike out there, too.

As I head down Grove, I hear, "Taxi!"

I look around.

"Taxi!"

On the other side of Hyde Street, I see two guys and a girl pushing a stroller with a clear plastic sheet draped over it. They're flagging every taxi that goes by, even though none have their top-lights on.

When they spot me, the mother and her companions cross the street. I pull over and hit my hazards.

A sense of civic duty kicks in. It's my job to get this family out of the elements. But as they get closer, I realize this isn't your typical family out for an evening promenade in the pouring rain. They all have scarred faces, missing teeth, hollow eyes and dingy clothes that suggest they spend most of their days sitting on the filthy sidewalks of San Francisco.

I'm beginning to wonder if there's really even a baby in that stroller.

I pop the trunk anyway and roll down the passenger side window.

One guy leans in. "Hey, can I charge this ride to meth?"

"What?"

"I have crank if you're interested ..."

"Uh, no. I'm fine."

The girl reaches into the stroller and removes an infant.

"We need to get to Hayes and Cen-

I DRIVE S.F.

tral," she tells me once she's inside the cab. "We only have 10 minutes to get there."

While the second guy tries to break the stroller down, the first one climbs into the backseat. He shoves something under the girl's ass and starts groping her. She holds the baby tightly and kisses him, glancing out the back window at the other guy struggling with the stroller.

"Go help him," she says finally.

Together, they wrestle the stroller for a few minutes. Then he returns.

"Is there a button we're supposed to push?" he asks, squeezing her right breast.

She kisses him lightly and smiles. "I can't believe you guys are having such a hard time with this. It's just a stroller."

He tries to get another kiss, but she rejects him.

"We only have seven minutes left."

He goes back to work.

"Sorry about this," she tells me, rocking the baby in her arms. Throughout the entire ordeal, the kid hasn't made a peep.

Outside, the two guys are wedging the entire stroller into the trunk as hard as they can.

"Do you have a rope or bungee cord?" the first one asks.

"No."

"Can you just drive like this?" the girl pleads.

"It's not going to fall out?" I ask.

"No, it's jammed in good."

"OK." What other choice do I have?

kelly DESSAINT

The first guy says goodbye, and the second one gets in. I take off down Market and turn onto Hayes.

"I don't understand," the guy says. "Why couldn't one of us have held the baby while you broke down the stroller?"

I was actually thinking the same thing at one point.

"It's been six months," she snaps.

"But we've only had this one for two weeks."

"Try two months."

When I pull up to their building, I get out to dislodge the stroller. I expect the guy to help but neither he nor the girl is exiting the cab. I walk around to see what's up.

They're searching for something underneath the seat.

The girl tries to make an excuse, but I know it's either a bindle or a rock.

"Get out," I say. "I'll help you."

I pull out the vinyl seat to reveal what's collected underneath. Among the dust, the crumbs, a tree air freshener, various pieces of papers, a couple business cards and a rubber band, there's a small rubber ball.

The guy quickly snatches it up.

The girl hands me two wet fivers. Just as I think my job is done, she asks if I can do them a favor.

"This is an assisted living facility, and we're past curfew ... So can you tell the manager why we're late?"

Sure. Why not? I follow them to the door.

"It's all my fault," I tell the manager. "The rain. Traffic. Sorry."

I rush back to my cab and out of the weather. I'm soaked but still ready to serve.

Kelly Dessaint is a San Francisco taxi driver. Write to Kelly at piltdownlad@gmail.com or visit his blog at www.idrivesf.com.

AIDING AND ABETTING PASSENGERS' VICES

So this hooker and an Irishman get in my cab at Post and Mason.
They're going to the Union Square Hotel.

"I know it's right down the street," the woman tells me. "But can you
drive around the block so we can get acquainted?"

"Alright." I hit the meter and continue down Post.

Despite the weather, she's scantily clad in a dress that's all va-va-
voom and Biff! Bang! Pow! He's a good-looking, young businessman
type, maybe in town for work and trying to squeeze in a little pleasure.

I keep the music faded to the front and turn up the volume to drown
out their conversation, which consists of her telling him over and over
how laid back San Francisco is.

I take a right onto Grant, then another at Geary. I don't want to venture
too far from the hotel in case they get to know each other quicker than
expected. I'm not making much on this ride anyway, just providing a
warm place for them to hash out the details of their transaction.

It's been a night of vices. Earlier, I did a round-trip from the Castro to
Polk Street so this guy could score blow. When I pulled up in front of the
bar, he asked me if I needed anything. He read off the menu of available
items, but I insisted my needs were covered. While he ran in to make the
deal, I kept the meter running. On the way back to the Castro, he did a

few bumps off the end of a key and offered me one.

Before that, I'd picked up three stoners from the Marriott in Fisherman's Wharf going to The Independent. From the moment they got into my cab, the smell of marijuana was overwhelming.

"Damn, you guys reek of pot!"

At first they acted surprised then started laughing and offered to smoke me out. After I turned them down, they begged me to drive as fast as possible down Gough. To amuse them, I tried to catch some air on the hills, but there was too much traffic.

I can't say it's been a profitable night, but at least it's been interesting. And now, here I am aiding and abetting prostitution…

At Mason, I take a left and complete a roundabout from Ellis to Powell. I pull up to the hotel and the woman gets out.

"Go around the block again," the man says.

I head up Powell and turn down the music.

"Tell me honestly," he asks. "If I take that woman up to my room, will I get arrested and kicked out of the country?"

I can't help but laugh. "Are you serious?" I look at his face in the rearview. It's obvious he's not joking.

"I need to know. Will anything happen to me?"

"Not as long as you don't kill her."

He thinks about that for a moment as I circle back to Geary.

"What would you do?" he asks, still skeptical.

"Me?" I pull over in front of Macy's. "I've seen some hot street-walkers in Union Square. I'm not going to lie. If you have the money, why the hell not?"

"So I'm safe from the police?"

"Man, the cops don't do shit around here except harass homeless peo-ple." I go on to list off all the sex workers I deal with in a cab: the trans hookers on Post Street, the dancers at the Gold Club with their regular clients who pay for college tuitions and new cars, the girls prowling DJ clubs looking for unsuspecting tech kids and the sleazy drive-thru action on Capp Street. Then there are the strip clubs and massage parlors where cab drivers get a finder's fee for steering customers. I even point out how they tried to pass a proposition in 2008 to decriminalize prostitution in the city, and it was barely defeated.

Finally, he seems convinced.

"Thanks." He slaps a $20 bill on the console. "I'll get out here."

The meter reads $7.90. I shove the twenty in my pocket and continue on Geary until a group of kids flag me outside Edinburgh Castle. They

get in and ask the number one question I get asked each weekend after 2am: "Do you know where we can get any alcohol?"

Since I've already assisted in various illicit activities, why not cap off my shift with a ride to an after hours club? I check the Hackers group to see which one is open and race down Van Ness.

"Faster!" they yell and I step on it.

LATE NIGHT LARRY ON HOPE

It's 3:30 a.m. I'm at Sixth and Mission. The place is deserted. The wind is blowing and trash is flying all over the place. It looks like the end of the world. As I head north on Sixth, I see a tall black man standing in the middle of Market Street screaming his head off. When I get closer, I notice he's wearing a pink wig.

Two cops in a squad car roll by, give him the once over, shake their heads and just keep driving.

As soon as he sees my cab, he waves me down. I think to myself, no one else is around. This is my only chance at a fare. There's no telling where this ride will take me, but you know, hope is better than nothing at all.

"What's wrong with you?" I ask him.

"22 cabs wouldn't pick me up!"

"Well, look at you! You're screaming like a lunatic. Get in the fucking cab already. Where you heading?"

"Take me to Hunter's Point!"

I stick out my hand. "Gimme $20!"

He hands over a $20 bill. All right. I think everything's cool and start driving.

"But wait..." the guy says. "I need to get some drugs first."

I shake my head. "Gimme ten more bucks!"

He hands over another bill and asks for $10 back.

I put the second $20 with the first one in my lap and hand the guy his change. And away we go, off to Ellis and Jones, which, as you all know, at that hour, is a post-apocalyptic nightmare straight out of some dystopian movie: shadowy characters lurking in the shadows, drugged out ghouls wandering around aimlessly, the gutters filled with trash and excrement...

I stop in the middle of the street. No point pulling over since there's no traffic. Several people approach my cab. The guy exchanges

money with a dealer who hands him a couple rocks.

"Where's the rest?" my pink-haired passenger asks.

"What are you talking about?" The dealer shrugs.

"Where is the rest?" He exits the cab and points a knife at the dealer. "Where's the rest of my shit?"

The dealer pulls out a gun.

As they start screaming at each other, the crowd moves in closer, and I just slowly... roll... away... Like I'm melting from the scene.

Once I'm clear, I gun it and the back door closes from the momentum.

Ten minutes later or so, I'm in SoMa. I look at the two $20s between my legs. One is actually a $100 bill!

If there's one thing this job has taught me, you never know what's going to happen.

THE PATRON SAINT OF LATE NIGHT DRUNKS

All good rides are alike, but each shitty ride is shitty in its own unique way. It's one of those nights. I've been driving empty for almost an hour, trolling the bars in North Beach as last call looms. With no takers, I head to Union Square, then venture on to Polk Street, where I quickly realize the error of my way and exit stage left to see what SoMa has to offer.

Somehow, I end up in the Financial. Brain dead, I'm cruising down Sutter when a hand goes up. Two guys. One comes to my window. The other is slumped on the curb like a bloated sack of trash. My first instinct is to drive away. Then I hear Daly City.

Our spokesperson's breath reeks of alcohol, but he seems mostly cognizant. I motion to his friend. "Is he okay?"

"He's not gonna throw up, I promise."

Whenever somebody tells me they're wasted companion is not going to vomit in my cab, I can't help but think they will.

"You know it's $100 if he does, right?" As a night cabbie, it's my job to transport the intoxicated citizens of the city home after hours—I am the patron saint of late night drunks. But I'm also like Charon. You have to pay for safe passage in my taxi.

"Don't worry. He got it all out. We just really need to get home. I'll take care of you. I swear."

Another empty promise, the "I'll take care of you" line usually means an extra dollar or two on top of the fare. I'm just hoping my desperation for a decent ride doesn't backfire on me. So far, after two years of driving nights, I have yet to clean up another person's puke. And I hope to keep my streak going.

I watch the guy drag his friend over and shove the pile of drunken flesh through the door and across my backseat.

He sits up front. "What's your name?"

"Kelly."

"Andrew. I really appreciate this. He's my boy and I can't leave him out here like this."

"No problem," I say, but immediately realize there is a problem. I haven't made it half a block when the most evil scent known to man rises up from the backseat and wraps itself around my head like a wrestler putting me in the sleeper hold.

"What the hell?" I demand, squeezing my nose.

"He shit himself."

"What the hell?" It's all I can think to say as I roll down my window.

"I know it's bad. Sorry."

"Has he just never had alcohol before? Cause…" I stick my head out the window for a second. "God damn!"

"I don't know what his problem is. We drank the same amount. I just gotta get him home. He's my boy."

At this point there's not much I can do but drive as quickly as possible. The fresh air doesn't help much. I remember the aromatherapy oil in my bag, grab the vile, put a few drops on a napkin and stick it in the vent. I turn on the heater and make sure the recirculate button is on. It does little to mitigate the stench though.

On 280, I'm driving so fast, the taximeter is rattling on the dash like it's about to fall off.

"You mind if I listen to some music?" Andrew asks.

I assume he's going to grab my auxiliary cord, but he puts in ear buds and raps along quietly to the music in his head.

I try to pretend like this isn't happening too, but the stink from the backseat keeps tapping me on the shoulder and punching me in the face.

Finally, at the John Daly Boulevard exit, he directs me to a house in the hills.

The meter reads $22.75.

"So…"

"Make it $50." He hands me his card.

I run it through my Square and the approval notice absolves them.

"Am I home?" the guy in the back mumbles as Andrew rousts him out of the cab.

"Yeah. Let's go, motherfucker." He pushes him towards the house.

I look in the backseat. There's only a little drool. Still, it's hard to tell if the odor is lingering or just banked in my olfactory memory.

To be on the safe side, I race back to the yard, grab the container of disinfectant wipes from the office and clean every surface the guy might have tainted.

Back on the prowl for rides, sure my cab smells lemony fresh, but when the next passenger asks how my night's going, I don't tell them this story.

Like the Sacrament of Penance, it's our dirty little secret.

COGS IN THE WHEELS OF CORRUPTION

As ambassadors of the city, cab drivers are both purveyors of myth and concierges of vice. From the tourist attractions to the ripped backsides, we navigate the orthodox and the underbelly to take you where you want to go.

Or at least point you towards the right transgression.

Naturally, most services come with the expectation of a gratuity. And once cash starts exchanging hands, everyone wants a piece of the action...

This weekend, after dropping off at the Sheraton in Fisherman's Wharf, the doorman says he has an airport for me. Then asks if I "take care of doormen."

I hesitate, remembering Colin's argument that we shouldn't have to bride doormen since they get tips from the hotel's guests. But it's a long ride, all the way from Fisherman's Wharf... so whatever. I fork over a fiver and he loads the passenger's suitcase.

On my way back to the city, I take the Vermont exit and check out Mighty. I pull in behind Juneaux. As we smoke cigarettes, he tells me he just took two guys to the massage parlor in the TL that pays $30 a head.

"Nothing like easy money," he says.

I've only taken a passenger to a massage parlor once. At the time, I didn't really know what I was doing. Since then, I've been trying to figure out the protocol, especially at the place with the $30 kickback.

We each light another cigarette and he lays out the details. Once I've got everything down, and we ascertain there's no business to be had at Mighty, we pitch our butts and drive off into the night.

Half an hour later, I'm on the throne at Public Works when a toothless, bearded man asks if I'll drive him to Eddy and Leavenworth. Along the way, we pick up a haggard woman carrying several bags. He directs me to the 7-Eleven on Market to buy condoms.

"What kind do you like?" he asks his companion. "Ribbed, flavored or colored?"

"I don't really care." She asks him to get pizza.

He returns with a Slurpee, a box of Trojans and a pack of Newports.

I drop them off at a fleabag on Leavenworth and cruise Union Square. Next to the Hilton, a guy flags me.

"Do you know of any massage parlors still open?" he asks.

Overcome with the serendipity of the situation, though somewhat remiss I didn't ask Junueax about the hours, I say, "Get in. We'll figure it out."

"I have an early flight," he tells me. "Hardly worth going to sleep now."

"That makes sense."

The high-paying massage parlor is just a few blocks away. I double-park outside, hit the hazards and collect all my valuables, per Juneaux's advice, since people watch the cabs going to the massage parlor, looking for an opportunity to smash and grab.

I walk the guy to the entrance and press the bell. Apparently, the woman in charge can see us, and my cab in the street, through the wide-angle camera positioned above the metal gate. She buzzes us in and we head down the stairs.

At the bottom, we enter a brightly lit parlor where several girls sit on a couch. They immediately perk up when we enter and display their goods.

A dragon lady sits behind a counter. You can tell she runs a tight ship. She collects $70 from the guy, which is just the entrance fee. The rest of the transaction takes place inside the room.

I'm standing against the wall several feet away, next to a door. On the other side I can hear a man grunting softly while a female voice coos, "Oh yeah, baby, fuck me good."

The air inside is like a sauna. At the end of a hallway, an old lady arranges white towels on a shelf.

I try to avoid making eye contact with the girls on the couch. Even with my taxi badge prominently displayed, I'm still a mark. An easy one at that. Before I entered this establishment, sex was the furthest thing from my mind. But now, with a buffet of pussy before me and a steamy atmosphere, I'm suddenly consumed with the thought of flesh for sale.

After the guy pays, he chooses a curly-haired hottie and they walk down the hallway.

The dragon lady calls me to the counter and hands me $30. I thank her and rush past the girls quickly, but not without a final sideways glance.

When I get back into my cab, a police car drives by slowly. The cop behind the wheel smirks at me. I can't help but wonder what percentage of each trick they get…

Whatever. We're all just cogs in the wheel of corruption. But as Tony Soprano said, "Shit runs downhill, money runs up."

With my filthy lucre, I head back into the night.

A GOOD NIGHT COMES AT A PRICE

"You know it's a slow night," Juneaux once joked, "when you're hoping somebody pukes in your taxi so you can collect that $100 cleaning fee."

Last Saturday, I'm racing back to the city from an Oakland ride. It's almost 2 a.m. and I'm only $80 in the black after making my nut. Due to intense competition, Saturdays have become one of the slowest nights of the week. I'll be lucky to break $100.

Once I've circled through SoMa to no avail, I pull behind a Town Taxi outside the Cat Club.

As I text Juneaux and Colin to find out where the action is, a group of people approach my cab. Someone opens my backdoor and shoves a very intoxicated guy inside.

"We found him lying in the middle of the street," a guy tells me.

Given his state of inebriation and the potential trouble, I'm inclined to follow cabstand etiquette and direct them to the taxi in front of me so I won't be guilty of backloading again. Then I hear his destination and my sense of protocol dissipates like smoke from that vape pen I found under my seat last week.

Livermore.

Once he's inside my cab, I drive a block and pull over. Before I get too far, I need to make sure I'm getting paid. I try talking to the guy but he's mostly incoherent. I hear a girl's voice. I notice he's in the middle of a FaceTime call. I take the guy's iPhone and describe the situation to the girl looking back at me.

Meanwhile, the guy gets out of the cab and unzips his pants.

"Is Ken alright?" she asks woefully.

"Well, Ken is currently peeing in the middle of Folsom Street."

"Oh god."

"Yeah." I ask where to take him and confirm I'll get paid when I get there. At first she wants to meet at the Stoneridge Mall in Pleasanton. I tell her the price: $175. She balks. I hear voices talking in the background and she suggests the Century Theater in Hayward instead. That's $125. Okay.

When I end the call, the Uber app pops up on the screen. Apparently, Ken was trying to request a car before he passed out. But Uber's surging. So his fare to Livermore would cost $246, which is a $200 ride in a taxi.

I usher Ken, who's wandering into an alley with his pants undone, back inside the cab and gun it toward the bridge.

I'm not even half way across the western span when Ken, without warning, leans forward and hurls onto the floorboard.

"Oh, fuck!" I roll down the windows as the retching continues.

After puking all over himself, Ken moans pathetically and passes out. Fuck! Fuck! Fuck! Now I'm hoping I don't get stiffed on the cleaning fee.

The smell isn't that bad, fortunately, but I'm still pushing the speed limit as I weave through the darkened hills on I-580.

Thirty minutes later, in front of the theater, I examine the mess. There's vomit everywhere: on the floorboard, on the backseat and all over Ken, sprawled out in his own sick.

I text Colin and Juneaux to let them know I finally found some action.

Five minutes later, a car pulls up. Two girls immediately start apologizing and thanking me for rescuing their friend.

The girl from the FaceTime call lures Ken out of my cab. He stumbles and falls down, covered in puke.

"It's going to be $225 total," I tell her. "$125 for the ride and a $100 cleaning fee."

She fishes Ken's wallet out of his pants and hands me a debit card. I run it on my Square. Declined. She hands me another. Declined. And another. Declined.

I try not to panic.

We both look at Ken, spread-eagle on the concrete, groaning.

"Is this your boyfriend?" I ask.

She hesitates. "Uhhh…"

"Can't he reimburse you later?"

She grimaces and hands me a card. The charge goes through. I sigh with relief and disgust as they roll Ken's sullied body into the backseat of their car.

The increasingly blurry lines of driving for hire

I was a Lyft driver for Halloween. The idea came to me at last week's barbeque. For some reason, driving around San Francisco, picking up fares with Lyft's iconic trade dress on my cab, seemed like an absolutely hilarious prank. Even if I just caused confusion, at the very least it would be a noteworthy social experiment.

So that Saturday, once it got dark, I fastened the fluffy pink Carstache

**kelly
DESSAINT**

Lyft sent me when I first signed up to the grill of National 182 and attached the Glowstache I'd received as a top-rated driver to the dash.

I created a Pandora station around The Cramps, Misfits and Ramones.

To augment my trickery, I planned to tell my passengers I didn't know where I was going and that it was 200 percent Prime Time all night.

I DRIVE S.F.

I figured everyone would laugh and throw piles of money at me for having such a clever costume.

On 16th Street, a girl dressed as a spider flagged me down.

"Can you take me to Geary and Fillmore, please?"

"Sorry, I'm a Lyft driver," I said merrily. "I don't know where that is."

"It's easy," she responded in all seriousness. "I'll direct you."

" ..."

From Japantown, I crawled down Polk Street behind a beat-up white limo. A few cab drivers looked at me like I was committing the greatest sin by "rocking the 'stache," as they say in Lyft parlance.

Trevor, the Street Ninja, impersonating Travis Bickle, cruised past me at one point cracking up.

"I'm a Lyft driver!" I yelled out the window. "Where am I? What street is this? Are we in SoMa?"

I stuck to the more congested parts of The City, where I knew my caricature would get the most exposure. Some Lyft drivers scowled at me. Others blew their horns or flashed

KELLY DESSAINT/SPECIAL TO S.F. EXAMINER
National 182 sports a pink Carstache on the grill and a Glowstache on the dash.

their high beams.

The majority of my passengers, though, didn't seem to notice or care. They just told me where they were going, and off I drove with my mouth shut.

So much for being a friend with a cab.

After dropping off a group of revelers at Bar None, I was heading deeper into the congestion of Union Street with The Stooges' "I Wanna Be Your Dog" at full blast when a guy darted out of the crowd.

"You!" He pointed at my cab, laughed and jumped in the backseat.

Barreling down Gough, we talked about irony and thrash metal. When I dropped him off on Valencia, he almost took off without paying.

"Hey, I'm only pretending to be a Lyft," I reminded him.

On my way to the Haight from the Mission with a fare, Other Larry pulled up next to me on Guerrero in Veterans 233.

"Nice fucking mustache!" he shouted.

"Look at me!" I jeered. "I'm a Lyft driver and I don't know what the fuck I'm doing!"

"Does it ever get old?" the guy in the backseat asked.

"What?"

"Making fun of Lyft."

"No."

On a ride through the back roads of the Western Addition, I tried to explain to another guy the tension between the Smartphone Hailed Internet Transportation Services and

cab drivers and why the Lyft mustaches on my taxi were so hilarious.

"You mean you can't do Lyft in a cab?" he asked. "I always assumed you guys were all the same."

The same?

Sure, the lines are blurry these days: Flywheel is an app and a taxi company; most Uber drivers are Lyft drivers and vice versa; decommissioned Yellow cabs are used as Uber-Lyft cars; Towncar drivers slap fake TCP numbers on their bumpers to access commercial lanes; out-of-town cabs come into The City all the time and pick up street hails; and now Uber-Lyft drivers are putting toplights on their Priuses.

According to a recent study from Northeastern University, the streets of San Francisco are congested with more than 10,000 vehicles for hire on average. During a holiday like Halloween, that number is considerably higher. But only taxicabs are required to follow rules and regulations. Everyone else is free to play make-believe all they want.

It doesn't even matter if the portrayal is convincing. The general population just wants the cheapest and most convenient ride available. Who provides the actual service, whether they're knockoffs or the real McCoy, is completely irrelevant. Especially on Halloween.

Kelly Dessaint is a San Francisco taxi driver. Write to him at piltdownlad@gmail. com and @piltdownlad.

LATE NIGHT LARRY ON PUKERS

2013 was just a brutal year for me. Someone threw up in the cab in January, someone in February, someone on March and someone in April. And here it is May 28th... I say to myself, I just might get through the month without anyone puking in my cab.

I pick up this couple. Drunk. Going to the city of Pinole. We're on the Bay Bridge and the girl starts moaning. And I say to myself, Goddamn it, she's going to throw up and there's nowhere to pull over. And I'm not going to make it through the month of May.

As I continue driving towards the East Bay, the moaning gets louder. Now, I never look in the backseat. But this time I did. And what do I see? She's not going to throw up. She's getting fucked! It's the wrong kind of moan!

What a lucky guy I am. I might make it through the month after all...

On we go. Finally, she has an orgasm and throws up all over the seat, the floor, the door, the window, the headrest... And then she rolls down the window and now it's inside the door.

What's worse, she was drinking red wine. So it's purple.

I got $200 out of them.

But it wasn't enough.

I DRIVE A TAXI SO YOU DON'T HAVE TO

There are days when I don't even want to think about driving a taxi. Days when I'd just as soon contemplate anything but what goes on behind the wheel of a cab at night in the city.

Given the option, I'd rather discuss this psychotic election cycle, the hunger strike outside the Mission police station, the fate of Syrian refugees or even my fucked up life. Anything but taxis...

Last Friday, I'm waiting outside the Art Bash at the San Francisco Museum of Modern Art when a hip, young couple get in. They're going to the Outer Richmond.

While they relax in the backseat and reflect on the highlights of the party, I turn left onto Market and right onto Turk. I catch all the green lights through the Tenderloin. I know I can't beat the red at Franklin, but push on to Masonic, where I'm stopped again, then over to Arguello, where I take a left and cruise down Fulton, adjusting my speed to catch

all the lights.

As I turn onto their street, they point out their building and I pull into the driveway.

"Ok, thanks for the ride." The guy gets out and walks around the back to open the door for his wife.

I roll down my window and sheepishly say, "Uhm, this isn't an Uber."

"Oh, I'm sorry!" he exclaims as he fumbles for his wallet. "It was such a smooth ride I forgot we jumped into a cab."

While I run his card, his wife laughs and I reassure him this happens all the time and not to worry about it, that it used to feel like an insult but now I take it as a compliment.

What they're saying is I'm not the stereotypical cab driver. I keep my car clean. I wash the outside and vacuum the interior each day before I leave the yard. I use aromatherapy to fill the air inside with peppermint and citrus. I don't talk on my phone while I drive. I don't blow the horn at other drivers (as much as I'd like to). I don't drive recklessly. I'm not argumentative. I gladly accept credit cards...

So yeah, I can see their confusion.

Sadly, I'm held to the standards of each shitty cab driver that came before me. And what's worse, I'm competing with most of them for the few fares left because most people prefer to take Uber and Lyft.

There are days when I ask myself why I do this job. When the exhaustion makes me want to weep. It's almost impossible to get enough rest between 12-hour taxi shifts, when the previous night hangs heavy on my soul as I try to reconcile the absurdity of what I'm doing.

There are days, technically mornings, when I walk through my front door after a long and wretched shift, exhausted and terrifyingly sober, head straight for the freezer with a tall glass and fill it full of ice, vodka and a little San Pellegrino. What follows is anyone's guess…

I drink and fight the inevitability of sleep. Because now I'm alive! I'm no longer scrunched up in the seat of a cab. I'm free! Free to rage against the dying of the light!

Sometimes I go on drunken Twitter rampages, post misguided rants on Facebook, text or call friends with normal schedules or end up babbling incoherently to a neighbor in the hallway at 3pm on my way to buy a pack of cigarettes at the liquor store.

I usually wake up later and piece together my activities through time stamps as I delete posts and tweets and send apologies to whomever I'd been texting or talking to on the phone the night before.

It can get a little embarrassing.

Of course nothing tops Colin's naked escapade at his girlfriend's house, when he apparently passed out and then sleepwalked into the kitchen, au naturel, grabbed a yoghurt from the fridge and sat down to eat it in front of the TV. That night, his girlfriend's mother was visiting and discovered him mid spoonful. Poor Jane. His argument that it was just an unfortunate side effect of exhaustion fell on deaf ears.

This is what happens when cab driving and life converges. It can get ugly. And truth be told, that's not anything worth exploring.

THE PERILS OF SHOPPING ON THE BLACK MARKET

I'm inbound on Market, trying to prevent a Yellow cab in the right lane from getting the jump on me, when a guy flags me at the Seventh Street Muni island stop. He opens my front door. I quickly stow my bag under my seat. With an Australian accent, he asks how much to Ocean Beach. I tell him around $20.

"Let's do it," he says.

I turn right on Sixth and start driving west.

His name is Hugh. He's from Sydney, in San Francisco working on some project for a tech firm. Spent the past two weeks sequestered in an incubator in the Mission. This is the first time he's been free to venture out and explore the city.

"So what have you been up to?" I ask.

"Well, I just lost $300 trying to buy weed."

"Why'd you think you could buy pot around here?" I ask, more nonplussed than he seems to be. They only sell crack and heroin in Mid-Market. Some pot dealers hang out by Jones Street, but they usually close up shop early.

Hugh shrugs. "I just wanted to celebrate turning in the first part of my project this morning."

He gave $150 to one guy who told him to wait. After fifteen minutes he asked the other guys standing around if they knew when their mate was returning. They laughed, told him, "That's not our mate." A second guy offered to help him out and Hugh handed over another $150. Of course, that guy never returned either.

As we're rolling over the hills on Fell Street, I say, "You should have just gone to Haight Street."

"Haight Street?"

"You've never heard of Haight-Ashbury? Where all the Sixties rock bands used to hang out? The hippie movement? Summer of Love? Flower Power?"

None of this rings a bell with my young fare.

"If you go up to Haight Street and walk around, someone is going to try to sell you weed. It'll be decent stuff and won't cost $150. More like $50."

To commiserate with him about getting snookered so badly, I tell Hugh about the time I got ripped off trying to score weed at night in Mid-Market back in 1994, when I was the resident concierge of vice at the Green Tortoise hostel in North Beach…

One night around midnight, someone asked me to get him a bag. Flashed a handful of cash. Even though I knew all the dealers I trusted on Haight Street would be off duty at that hour, I couldn't resist the opportunity to make a quick buck.

I went down to the UN Plaza where the dealers used to hit you up when you get off BART. I didn't see many people around but eventually caught the eye of a guy sitting on a bench.

I told him what I wanted but all he had was crack. I said no thanks but he had a "you ask, you buy" policy because he insisted I take what he was selling.

I started walking away. Fast.

"Hey, come back here, motherfucker!" he shouted.

I heard his footsteps behind me as I ran towards the Civic Center BART. I went down the broken escalator three stairs at a time. At the bottom, as I tried to figure out which hallway led to the trains, I hesitated for a few seconds.

That's all it took.

I didn't even see it coming. Next thing I knew I was sliding across the tiles. The guy lifted me up by my jacket with one hand and hit me in the jaw with the other.

"Give me back my shit!" he yelled, slamming me into the ground and socking me a second time.

I saw a lady on a pay phone a few yards away. I tried screaming for help, but a second blow shut my mouth.

I knew what he wanted so I finally handed over the $20 bill to get him off me…

"And I didn't even get the crack!" I tell Hugh as we reach Ocean Beach.

I pull into the lot and park the cab. We walk out onto the sand and smoke cigarettes, listening to the waves crash on the shore as a bonfire rages in the distance.

"Haight Street, you say?" Hugh asks as we head back downtown.

"Yeah, catch the 6 or the 7 bus on Market. Get off at Masonic and just start walking around."

WHAT WE TALK ABOUT WHEN WE TALK ABOUT UBER AND LYFT

It's 2:35 a.m. and I'm looking for a cabstand showing signs of life. Everyone's in some kind of motion, either trying to go home or get to an after-hours joint.

In front of 1015 Folsom, a large crowd is milling about in the street among several dozen unmarked sedans blocking the flow of traffic while

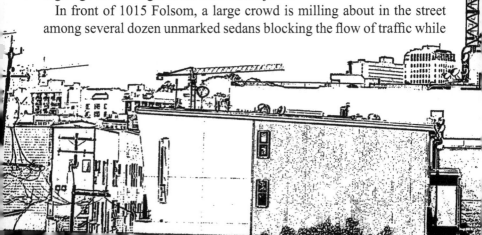

a few taxis wait patiently outside the club.

As I slow down to suss out the situation, a young guy approaches my window. He wants to know the fare to Berkeley.

"Around $35-$40," I tell him. "Plus the bridge toll."

"But Lyft is only $20." He holds up his phone as proof.

"Then take Lyft." I roll up my window but he has another question.

"Why cabs are so expensive?" he asks. "Don't you guys want to be competitive with Uber and Lyft?"

"The city determines taxi rates," I tell him. "I don't have any control over them. Neither does my cab company."

"Really?" he asks, genuinely surprised.

"You think we just charge more because we're bad at business?"

He's about to respond when another guy approaches my cab and asks if I'll take him to the Richmond District for $10.

"You gotta be kidding me?" I laugh. "Sorry, that's a $20 ride."

"But an UberPool is only $7."

"Then take Uber!" I say abruptly.

"I would," the guy tells me. "But my phone's dead."

"You know what, then," I say with a smirk. "The fare's now $30. My cab just went into surge pricing."

The guy scoffs while the first one laughs.

"Come on," Mr. Richmond pleads. "None of these taxis are going anywhere anytime soon."

"That may be true, but I still have my dignity. Why don't you ask another cab driver?"

"I asked them all. You're the last in line."

"Then the price to the Richmond is now $40. My surge multiplier just went up!"

"Come on!"

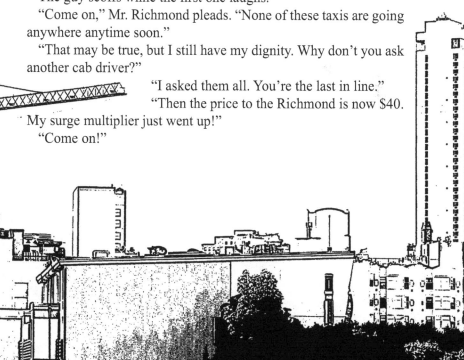

"Tell me something," I address the two of them. "Do you guys really think it's acceptable for these companies to charge half the price of a taxi and justify it by calling it a disruptive business model? You know that's bullshit, right? That's not disruption. It's predatory pricing, plain and simple. And who pays for all these cheap rides? Not you. Not Uber. Not Lyft. It's their drivers who get screwed so you guys can get a good deal."

"Nobody is forced to do anything," Mr. Berkeley points out.

"Because jobs grow on job trees?" I ask. "I think most people who decide to use their own cars as taxicabs are doing so out of desperation."

"Everyone has options," adds Mr. Richmond.

I decide to alter my approach. "So do you guys support Bernie Sanders?"

"Of course!" Mr. Berkeley declares. "Love him!"

"Bernie's my man!" says Mr. Richmond.

"Then why are you participating in the exploitation of workers? Isn't that something Bernie is fighting against?"

They both shrug, not seeing the connection.

"The people who drive for Uber and Lyft don't make shit and assume all the risk involved with driving a car on the congested streets of San Francisco just to make four or five bucks off a $7 ride. You think that's cool?"

"I've never heard a driver complain."

"You hold a rating over their heads," I say. "They're afraid of losing their jobs."

"But..."

"Well..."

"Look, you guys are obviously confused about what being progressive means. This new gig economy is regressive. It pushes the most vulnerable members of our society into wage slavery, where they're paid for piecework rather than given an opportunity to secure a stable income. And what's worse, instead of seeing their profits increase by working more, due to the constant Uber/Lyft price wars, they actually make less in the process. How can you support a system like that?"

"But if people stopped using these services," says Mr. Berkeley, "it'll hurt the drivers more because they won't have a job left."

"Yeah, less of something's better than nothing!" Mr. Richmond pipes in.

I'm about to launch into another tirade when I notice the time. It's 3:15. I've already wasted over half an hour arguing with these guys. I might as well be making some money along the way.

"Guess what? My cab just turned into a TaxiPool. I'll do $10 to the Richmond and $25 to Berkeley. But, goddamn it, you better give me decent tips. Get in and let's go."

I don't even bother hitting the meter as I speed away.

A HELL RIDE INTO THE PENINSULA

The cashier at the ARCO on Fourteenth and Mission is a funny guy. When he's not scolding me for giving change to the panhandlers who loiter outside his thick Plexiglas window, he asks me while counting bills with long, curly nails, "Busy? Busy?"

You can usually tell how lucrative a night has been by how much you spend on gas at the end of your shift. Unless you've been short tanked by a day driver.

On Thursday, I pumped $13 into 182, which included an SFO run and a trip to Berkeley.

On Friday, I dropped $20.

Apparently, there was some festival or something in Golden Gate Park, but I just worked the city as usual...

Around midnight, I'm in the Mission. I approach a woman with her arm extended on Sixteenth Street. She doesn't seem that excited to see me, so I ask, "Do you need a taxi?"

"I'm going to Oakland," she says.

"No problem."

Several hours later, a guy flags me at the corner of 18th and Castro. At first he's tells me 442 Natoma, then asks how much to Palo Alto. We negotiate a price and he hands me his debit card.

"I know you want me to pay up front cause you towelheads don't trust black folks."

"Whoa!" I hit the lights and say, "You can pay at the end of the ride if you like, but don't be so quick to judge!"

"Oh, you're a cute hippy boy!" he responds gleefully.

It's obvious he's wasted. Before I'm even on the Central Freeway, he asks if he can suck my dick. I laugh it off, but he persists. Vehemently. No matter how many times I turn down his offer and try to change the subject, he doesn't let up. Over and over, all the way down 101, he continuously asks to suck my dick.

"I just know you're going to let me suck your dick…"

"Uhm, no."

"Then shut up," he says. "Your voice is turning me on."

I shut up. Then he asks me a random question and returns to the topic of sucking my dick. When I reject his advances for the umpteenth time, he tells to shut up again.

"Stop asking me questions then!" I shout.

I'm driving so fast, at one point, he tells me to slow down. I just keep counting down the cities: Burlingame… San Mateo… Belmont… Redwood City… Menlo Park… Palo Alto!

Just when I think this ride is almost over, he decides to give me a tour of his neighborhood, showing me where he grew up and where his relatives live.

At each spot, I ask with increasing urgency, "Is this where I'm dropping you off?"

"I bet you have sweaty, stinky balls," he says, ignoring my pleas to reach his destination. "But I'll still suck your dick."

"Hey, don't talk about my balls like that!"

I don't know where the hell I am. It's dark. There are trees everywhere! So many damn trees! There are no sidewalks. The houses have white picket fences and lawns. And what are those, cul-de-sacs?

Finally, he tells me he's getting out at the next stop. He tips me $20 and asks if I'll let him suck my dick for another $20.

I quickly speed away, exhausted and weary. I try to find the freeway but I get lost. All these trees are disorienting!

That's when I realize I need food. As I continue driving north on surface streets, I see a Carl's Jr. with an OPEN sign. I haven't eaten at a

Carl's Jr. in 20 years maybe, but I'm starving and figure, what the hell. It won't kill me.

I pull up to the speaker. The cashier tells me to continue on to the window, where he's explaining to a woman in the car in front of me that they're out of beef. (!) She has coupons though. For burgers. (!!) An extensive process of haggling over semantics ensues during which she tells the cashier she drives for Uber. (!!!) After spending ten minutes ordering two chicken sandwiches, (!!!!) she goes on to talk about how cool it is driving for Uber, (!!!!!) that she loves all the extra spending money, (!!!!!!) but doesn't work the city because the drunk bar kids puke in your car. (!!!!!!!)

"You have to carry buckets with you or your backseat fills up with vomit," she tells him. "Can you imagine the smell?" (????????)

By the time it's my turn to order, I'm ready to blow my brains out. The cashier, looking somewhat dismayed, goes into his spiel about not having beef, but I cut him off.

"Just give me a chicken sandwich. I don't care which one. And some fries."

Up ahead I see a sign for Highway 101. I grab the bag of crappy food and put the pedal to the metal.

LATE NIGHT LARRY STORY ON ORGASMS

In 1997, I finally put a sign on the back of my headrest that read, "NO ORGASMS!"

Things were just getting too dangerous. Like this one Sunday night...

I'm driving through downtown. And there isn't anyone anywhere. Somehow, I manage to find a fare. A couple. The guy is dressed in leather. The girl has on a miniskirt.

They're going to Hercules. From the early conversation, I realize they've just met. We get on the bridge – and he's a smart guy for waiting until I'm on the bridge before he pops the question:

"Hey cabbie!" he says to me. "You don't mind if I fuck this bitch, do ya?"

Those are his exact words.

So I say, "We don't have any fucking rules in this cab!"

And away we go. I have the house music cranked. Everything starts out mellow. They're having a good time. Then things start to get happy.

We run across two girls in a Volkswagen and she presses her boobs on the window.

We run across a truck driver and they put on a show for him too.

But that's just the beginning...

Things get serious when he pins the girl behind my seat.

We're going 80 miles per hour in the fast lane while he starts fucking the shit out of her. And I'm getting slammed forward with each thrust.

At 80 mph!

My head is practically bouncing off the steering wheel.

Then she has this massive orgasm. She wraps her arm around my neck. And she's screaming in my ear.

Well, I knock it down to 65. Cause, you know... safety first.

When we finally get to Hercules, I turn around to see who I've just had sex with. And she clams up. She covers herself with her hands and turns away so I can't see her face.

After all that, now she's shy.

WHEN THE DRIVING'S OVER, THE REAL SLOG BEGINS

Sometimes it seems like your night isn't over until you've crested all the hills in San Francisco and seen each low point the city has to offer.

And although you've driven these streets long enough to have memorized almost every pothole, the way the light changes, even at night, depending on the weather and the cycles of the moon, it's like you're taking it all in for the very first time.

And you're feeling good tonight, jacked up on strong coffee.

And if you're lucky, one ride follows the next, like jigsaw puzzle pieces falling into place. One minute you're working the swanky hotels on Snob Hill, the next you're dropping off in the oft-forgotten Bayview, where urban detritus collects like dust bunnies under a credenza.

And you've seen it all, cause you're a cab driver, or at least you've seen most of it, although in reality, you don't know fuck all. But tonight you'll transport everyone from the opera crowd in their frocks and tuxes to the skeezers heading to some fleabag in the Tenderloin.

And when it gets late, you'll cruise Valencia looking for taqueria workers or millennials brave enough to take a cab. Maybe you'll get a Daly City, a Lake Merced or a ride out to the Avenues.

And then you'll race back to the Castro before last call.

And if you strike out there, you can head down to the Mission again, circling your way to SoMa, hoping for someone going further than a few clicks past a meter drop.

And once the venues still open after 2 a.m. are stacked with cabs and the streets are so lonely they make you weep, there's nothing left to do but meander back to the yard, hidden among the deserted warehouses off Bayshore Boulevard.

And it would seem, now that your shift is over, that your work here is done. Soon, you'll be home in Oakland, with a vodka drink in one hand and a cigarette in the other. But you don't have a car anymore. You're at the mercy of public transportation.

And since the first BART train doesn't hit 24th Street until 4:20, you gas up at the Chevron where you don't have to prepay, turn in your cab and wait outside the office smoking with the other drivers, building up a head of steam to make the thirty-minute walk to the station.

And if the opportunity for a free ride comes along, you seize it. Otherwise, ten minutes to the hour, you head down the alley to Jerrold, then under the hairball, through the homeless encampment, past the tents and barely-covered bodies sleeping on the cold ground.

And you watch your feet as they move across the asphalt layered with decades of soot and human excrement, mindful not to step into anything fresh, or stumble on the trash scattered among chucks of concrete, broken glass and discarded food.

And you march with determination, ready to outmaneuver rats or anyone looking to mug a cab driver, that hardearned wad of bills stashed in your boot.

And you crisscross the neighborhood, quiet and spooky so early in the morning. Your shadow splits as you pass a streetlight, then it creeps back up on you at the next one.

And there's just one car on the road, yet somehow, when you step off the curb, it comes straight at you.

And in the distance you see figures. No telling if they're friend or foe, but you keep your hand in your pocket anyway, your apartment keys between each finger, in case you need to go Wolverine on someone's ass.

And then, finally, you reach the BART station.

And you're grateful the escalator is working so you can stand for a minute while you pull out your Clipper card.

And you're even more grateful you have enough money on it so you don't have to deal with the ticket kiosk.

And there are only two other people on the dais, but you don't think about them cause you're too exhausted.

And when your train comes, the wind almost knocks you down. The doors slide open. You find a seat that doesn't reek of piss.

And you know there's another twenty-minute walk at the end of this train ride.

And those last twenty minutes are the worst. You dread them during the entire trip, holding your head in your hand with your elbow resting against the window as the train barrels underground.

And then it emerges into what's left of the East Bay night.

And you're almost home. You're almost home.

And that's all you can think about
     until it's time
          to make the final slog
            up
            Telegraph
               Ave.

The wrong way to deal with a prostitute

I t's 3 a.m. The streets are gloriously free of traffic. As I'm heading back to Public Works, a man waves me down at 15th and South Van Ness. He isn't going far, no doubt on his way home from work, when the last few blocks can feel like torture. I pull up to his place on Folsom just as the meter hits $5.15.

"Give me $5," I tell him.

He hands me a $20. "Make it $10."

While I'm sifting through my wad of bills, a scantily clad woman approaches my cab and tries to open the back door.

kelly DESSAINT

"¡Pinche puta!" the man shouts and slams the door shut.

She looks at me imploringly through the window. I hand the man his change. He exits, spewing more insults in Spanish.

"You don't have to be rude, Chubby," the woman says before asking me, "Can we get a ride?"

Beside her is a young Latino carrying a plastic bag in the shape of a 12-pack.

"Sure. Where to?"

"Balboa Park," the guy slurs. Then he asks me to play music and cracks open a beer.

"What are you doing?" the woman demands. "You can't drink alcohol in the back of a taxi."

"Yes, I can," he says. "I know the law."

"Maybe this gentleman doesn't want you drinking in his cab."

I'm about to take his side, but upon exchanging glances with the woman in the rearview, I keep my mouth shut. It's obvious she's a professional.

After catching a few lights down Folsom, I take a right toward Guerrero.

"No, go to Persia and Mission," he says.

While I'm waiting to turn left onto Mission, he changes his destination again to San Jose and Geneva.

OK. I head back toward Guerrero.

"Don't you like me?" he asks the woman over the hip-hop blasting at his request. "You don't say anything."

"We'll talk once it's just the two of us," she tells him. "Maybe you should stop drinking so much."

He laughs and cracks open another.

"Sir, this is not how you deal with a prostitute. You can't take me out in the middle of nowhere and try to trick me."

COURTESY PHOTO

When I get to Geneva, he's not sure whether to go left or right. I turn the music down.

"Go right," he says finally. "To Ocean Avenue."

"OK, sir," the woman snaps. "That's the fourth address you've given. I've had enough of this shit. Driver, take us back to 18th and Capp."

I glance in the rearview. Her eyes are like razorblades. I make a quick left onto Interstate 280.

The guy begins to protest vehemently. "Where are you going?"

"Sir, this is not how you deal with a prostitute," she tells him, as if he's a small child. "You can't take me out in the middle of nowhere and try to trick me."

"Why are you listening to her?" he shouts at me. "I'm the one paying."

I say nothing and drive.

"If you listen to her, I won't pay!"

"Oh, you're going to pay the man." The woman reads him the riot act. "He probably has a family at home that he needs to take care of, and you're wasting his time."

"I'll call the police then."

"Call the cops." She laughs. "You're just staring at your damn home screen. You're too drunk to even make a call."

"I'm not paying shit."

At a red light, he tries to bail.

"You better stay in this taxi!" she yells. "Keep your hands off me!"

He punches the back of the passenger seat.

Just as things start to get ugly, I pull over at 23rd and Mission.

"Now, pay the man!" she orders.

The meter reads $24.40.

"25 bucks! Now!"

The guy makes a grandiose gesture of handing me the money while mumbling bitterly. As she walks away, he steps out of the cab to yell at her and

then gets back in.

"Take me to Capp," he demands.

"C'mon, man," I say. "I don't have time for this shit. It's late."

"But I want a girl," he whines. "Please, help me." His eyes are full of confused desperation.

Reluctantly, I drive to 20th and Capp, but there are no girls standing around.

"It's too late," I point out.

"I'll find one." He exits the cab and disappears around the corner.

I'm about to take off when I notice his 12-pack is on the floorboard. At this hour, an ice cold 12-pack of Modelo is like gold. So why leave it in my cab? Does he think I'll wait for him?

I consider tossing the beer out on the street, but then again ... it's not like he tipped me.

Kelly Dessaint is a San Francisco taxi driver. His zine, "Behind the Wheel," is available at bookstores throughout The City. Write to Kelly at piltdownlud@gmail. com or visit his blog at www.idrivesf.com.

PILTDOWNLAD

NO. 11

$7.00
cash
or trade

The fourth installment
in the **Behind the Wheel** series

From the creator
of the "I Drive SF"
column.

A ribald journey
into the reality
of driving
a San Francisco
taxicab.

BEHIND THE WHEEL
THE THIN CHECKERED LINE
4

**THE
UNEXPURGATED
UNCENSORED
AND TOTALLY
UNNECESSARY

I DRIVE S.F.**

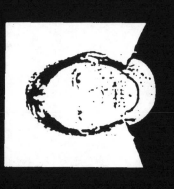

VETERANS

SAN FRANCISCO TAXI DRIVER

BEHIND THE WHEEL 4

THE WAY OF THE TAXI

◎ Cab to the Yard 283
◎ Gridlock is My Business 289
◎ The Slumlord of Haight-Ashbury 291
◎ Felicia the Freeloader 296
◎ A Taxi-Driving Hero Ain't Nothing to Be 304

A STORY WITH WHEELS

◎ When I Was a Green Pea 306
◎ Looking for a Story 311
◎ Personal Economics 315

NAVIGATING THE UBER EFFECT

◎ The S.H.I.T.S. 322
◎ Just Another Manic Mantra 323
◎ Fear and Loathing on Talk Radio 326
◎ The Poor Man's Taxi Driver 330
◎ The Uber-iquity of Convenience 333

THE DEATH OF CAB CULTURE

◎ The Taxi Driver's Worst Enemy 339
◎ Hell Is Other Cab Drivers 343
◎ Canary in the Coal Mine 345

SAN FRANCISCO HAS NEVER BEEN WHAT IT USED TO BE

◎ The New Scourge 347
◎ Tub Thumping for a Lost Cause 351
◎ The World's A Mess - It's in My Cab 355
◎ Requiem for Valencia Street 357

THE THIN CHECKERED LINE

taxi driving is not a crime

First Printing, December 2018
Second Printing, November 2019

Cover: Late Night Larry behind the wheel of Veterans 327 on Larkin Street in the Tenderloin. Photo by Trevor Johnson.

Some portions of this zine originally appeared in the *S.F. Examiner*.

PART ONE
THE WAY OF THE TAXI

CAB TO THE YARD

I emerge bleary-eyed from the 24th Street BART station and immediately recoil from the onslaught of sunlight and heat. The same climate I was hoping to leave behind in Oakland has followed me across the Bay.

Dazed and sweaty, I hobble past vulgar pigeons and suppliant palms, caked with the grease of a thousand spare transactions, their plaintive requests a far cry from the proselytizing auctioneer across the plaza, shrieking the word of Jesuchristo at the rush hour commuters through a beat-up Peavey amp plugged into a battery charger.

With a jacket wrapped around my waist and a hoodie draped across an overloaded shoulder bag, I'm looking more vagrant than working stiff.

Running late, as usual. Still recovering from my last taxi shift and the physical toll of not getting enough sleep.

It seems my six-month-old daughter has developed a bad case of FOMO, a condition I only recently learned about from the TV show "Broad City." FOMO, or Fear Of Missing Out, is what compels my little party girl to think that if she closes her eyes for half a second, the most fantastic, amazing, life-shattering event will occur. And she won't be awake to experience it.

My greatest challenge living with an infant is the need to be quiet. Besides a penchant for pontificating wildly, I'm clumsy as hell. I drop glassware as a matter of course and trip over anything that isn't crushed beneath my size-11 Fluevogs. Before the kid showed up, I deluded myself with a chimeric notion of putting her to sleep to the sound of my voice.

One of the many idealized fantasies crushed by the reality of living with a newborn.

She's a good sleeper, but the smallest noise rouses her. Like opening the refrigerator door. Or piercing the plastic on a microwavable meal with a fork. Or turning on the bathroom faucet. Or the faint clink of ice cubes hitting the bottom of an empty glass.

One false move or a single errant commotion and I'll be spending the next hour rocking her back to sleep. When she's finally out, I try to get a few hours of shuteye before waking up, getting ready for work and taking BART into the city.

Even though I usually walk or take the bus to the National cab yard in the Bayview, today I'm hoping to avoid the long trek by taking a taxi.

At the corner of Mission and 24th, I look for a passing cab. I scan up and down Mission. Then east and west on 24th. But there's not a single taxi in sight. So I phone National dispatch.

Before hanging up, Artur, the dispatcher, puts the order out over the radio: "Possible, 24th and Mission."

Possible? Fuck that. I'm no Possible. Need. I'm a Need. I need a cab!

I smoke an American Spirit in the shade of McDonald's, pitch the butt into the gutter and call Artur back.

"Nobody checked in. Sorry."

I walk to the corner of South Van Ness, muttering expletives, and try to flag a Citywide taxi heading my way. It blows right past me. A Luxor driver slows down long enough to shake his head before speeding off.

"But I'm a taxi driver too," I say out loud.

Being a taxi driver, I know these guys are ending their shifts and in a hurry to return their cabs. Otherwise it's a dollar a minute. Even though picking me up won't impede this objective, seeing as how most of the cab yards are in the same vicinity, how do I convey this to the cabs speeding past me and my outstretched arm?

I consider making a sign: "S.F. Cab Yards or Bust."

After three more taxis pass me by, I light a cigarette and start walking.

I weave through the crowded sidewalk, evading local shoppers, tourists Instagram-ing artful window displays, rowdy packs of school kids in matching uniforms and tech workers in company-branded t-shirts and shoulders bags staring into their iPhones.

Despite my foul mood, I can't help but succumb to the exuberant atmosphere of Calle 24. As I march down the street, each block seems to have its own kinetic identity, its own corner store, produce market, Mexicatessen, taqeuria, lavenderia, panderia and nail salon.

The street radiates such a heavy Latinx vibe, even the influx of high-end restaurants and hipster coffeehouses are easy to ignore among the harlequin murals that cover every available surface – the visible testament of a culture that refuses to be whitewashed.

At Bryant, I cut through the neighborhood on the shady side of the street, towards Army, where rush hour traffic is a steady roar and the sun beats down relentlessly.

Among the commuters, taxicabs from half a dozen color schemes race towards Mission Street, while those headed in the opposite direction speed into the Hairball.

Soon, I reach the pathway under the knot of freeway overpasses and wander into the post-apocalyptic Hobo Jungle.

The narrow pathway is made tighter by a row of shopping carts, overflowing with possessions and recyclables, and a small village of tents. I tread carefully through the encampment, avoiding the busted household goods, streaks of mud, gravel, murky puddles, orange syringe caps, discarded clothing, papers and 49ers and Giants paraphernalia.

Out from under the twisted overpasses, I'm back in the radiation on Bayshore until the final jaunt down Jerrold, lined with ramshackle RVs and campers, to Upton Alley: the home stretch.

I stumble into the National office, sweat pouring down my back. My head is spinning. I feel ill.

Artur looks up from the dispatch computer. "What happened to you?"

"You know, it's a goddamned sad state of affairs when a taxi driver can't even get a fucking cab in this town!" I bleat, collapsing into a chair. "Sadder still, when it's a cab to the yard."

Tomas, a West African driver, stops counting his money and laughs heartedly. "Oh, you're still around," he says.

"Where else would I be?" I respond.

"Figured you'd be long gone by now."

"Nah, man," I say. "I plan to go down with the rest of the rats on this sinking ship."

Tomas' laughter bounces off the walls. "Why haven't I seen your column in the *Chronicle* lately?"

"Cause it's in the *Examiner*."

Tomas shrugs. "So when you gonna write something that actually helps us fight Uber?"

Now it's my turn to erupt with a bellyful of laughter. "How do you propose I do that? With a well-crafted sentence?"

Tomas isn't the only taxi driver with this bizarre notion that my weekly 700-word contribution to the *Examiner* has the power to sway public opinion. Most Uber and Lyft users don't get their news from traditional sources like local newspapers. Besides, if all I did was shit on Uber and Lyft each week, I wouldn't have a column for very long. But Tomas doesn't care about these trivialities and resumes counting his money.

At the window, Artur hands me the key and medallion to 2972.

"A fucking spare?" I ask incredulously. "Where's 215?"

"Shopped. The hybrid battery is fucked up."

"This isn't the one Parker lived in?"

"No, that was 2409."

I scowl dubiously over my glasses before handing Artur a fiver.

Walking across the lot, I expect to be disappointed. There's nothing worse than rolling in a piece of shit spare.

Several months ago, I lost my regular cab. Since then, I've been back at the window playing taxicab roulette.

From my earliest days at National, I cajoled and greased the palms of each cashier for a taxi that was clean and ran well, happily paying extra for National 182, a Ford Fusion that met the above criteria and wasn't assigned to a regular driver. For almost two years, 182 was my trusted ride, until the medallion owner took it out of circulation.

After that, they put me on 1462, the only National cab with an ad topper. I hated driving around with a glowing advertisement for a tech company above me. Plus, the right speakers weren't installed properly. So when Vic, the medallion holder/day driver, switched to a 24-hour lease, I was almost relieved.

Then I ended up with Veterans 215. Even though I'm not too keen on Camrys, it's relatively clean. Although the longer it stays in general circulation, the faster it deteriorates. Taxis are operated 24/7 and driven hard on San Francisco's ripped-up streets, rife with potholes and littered with jettisoned obstacles. They break down constantly. If it's not a faulty chassis, it's the hybrid system. Which, now that I think about it, explains why 215 has been guzzling more gas than normal. So perhaps waiting for the mechanics to replace the battery is worth the inconvenience of driving a spare for a short while. Sort of. ⊙

GRIDLOCK IS MY BUSINESS

For some stupid reason, I always begin my shifts at Caltrain. Fourth and Townsend is not only a bustling hub for commuters heading to and returning from Silicon Valley, but also a constant construction zone. Even without the massive influx of traffic converging into the area, the perennially delayed track extension to the new Transbay Terminal guarantees a total and complete, almost impenetrable, choke point.

During morning and afternoon rush hours, thousands of people who work in the city and live in the Peninsula arrive at the Caltrain station via Uber/Lyfts, Muni trolleybuses, corporate shuttles and private jitneys, while those returning home from their Silicon Valley jobs exit the station and jump into Uber/Lyfts, Muni trolleybuses, corporate shuttles and private jitneys. (Occasionally, someone will even take a taxi.) With all these vehicles for hire competing with the regular commuter traffic trying to access I-280 south at King Street, the end result is a clusterfuck of epic proportions that begs the question: why would anyone knowingly subject themselves to the inevitable quagmire if they had another option? I could, for example, go to the airport. Or work the Financial. Or the Union Square hotels.

I'm a creature of habit, though, and there's a cabstand outside the train station on Townsend. If no taxis are in the cabstand, is it still a cabstand? Or does it become a random loading zone for Uber/Lyfts? Or a new turn lane for the cars trying to get on the freeway?

After leaving the yard in my latest jalopy with Thee Oh Sees blasting (at least the CD player works), I head over Potrero Hill on Rhode Island to the roundabout at Eighth Street, then inch down Townsend towards the sanctuary of the cabstand. I pull behind a Luxor just as the 5:42 train arrives. Within minutes, I'm loaded and fighting to get back into the maelstrom.

My attempt to squeeze in front of a Acura is met with resistance from the driver who rides the ass of a Honda. When the light turns green, I merge forcefully anyway, despite the honking, and interject the front of my taxi between his bumper and the Honda.

"Do you not understand how taxis work?" I yell out my window. "This isn't my car. I don't give a shit if you hit me. In fact, please, go ahead and

hit me so I can go home and get some sleep."

The Acura driver screams something back but I ignore him. Spot an opening to the right and seize the opportunity like a running back charging towards the end zone. At the corner, a sympathetic PCO directing traffic motions me through the intersection just as the light turns red.

"So long, suckas!" I swerve past a few slowpokes into the left turn lane at Third Street. "Sorry about all that," I tell the well-dressed lady in back.

"I don't know how you guys deal with all this traffic," she says, seemingly unfazed by my aggressive driving.

"You definitely need a few screws loose," I deadpan.

She laughs.

"And nerves of steel," I add.

A zen-like approach to traffic also helps. Or just a bad attitude. Whatever it takes to survive the mean streets of San Francisco, where it's every driver, pedestrian, bicyclist, Muni and cable car operator for themselves.

Traffic is war. And every other driver is the enemy. Any display of courtesy is a sign of weakness. Letting someone merge in front of you means defeat. The ultimate failure would be sacrificing a single inch of road to another vehicle.

Bay Area drivers are the absolute worst. Most seem to take great pleasure in impeding your trajectory. Hardly anyone cuts you any slack. The competition to get through intersections, make turns, find parking spaces, or even change lanes is on par with a sporting event, as if beating a red light is a gold medal event.

During rush hour, driving in downtown is like swimming laps in a crowded kiddie pool. To get from Point A to Point B, you have to bypass a vast array of conveyances. From the city's large fleet of trolleybuses, to oversized tech shuttles, double-decker sightseeing buses, Chariot mini-buses and assorted private hospital, university and corporate jitneys, as well as 100,000 super commuters.

Throw an additional thirty-thousand Uber/Lyft drivers into the mix and you have a perfect recipe for horrific gridlock. While the SFMTA estimates that only about 6,000 of these Uber/Lyft drivers, who venture here from far off locations like the Central Valley, Los Angeles and even other states, operate in the city at any given time, most of these car-petbaggers barely know how to negotiate the unique conditions on the streets of San Francisco, much less the proper methods for picking up and dropping off passengers without making traffic even worse.

In the midst of this vehicular morass, you have packs of bicyclists blowing through intersections, motorcycles and mopeds mainlining through the snarl-up, jaywalkers stumbling recklessly into the street with their faces glued to hand-held devices, daredevils on kick scooters and skateboarders, and their more technologically-advanced thrill-seeking compatriots speeding through the mêlée on electric bicycles, electric skateboards, electric scooters, electric unicycles, hoverboards, segways and other self-balancing devices that propel the human rabble through the concrete jungle at rush hour…

Yeah, it definitely requires a special brand of callous indifference to your own mental health to drive a taxi on the streets of San Francisco, but oh, the places you'll go and ah, the things you'll see, ◉

THE SLUMLORD OF HAIGHT-ASHBURY

After escaping the congestion in SoMa, I wind through the Financial District. All the cabstands are stacked, though, so I try my luck in Union Square. On Market, I circumvent the malicious attempt of a Muni driver to prevent me from accessing the transit lane. Cruise past crowded sidewalks. But not a single arm reaches out for my services. Until Fifth Street, where a young professional flags me and gets in before the bus catches up with me.

ID	1482	Driver	DESSAINT					GAS	Gals.	$ 18+

Month	Day	Year	Vehicle License No.	Cab No.		Medallion No.		GATES	$ 103
12	10	18		82		82			

Time Out		Total Miles	Paid Miles	Units	Trips	Company Revenue	$
2:45 PM	In					Driver Revenue	$ 302
Time In							
5:12 AM	Out					Gross Turn In	$
Hours Worked						Signature	
13.5	Dif						

Trip No. Pass.	No. Pass.	TIME IN	TIME OUT	FROM	TO	AMOUNT	
1				HYATT REGENCY	UNION SQUARE	$	13
2				S/ FRAN	9TH / VN	$	20
3				VN / CLAY	19 / CASTRO	$	14
4				37 / LAWTON	FL 4	$	30
5				HYATT REGENCY	DIVIS / BUS	$	20
6				GEARY / MASONIC	R / COLLINGWOOD	$	11
7				PIER 16	S/ MISSION	$	15
8				OFELLA	HOFFMAN	$	75
9		168		FL 4	37 / LAWTON	$	30
10				LARKIN / EDDY	TS	$	7
11				BG	BART	$	12
12				VN / POST	LOMBARD / LARKIN	$	8
13				HYDE / McALI	OCEAN BEACH	$	45
14				550 BARNEW	15 / NOE PEPO	$	15
15				S BARN	37 / MARKET	$	14
16				S BARN	6 / PT HOTEL	$	15
17				MEZZANINE	17 / EUREKA	$	13
18				S60 FRAN	DNA	$	11
19		308		S BARN	CAL / RUSTON	$	20
20							
21				SLOW	2 MOTOR	226	
22				4 DINNER	CO - 77/5		
23				4 CIGS	$168		77

DRIVE CAREFULLY.   DRESS NEATLY   BE COURTEOUS

He's going to the Marina. I make a quick right onto Turk and head towards Franklin.

At Larkin, I instinctively glance up at the outspoken billboard on the corner connected to the Kahn and Keville tire shop that Herb Caen once called "the world's largest fortune cookie."

Since Trump's election, the billboard has reflected the collective despair of progressive San Franciscans.

First there was a quote from Lily Tomlin: "Behind every failure there is an opportunity someone wishes they had missed."

The following one, "Where is Mark Felt?" was equally vague, but only insofar as it made you Google "Mark Felt."

The latest one, though, is anything but ambiguous: "Build the wall on the internet and make Russia pay for it."

I'm inclined to explain the source for my laughter to the guy in back, but it's hard to tell who shares your political views anymore. Even in San Francisco. Hell, especially in San Francisco.

With the tech boom still booming and the subsequent rent hikes, the demographics in the city have become young, white and, seemingly, more conservative.

Reality these days is so sterile. And why not? There's no resistance in paying an exorbitant amount of money to live here and work in an industry that embraces corporate culture.

At least this billboard exists. Although it'll soon be gone too…

I take a left on Sutter, cross the Van Ness ruins and join the funeral procession on Franklin. In silence.

Compared to the traffic jams south of Market, the snarl-up on Franklin seems quaint. From the top of Pac Heights, I coast through the lights until the Lombard death match. Then, the end of ride procedure:

Awkward remark. ("Wasn't sure we were going to make it there for awhile." Hehe.) Run credit card. Exchange pleasantries. Struggle with door lock. Awkward remark. ("You don't really want to go home, do you?") Standard farewell. Drive away.

I instinctively clear they taximeter and tap my Flywheel phone to become "available." Even though I log in to the app religiously at the start of each shift and stay available unless I'm unable to accept orders, the Android phone attached to the a/c vent hasn't chirped in so long I sometimes forget it's there.

So after going online, I'm shocked to get an immediate ride request for Beach and Cervantes. And with a $9 guaranteed tip!

I quickly hit accept and head towards the part of the Marina that looks like it was designed by a drunken cartographer. When I pull up, an older gentleman is outside waiting for me.

"Market and Jones," he says curtly. "The Aida Hotel."

"No problem." I hit the meter. "By the way, thanks for the $9 tip."

"That's to make sure you fuckers show up!" he snaps.

I respond with an audible gulp.

"What route you planning to take?" he demands.

"Uhhhhh…"

Before my scrambled brains can conjure up a detailed trajectory, he gives me directions:

"Take Van Ness to Broadway, right on Larkin, left on Washington and then Hyde to Golden Gate."

"Sounds good," I say cheerfully.

"No offense, kid," he says. "I've lived in San Francisco forty-five years. I can get around better than most cabbies."

"That's a long time," I remark absently, turning left onto Lombard.

"I moved to San Francisco in 1963. From Sicily. Wasn't much older than you when I got here. Hardly a dollar in my pocket. Took any job that paid, until I'd saved up enough money to buy my first apartment building on Haight Street."

"How much did apartment buildings go for back then?" I ask, merging into the turn lane at Broadway. It still feels like he's yelling at me but at least the codger is talkative, which makes the ride go faster.

"$40,000," he says. "The old lady who owned it before me lost it to the bank because she was renting to a bunch of deadbeats who never paid their rent."

"Fucking hippies." I laugh.

"After I signed the papers, I went down there and said, 'I'm the new owner.' And these long-haired dopers just went, 'Far out, man.' I told them I'd be back in a week for the rent. Of course when I returned, no one had any money. So I offered them a deal. Said, if you can't afford the rent, there's a cheaper unit that just opened up in the basement. Under six feet of concrete. Said, if I don't get my money, I'll have you fitted for Sicilian neckties. If you know what I mean."

"They paid up, right?"

"What do you think?"

I can't tell if this guy is full of shit or not – his deadpan delivery is too cryptic for a joke – but laugh anyway.

"Look at this traffic!" he shouts.

As we descend Nob Hill, there's nothing but the usual sea of brake lights ahead.

"Better take Bush to Jones," he commands, then goes on to tell me that once his tenants started paying rent, he was able to buy another building. Then another. And another. He kept buying rundown Victorians in the Haight and Western Addition, along with old hotels in the Tenderloin, until he'd acquired over fifty properties in the city, including the Aida.

"I like buildings nobody else wants. While others may see a rathole, I see dollar signs."

Just as I'm about to ask him if he's looking to adopt an heir, he makes a comment about some black kids standing outside a corner store.

Whoa!

"That's what happens when you have someone like Obama in the White House for eight years."

Someone like Obama? Uhhhh…

"Worst president in history!"

Oh, man. I start desperately looking for an opening in the congestion.

"Thankfully, we got Trump now."

What the fuck? This ride needs to end. Now!

I cut off a discombobulated Lyft driver in the right lane.

"Let's just hope he gets rid of all these damn foreigners and kicks all the deadbeats off welfare."

Ugh. I swerve recklessly in front of another slowpoke. Outta my way!

"All my taxes going to support these lowlifes."

At Eddy, I charge into the turn-only lane and continue straight to Market, pulling over on the right, across from the Aida.

"So, uh… thanks for the tip."

"I appreciate the ride, kid. If you ever have any passengers in need of an inexpensive, but clean, hotel, bring them by. But only if they have money. We don't take any deadbeats here." ◉

FELICIA THE FREELOADER

I play the radio loud. It's the only way to decipher cross streets when Artur calls out dispatch orders in his overworked and underpaid drawl.

The Russian accent doesn't help. Especially if the two-way starts cracking up.

When it comes to regular callers, Artur will browbeat drivers on the air to get the orders filled, calling out the cross streets repeatedly or singling out nearby cabs like a school teacher trying to get the class to answer a question nobody knows.

I've just dropped in the Castro, and now heading inbound on Market, as Artur tries filling an order at Geary and Webster.

For the next several minutes, Artur's voice gets increasingly choleric: "Drivers! Geary and Webster! Somebody go pick her up! This is a regular customer! Come on!"

Even though I'm not close, I check in. "2972. Market and Sanchez."

"2972. Thank you. Go get Marina at the Safeway, please. You got a bonus load coming."

With the promise of ten dollars off my gate, I swerve into the left turn lane, figuring that Steiner through the Western Addition is my best – and fastest – bet. But there's an Uber with Nevada plates in front of me. The light goes from green to yellow and then red, but the driver doesn't move.

"Goddamn it!" Just my luck. Stuck behind a bonehead out-of-towner.

After waiting an eternity for the lights to cycle back to green, the Uber driver moves forward slightly into the intersection. But when the light changes to yellow he makes no attempt to turn.

I lay on the horn and yell out my window, "You have to get out of the intersection! Turn! Turn!"

But he doesn't turn.

Now, I'm not about to get stuck in the middle of Market Street like some rube. So I jerk the steering wheel to get around him, cutting off a car trying to beat the light. As they blow their horn at me, I whip around the front of the Uber driver, who seems content to just sit there blocking traffic, and aim towards Sanchez. But not before a Lyft makes an illegal right in front of me.

Another out-of-towner, this one from Fairfield, is going 5 mph. I'm right on his bumper, letting him know he needs to step on the gas, but as is often the case when you tailgate someone, he goes even slower.

I abandon the Steiner plan, turn left at 14th and take Divisadero to Geary.

Around Ellis, Artur is back on the two-way. "2972. How long for Geary and Webster?"

"Almost there," I say, stretching, of course. Hit Geary and take a hard right.

A few minutes later, I grab the mic. "This is 2972. I'm pulling up to the Safeway now."

Near the entrance I spot an elderly woman with a walker and three bags of groceries. She waves at me.

I flip a U-y, pop the trunk and hop out of the cab.

Even though the woman is more than happy to see me, I apologize for the wait and open the passenger door, quickly stowing her groceries. Once she's secure in the backseat, I fold up her walker and place it next to the bags.

"Golden Gate, between Steiner and Fillmore."

When we get to her building, there's no loading zone. She tries to tell me something, perhaps directing me to a place to pull over, but her English isn't very good and my Russian is even worse. I hit my hazards, unleashing a maelstrom of horns. Fuck it. My turn to block traffic.

The woman hands me a paratransit card and bunch of loose change. "For tip," she says.

"No, that's not necessary," I protest. "You had to wait so long."

I try to give it back but she insists.

"For taking bags to elevator. Yes?"

"Oh, no problem." I drop the coins into the cup holder.

After running the card, I get out to retrieve her walker and groceries from the trunk amid the clamor of blaring horns.

I want so badly to hold the walker in the air and shout, "Old people still have rights in this city!" But instead, I focus on helping this woman get home with her groceries.

Later that afternoon, around 6 p.m., I'm sitting on the throne at the Hilton Union Square, watching the madness of rush hour traffic in front of the hotel. As cars trying to drop off and pick up contend with a single interloper who didn't utilize the loading zone properly, forcing every other vehicle behind him to wait in the street akimbo while the 38 bus, followed closely by a 38R, comes barreling down O'Farrell, horn blasting, and all the stymied doormen can do is push around empty luggage carts hoping that somebody – anybody – will need help checking in, but the tourists move through the bedlam fearlessly, phones held aloft, like seasoned globetrotters.

When Artur calls out a radio order for Market and Sixth, there's a break in the congestion, so I grab the mic, press the button, wait for two beeps and check in:

"2972. I'm at O'Farrell and Mason."

"I read you, 2972," Artur responds. "Go pick up Felicia."

Artur sends the order to my tablet and I head down Ellis to Jones. As soon as I cross Market, a woman waves me down.

"I need to go to the Travelodge on Valencia and Market," Felicia tells me.

"Sure thing," I say, merging into traffic and taking a right onto Mission.

"Hey, aren't you the guy who writes for the paper?"

"Oh, you read the *Examiner*?" I'm never sure how to respond when people recognize me from the column. It's not something I advertise in the cab, or even bring up. I usually just say something awkward.

"Oh wow! I can't believe it's you!"

"Yeah, it's me. I really drive a cab."

"Oh, you better not put me on blast!" she unleashes a protracted cackle.

"Why would I do that?" I laugh.

"Oh, I'm just so nervous. I'm trying to find my stepbrother. Well, I call him my stepbrother but he's really my brother. How do I look?"

"You look all right."

"Do I smell like booze?"

"Not that I can tell."

"I can't believe you're the guy from the paper… Oh, man, I remember one of your stories about this … uh, this lady and she did… oh man, I forget what she… Then something else happened to her…"

When I turn onto McCoppin, Felicia has me stop next to some tents and asks the people inside if they've seen her brother Pickle. They have not.

"What about Droopy?"

"No."

She gets back into the cab. "Can you take a left?"

I turn onto Stevenson.

"Go slow."

She looks between the parked cars.

As I approach the skate park, she tells me to stop. "Hey!" she calls out to a skater jumping over the fence.

"You seen Pickle?"

The guy shrugs and walks away.

"Okay, go to the end of the alley."

Before I get to Duboce, Felicia asks another seemingly random guy. "You seen Pickle? What about Droopy?"

The guy walks to the passenger side of the cab. They talk for a minute and she asks me for a dollar. "I'll reimburse you."

At this point, I'm ready for this ride to be over and willing to do what it takes to make that happen.

"Okay, take a right," she says. "Go slow!"

I cruise past the dog park while she looks through the fence. Then she wants to go right.

Halfway down the block, she screams, "STOP! There he is!"

I slam on the brakes.

"Don't leave! Please don't leave!"

While Felicia talks to the guy, she holds the door open. So it's not like I can take off, even though I really want to.

"Oh my god, I can't believe I found him," she gushes when she gets back in the cab. "That's my brother. Well, more like kissing brothers."

"That's cool, but..." I glance at the $18.40 on the meter and sigh.

"Can you just wait a little bit? He'll be right back. Please?"

A few minutes pass. She gets out of the cab. Wanders down Stevenson. I drive away. Clearing the meter, I get on the radio.

"This is 2972, do you copy?"

"2972, I read you. What's your over?"

I tell Artur what just happened. He says Felicia had burned another National driver the day before.

"So then why'd you send me to pick her up?"

"You gotta give people a second chance, right?"

I respond with a serious of disgusted sounds.

"But that's it," Artur says. "She's cut off."

After promising me a second bonus load, I hang up the mic and search for another fare ...

That night, around 1:30 a.m., Jesse puts an order out on the radio.

"Sixth and Market," he says. "Who's for Sixth and Market?"

I'm at South Van Ness and Division, but there's no way I'm checking in for that order, even if Jesse said it was an SFO.

"474, I read you," Jesse says on air. "Anyone else?"

474 is Mary. I consider texting her to watch out for Felicia, but a pair of waving arms on the corner of Folsom and 11th takes precedent.

Fifteen minutes later, Jesse's voice is the radio again.

"Yeah, 474. What's going on?"

Since you just hear the dispatcher's side of the conversation on the two-way, I can only imagine what happened to Mary.

Later, while cashing out at the office, Jesse gives me the details...

Of course, Felicia stiffed Mary as well. To the tune of $21.65. But I doubt Mary was stupid enough to hand over personal money. Unlike yours truly. King Dipshit.

"I told her, never call here again," Jesse says. "She's blacklisted."

"Artur already blacklisted her," I point out. "When she ripped me off this afternoon."

"Well, unlike fucking Artur," Jesse gestures towards a sheet of printer paper covered with a magic marker scrawl above the cashier's window. "I made a sign." ◉

A TAXI DRIVING HERO AIN'T NOTHING TO BE

On my way home to Oakland, I stop by the 24-hour Walgreens on Telegraph to pick up some Advil, a jug of water and a couple candy bars. You know… the breakfast of champions.

It's 3:30 a.m. and I'm the only customer in line. But the cashier is M.I.A. and the security guard is preoccupied with a phone call, forcing me to look for someone in charge. I find a likely suspect in the hair products aisle.

The woman is apologetic and mentions something about being tired and distracted.

"It's totally not a problem," I say, handing her one my hard-earned twenties. "I work nights too."

"Really?"

"Yeah, I got off early today, but I usually work until 6 a.m."

"What do you do?" she asks.

"Taxi."

I can tell by her accent, and the demographics of the neighborhood, she's Ethiopian or Eritrean. Probably has more than a few relatives involved in the cab industry. But that doesn't prevent her from expressing surprise, seeing as how I'm a – seemingly – young white guy.

Before she can inquire further, a panhandler outside the store gets into a shouting match with a second panhandler encroaching on his turf. While the security guard grudgingly puts his phone conversation on hold, I skate past the commotion and beat it home.

As soon as I enter the building, the familiar wail of my one-year-old reverberates down the hallway. How the neighbors don't hear this late-night shrieking is a complete mystery, but whenever we ask, they steadfastly insist it's inaudible. They're obviously just being nice, since you can't really complain about a child crying.

For the next hour or so, I hang out with my daughter as she toddles around the apartment until she's yawning and rubbing her eyes. Then I strap her in the BabyBjörn and rock her to sleep to The Kinks.

After putting her in the bed with Irina, I go out back for a smoke and try to bang out a few words on the computer before I'm yawning and rubbing my own eyes.

Finally horizontal, I pull out my phone and scroll through Twitter, passing up the usual barrage of outrage and indignation, the atrocities and injustices, the braggadocio and dumb jokes. I click on a few taxi-related articles.

As a general rule, I never read comments. Especially comments on my own stuff, either on the *Examiner* site or social media. But when someone tags you in a Facebook post, it's hard to avoid the nastiness. Which is how I stumble upon this bitter perspective:

"I guess writing this column is the only reason you still drive."

I click reply and type, "What the fuck does that even mean? As opposed to doing what? Getting back on track with my fledging astrophysics gig?"

Does this person think I'm independently wealthy? That the *Examiner* is paying me the big bucks for my 700 words a week, which I invariably turn in late because I'm too exhausted from driving a taxi all week to write about driving a taxi?

Before clicking submit, though, I delete the response. Type out, "You sound like my wife." Then replace "wife" with "mother in law." And delete that too.

Instead, I turn off my phone and roll over. As I watch my daughter sleep under the muted glow of a nightlight, my mind spins, processing this notion that I'm supposed to be more than a taxi driver. Why? Because I'm white? American? College educated?

Who makes these rules?

My in-laws think I'm wasting my time driving a taxi. They emigrated from Ukraine after the fall of the Soviet Union to give their daughter the chance for a future that was brighter than the one left in the wake of communism. To them, success is measured in how much money you make, your job title and the brand names of your possessions.

Irina is more Americanized, but since becoming a mother, she's developed this fear that if we don't have enough money, we'll end up on the streets. Her frustrations definitely feel justified at times.

Since she's taking care of the baby full time, Irina isn't taking on very many freelance projects. And taxi driving doesn't always fill the gap. Good weeks are all too frequently attenuated by bad weeks. The longer hours required to make up the difference put the burden of childcare mostly on her. And I don't get to see my kid that often.

At the end of the day, all I can do is reassure her – and myself – that all this matters, and the sacrifices made today will pay off in the future. But try telling that to my mother in law.

Or a bunch of assholes on the internet. ◉

PART TWO

A STORY WITH WHEELS

WHEN I WAS A GREEN PEA

After taking a family of chatty tourists from the Orpheum to the Hyatt Regency, I head down Market Street. It's 11:30 p.m. and the sidewalks are deserted. Besides the lumps of humans sleeping in the nooks of financial towers and rats scurrying across the red brick and down tree grates.

In the distance, someone is playing Marco Polo. Or at least that's what it sounds like. Two names, repeated one after another, reverberating against the glass facades of 101 Cal, 333 Market, One Bush and 455 Market.

Out of boredom, my mind conjures up a movie scene. A homicidal ghost from the Barbary Coast days is on the prowl in the Financial District, hunting innocent victims in the shadows of past haunts…

To lighten the mood, I turn up the Elvis Costello and take a right on Sutter, towards Union Square. Might as well head to where there's neon.

Waiting for the signal at Mason, I see a light flicker up ahead in the middle of the block. Assuming a hotel doorman is summoning me, I flash my high beams in acknowledgment.

When I pull up, there is no hotel. And no doorman. Just two young women, who quickly climb into my cab.

"Sorry, it's a short ride," the first one says. "Pine and Larkin."

Smiling to hide my disappointment, I hit the meter. "No problem."

"What did you think of our flashlight?" the other woman asks.

"It's effective," I respond.

"I bet you thought it was a doorman and you're bummed you didn't get an airport."

Both women cackle.

I laugh along. At least snarky drunks are good for changing the mood, like dialing in a new station on the radio.

"I haven't been to the airport in so long," I say, casually. "I'm not even sure where it is anymore."

"How long have you been driving a cab?"

I've lost track of which woman is talking. Pine Street is dark through this part of Nob Hill and their boozy voices have merged into one.

"About five years," I respond to the collective inquiry. "Not that long, but it feels like an eternity."

"You're practically still a green pea!"

"Oh, how cute!"

They laugh.

"My father drove for Yellow. After thirty years, he saw the writing on the wall and sold his medallion, right as Uber and Lyft showed up."

"Lucky him," I say. "Better to retire than suffer."

"Or swtich sides," suggests the other voice.

"Fuck that!"

"You ever thought about going over to the dark side?" she asks me.

"Hell no!" I lie, refusing to admit that I did the Uber/Lyft thing for eleven months prior to driving a cab. It's too embarassing.

"Just so you know… I've never ridden in one. Nor will I ever. I don't care how cheap they are."

"You're definitely in the minority there," I mumble.

"Must suck to lose all that business though."

"Sometimes the sun shines on a taxi driver's ass." I laugh. "Just last night two young girls got into my cab at the Great Northern – a DJ club – going to San Carlos. I wanted to ask, 'Have you ever taken a cab to San Carlos?' But they didn't flinch when it came time to pay. $85."

"Shouldn't it have been more with meter and a half?"

"I usually do straight meter at night."

"What's wrong with you, noob? That's how you make money!"

"Ah, they were just kids," I defend my actions. "Probably didn't even know what meter and half is."

"Bullshit. They know how much it costs to get home."

"Still... a long ride is a blessing at that hour. It made my night."

"You shouldn't be so nice," one of the women says.

"You won't make it as a cab driver with that attitude," says the other. Their joint laughter is cut short when I turn right onto Larkin.

"This is us over here on the right."

I hit the hazards and the overhead light.

"I only have a credit card," the second woman tells me.

"That's fine," I say, inserting the Square reader into my phone.

"Come on, noob!" snaps the first woman. "You're supposed to say your card reader is broken."

"Of course we have cash." The other woman hands me a $20 bill. "Do you have change?"

I pull out my lower denominations hesitantly, not sure if she's tricking me again. Should I claim to only have a few bucks and force her to give me a bigger tip? Since that's the standard cab driver MO?

"Just give me $10 back," she responds, as if reading my mind. "Alright, noob. You have a good night."

"Good luck out there."

"Yeah, yeah, yeah..."

I pocket the bill, wave goodbye and clear out the meter, slowly dragging out time until the women are securely behind their gate. Then I take a right on California and head down Hyde towards Geary Street.

I cruise past Whiskey Thieves and the Ha-Ra, looking for signs of life. After a cursory glance at Edinburgh Castle, I take a left on Polk to check out the strip clubs before heading to SoMa.

While driving empty, I keep thinking about the two ladies calling me a "green pea" and their barrage of advice on how to become a good horrible cab driver.

They were obviously joking, but it makes me think about my first days as a driver for hire in San Francisco, back when I was a deer-in-the-headlights Lyft driver...

Most of my early passengers would regale me with their nightmare experiences dealing with the city's taxi service, which mirrored the ladies' acerbic suggestions: not accepting credit cards, refusing non-airport rides, talking on the phone incessantly and freaking out if you even remotely questioned their route.

It seemed like you weren't a real San Franciscan unless you had a bunch

ID								
1482	Driver: DESSAINT KEVY			GAS	Gals.	$ 15	
Month/Day/Year 5-13/17	Vehicle License No./Cab No. 788	Medallion No. 333		GATES		$ 105	
Time Out 4:15 PM		Total Miles	Paid Miles	Units	Trips	Company Revenue	$	
Time In 2:45 AM	In					Driver Revenue	$ 120 84	
	Out					Gross Turn In	$	
Hours Worked 11	Diff					Signature		

Trip	No. Pass.	TIME IN	TIME OUT	FROM	TO	AMOUNT	TIPS
1				CALTRAIN	SHRADER / FULTON	21 80	
2				W HOTEL	WESTN / ST FRANCIS	1 80	
3				WST FRANCIS	LYON / PACIFIC	16 00	
4				SUTTER / FRANKLIN	333 BUSH	15 30	
5				CALTRAIN	CLAY / VAN NESS	15 00	
6				VALENCIA / 23	MONARCH	15 38	
7			W	WST FRANCIS	EDDY / HYDE	11 00	
8				ST. FRANCIS	HARLOT	6 70	14 38
9				7TH / MARKET	22 / MISSION	08 00	
10				OPERA	CLAY / LAGUNA	13 00	
11				OFARREL / VN	GEARY / POWEL	16 00	7 70
12				OFARREL / MASON	W HOTEL	10 00	
13				3 / HOWARD	W / TROMBO 10	22 00	8 00
14				MISSION / NM	21 / FOLSOM	85 00	15
15				MARKET / LAGUNA	24 / MISSION	19 00	14 70
16				19 / MISSION	BRYANT / ARMY	10 00	
17				22 / MISSION	BUSH / WEBSTER	14 76	
18				CAT CLUB	HAIGHT / PIERCE	11 00	
19				MAKEOUT ROOM	14 / MISSION	8 00	
20							
21				10 - TIPS	740. 84		
22				11 - GIGS			
23				15 - DINNER	84 MEOW		

DRIVE CAREFULLY   DRESS NEATLY   BE COURTEOUS

of horror stories about taking taxis. People talked about missing flights, losing jobs, getting stuck in the rain and – pretty much – left for dead.

The people who got into my Jetta were so thrilled to have a ride they didn't care that I barely knew how to get around. Or refused to attach that hideous pink mustache to the grill of my Jetta.

Not that I didn't run into occasional problems …

On my first day, I got a ride request for an address in Showcase Square. As I'm promptly driving to the pinned location in the app, the woman who ordered the Lyft calls to inform me that she's actually a few blocks away.

"I'm at BoConcept," she says.

Of course, I have no idea what BoConcept is, where it is, or even how to spell it. "Is that 'b-e-a-u-x'?"

"It's called BoConcept!" she snaps. "Shouldn't you know where that is? What's wrong with you?"

"Sorry, it's my first day."

"Oh, great! Just my luck!"

As she proceeds to scream at me, then hang up and call back several times, I'm frantically typing "concept" into Google Maps, talking to her on speakerphone and navigating unfamiliar streets at the same time.

Eventually she decides to cancel the request and get another driver. Which is fine with me. I'm more than happy to end this futile quest.

A minute later, though, she calls back. If she cancels the ride, she gets charged five dollars. She wants me to cancel on my end. Except I don't know how. It's my first day!

"Why don't I just pick you up?" I respond. "Can you please just spell the name of the place where you are?"

Just then, I enter a roundabout and see the store she's standing in front of. She climbs into the back of my Jetta with a huff, and despite my attempt to make a joke about not giving me a bad rating, she makes a phone call and complains loudly to the person on the other end about her "clueless Lyft driver." ◉

LOOKING FOR A STORY

After my horrendous first day as a Lyft driver, I wanted to drive back to Oakland and fill out an application at Trader Joe's. But the decision to use our Jetta as a taxicab in San Francisco was about more than just making a few extra bucks.

I was looking for a story.

What started out as a lark rapidly took on a life of its own. Originally, I just wanted to document the Uber/Lyft trend, explore San Francisco, have some interesting adventures to write about, make a zine about the experience and move on with my life. But as I delved further into the vehicle for hire debate, I found myself in the front seat of a story that was bigger than just gypsy cabs.

The city was going through a period of major upheaval. The extravagant displays of tech money only served to magnify the abject poverty that was laid bare.

The tension was palpable. On my first day driving for Lyft, there was a five-alarm fire in the Mission Bay. As I desperately tried to navigate the city and figure out the app, a small trail of smoke over a construction site quickly spread across the sky from Mission Bay into SoMa, downtown and the Mission.

It all seemed to make sense.

The confusion. The madness. The fires.

San Francisco had become a war zone.

There were battles raging across the city. Between long-term residents and fresh transplants. Between tech workers and non-tech workers. Between renters and owners. Between people leasing their apartments to strangers on the internet and the neighbors who didn't want to live next door to Airbnb flophouses. And between tradition taxicabs and these new services that paired random drivers and passengers through apps.

Inspired by Gonzo Journalism, I charged headlong into the fray, with a stack of Moleskins. The narrative practically wrote itself. Like a prospector who'd struck it rich, I just held my pan in the creek and collected nugget after nugget of golden material.

My passengers had no clue their words and actions had any significance to me. But they were actually telling the story of the new San Francisco as they complained about the weather, the fog, the hills, the filth, the bums, the dating scene and how there aren't enough restaurants open late at night when the bars close.

Most of all, they talked about money. VC capital. Billion dollar valuations. Funding rounds.

Everyone had an app.

It was 2014 and startup culture was all the rage. Overly hyped apps were popping up weekly to make people's lives more convenient. And commerce was the driving force behind this new tech boom.

One night I was driving up Franklin and this guy stuck his head out the window and screamed into the wind, "I've made thirty million dollars so far this year!" Then he commandeered my stereo and really got the party started...

Despite its popularity, I assumed the whole "rideshare" phenomenon was a passing fad. Since it was technically illegal, how long could it possibly last?

Around the time I was finishing up the first Lyft zine, I had a dream that City Hall passed a law outlawing Uber and Lyft. I woke up in a panic. All my work! The writing! Designing a 60-page zine! Wasted!

In reality, this was only the beginning of a massive shift in public transportation, as well as employment, by changing how those two things are defined.

The rise of Uber and Lyft was founded on a semantic loophole. By creating a new denotation for taxis – ridesharing – they were able to barge into cities around the world and disregard local regulations. Since they claimed to be a technology company and not a taxi company, the rules governing taxicabs, they argued, didn't apply to them.

Utilizing doublespeak, these young entrepreneurs disguised their nefarious intentions behind innocuous smokescreens. Like, "sharing."

Of course, nothing is shared when you Uber and Lyft. Or when you Airbnb. If you're paying someone to drive you to work, whether it's in an unmarked sedan or a multi-colored vehicle with a toplight and a phone number on the side, if a meter is running, you're taking a taxi. The same is true if you're charging people money to sleep in your bed.

Now that it's been a few years, anyone with half a brain knows the "sharing economy" is just a predatory business model designed to push workers' rights back to the 19th century. But its proponents were able to sustain their bullshit long enough until the services were entrenched in the public mindset. By the time politicians were able to include these new definitions in transportation laws, the concept of riding in strangers' cars had become such a huge part of daily city life that it was too late to eradicate Uber and Lyft.

The will of the people ensured their success.

While this drama played out in the media and in courtrooms and boardrooms and wherever else dirty deals go down, I tried to document the experience on the street through zines and multiple blog posts.

After blogging on several platforms, the editor at Disinfo.com approached me about contributing to their site. Then, a few months later, I started writing for Broke-Ass Stuart's website.

When "Night of the Living Taxi," a blogpost about Flywheel's successful attempt to beat Uber and Lyft at their own game on New Year's Eve went viral, several media outlets contacted me, including Joe Fitzgerald-Rodriguez from the *San Francisco Examiner*.

We must have had a good chat because a few weeks later, he asked if I was interested in writing for the newspaper.

Michael Howerton, the Editor in Chief at the time, was looking to revive the Night Cabbie, a column from the Nineties written by an anonymous taxi driver. Howerton's idea was to present a modern take, from the perspective of an Uber driver.

By this time I'd already switched a taxi. And it was becoming obvious that nobody cared about taxi drivers. People wanted to read about Uber and Lyft drivers. The hip new thing.

I didn't want to lose my shot at a column, though. So I read everything online by the Night Cabbie. Most taxi drivers around the National/Veterans yard were familiar his work. As it turned out, he actually drove for Veterans. Used to be finance guy. Late Night Larry, who also worked in the Financial prior to driving a cab, was the one who encouraged him to drive a taxi when he got burnt out and needed a change.

Once I revealed the possibility of reviving the column, everyone had advice, usually criticizing some aspect of how the Night Cabbie documented the taxi driving experience and pointing out what not to do.

Since the only way to pull off the column would be to present both sides of the reality, I cobbled together a counter pitch:

"I Drive SF is a hard-edged take on the current state of driving for hire in San Francisco, from the perspective of a nighttime taxi driver who chose the cabbie's life after ten months of driving for Uber and Lyft. With comparisons between the ride-hail and taxi experiences, interesting rides and encounters, unavoidable commentary on the impact of the latest tech boom and various historical and cultural observations on the changing city. Sprinkled with maybe too much personal information: accepting a life in Oakland, my high blood pressure, thrash metal, manic interactions with longtime cab drivers and the wife's existential quest to find a job with meaning… A portrait of the Bay Area in flux."

Two weeks later, I met Michael for coffee in Mint Alley.

The first installment came out on May Day.

Just like that, I had my story, along with a forum to reach a wider audience.

That's when things got ugly. ◉

PERSONAL ECONOMICS

The last thing Irina said before walking out the door was, "I'm so fucking sick of hearing about taxis and Uber and Lyft! It's always Uber this! And taxi that! Blah blah fucking blah."

Now I'm not about to blame San Francisco's transportation problems for ruining my marriage. I've done a pretty good job of that myself. But my obsession with documenting the two startups and driving a taxi didn't help.

At first, Irina enjoyed hearing my crazy road stories when I got home late from driving for Uber and Lyft. She usually waited up for me and drifted off to sleep while I regaled her with the details of my rides. But eventually, she got bored. Because, she pointed out, they were all the same story with only slight variations.

After a night of driving in the city, though, the impulse to purge the experience from your brain is like a gag reflex from drinking too much cheap booze.

I can only assume most, if not all, fulltime drivers go through a similar predicament, regardless of whether they drive an Uber/Lyft, a limo or a

taxi. Or any combination thereof.

Driving isn't an easy job. It takes a toll on every aspect of your life. That's why drivers flock to Facebook groups, Twitter and start blogs to express our frustrations, air grievances, share the occasional positive anecdote and offer advice to newbies. Because if you're smart, you spare loved ones the mental garbage collected during long shifts and fertilize social media with it instead.

Eventually, the driving and the writing – as well as all the baggage we brought from LA – created a wedge between us. Things kept getting worse until Irina left.

Devastated, I went on an epic bender.

After circling the drain for three weeks, it was time to get back to work or just keep going until I ended up living under an overpass.

Over the next several months, I drove the cab, to varying degrees of success, and managed to turn in a column each week. The dissolution of my marriage featured heavily in the pages of the *Examiner* as I tried to sort out the mess and make sense of what was left.

Irina was in LA for eight months until she came back to Oakland.

For better or for worse, it seemed our story wasn't over yet.

A few weeks later, we were sitting at the kitchen table one night, drinking and drugging and figuring out the whole reconciliation thing when she said, "It's funny, I don't really feel like drinking wine anymore. This cigarette tastes awful. And I've been having these weird cravings..."

"Maybe you're pregnant," I blurted out.

We both cracked up.

For several years, back when we were living in downtown LA, we tried to have a baby. Even going to a fertility doctor while she had amazing health insurance through her job at Disney. And paid maternity leave. It was an ideal time to have a kid. Besides the fact that I'd always wanted a Kelly Junior, all her friends were having kids. At 33, her biological clock was like a time bomb. We were determined to procreate. I was on call for baby-making duty around the clock.

To cover all bases, I even provided a specimen in a cup.

We tried everything but nothing worked. Eventually, we assumed it was impossible. After Irina was laid off from Disney, we gave up. Started partying more and pursuing harebrained ideas. Like moving to the Bay Area. Might as well have fun, we figured... If something happens, something happens. Still, despite not really talking about it, the disappointment was an underlying point of contention in our relationship. How do you come to terms with the reality that after eight years of

318 · **Dispatches from Behind the Wheel**

marriage this is all there will be?

So that night, sitting at the kitchen table, drinks in one hand, smokes in the other and a plate of drugs in between, the possibility that she could be pregnant now, after all this time – through all the hardships – was… actually, pretty fucking funny.

Now that our marriage was in shambles?

Now that all the pain we'd inflicted on each other had reached a very public crescendo?

Now that we'd been separated for eight months and still haven't decided if there was actually anything worth salvaging?

Now?

Now the universe decides my boys and her girls can make a baby?

The absurdity was beyond incongruous!

After laughing for a while, we began to wonder… What if?

"Maybe you should pee on a stick," I suggested, then chugged my vodka drink and laughed nervously.

The next day she showed me the plastic wand.

"No fucking way!" I exclaimed. "Try it again."

The results were the same.

"What about another brand?" I asked. "Did you get the generic kind? You're always getting the generic shit. We need a name brand for this!"

Four days later, in an exam room at Sutter Health in Berkeley, the ob/gyn cheerfully lubed up a wand and a few minutes later we saw what looked like a bean on the monitor. That's when it became real.

For the next seven months, in the cascading waves of acceptance and fear of what becoming a parent meant, we didn't talk about the fear of bringing a child into an already tenable situation. This is what we wanted. The Fates be damned.

On January 5th, we set up camp at Alta Bates Hospital in Berkeley to wait for the birth of our daughter, who arrived, reluctantly, three days later.

Weighing in at eight pounds, twelve ounces, with a head of dark hair, just like her mother, and inquisitive eyes that darted around the room, her first bewildered take on the world akin to my own: WHAT THE FUCK? WHAT THE FUCK? WHAT THE FUCK?

As she looked at me for answers, I could only sob in ecstatic wonder. At that moment, the little creature in my arms was all that mattered.

Despite a complicated labor that left the hospital room looking like a murder scene, the joyous surge of pride at seeing my daughter born was a very real reminder that life is full of twists and turns.

The following day, while filling out the birth certificate, the nurse asked my profession. I paused and thought of the birth certificates of the fathers that came before me: My paternal grandfather was a general laborer. My mom's dad, a miner. My old man was listed as a clerk, even though he was in the Army.

"Writer," I told her.

Sure, it's a full time gig that pays slave wages – barely enough to support a geriatric cat, much less a growing child – but would it have been more honest to say taxi driver?

"You mean like Uber?"

That's how most people usually respond.

No, not like Uber. I drive a cab in San Francisco, which, up until a few years ago, was a legitimate, blue-collar job, in a city where blue-collar jobs used to mean something.

The taxi industry is full of men and women who've raised both daughters and sons in the city, who've provided for their families, bought houses, traveled, paid for college and medical expenses, and still do, as taxi drivers.

It's hard to imagine now that the profession has been diluted by Silicon Valley eggheads who believe robots can do any job better, and the Millennials who bemoan the lack of decent jobs and yet celebrate the systematic dismantling of one decent job after another in their constant pursuit of convenience.

Which is why I thank the stars my daughter was born under Obama's administration, so we were covered for maternity care through the Affordable Care Act. Otherwise, what? Google how to give a DIY caesarean?

After the nurses yanked our daughter away, they washed her hair and gave her some vaccinations. When we asked, out of curiosity, why they give newborns so many shots, the nurses told us that for some babies, this is the only time they receive medical care, unless it's an emergency.

That made me think long and hard about becoming a parent.

It's already normal to worry about providing for a child. As someone trying to make money in an industry that's being attacked by unscrupulous companies that eschew regulation through semantic subterfuge, it seems perfectly reasonable to freak the fuck out. But I think of my laborer grandfather, who was essentially a drunk, my miner grandfather, who, after contracting black lung, tried his luck at farming before moving to LA to be a janitor, and my dad, who sacrificed his true identity as a gay man to raise a bunch of kids, ultimately ruining his life, my mother's life and severely fucking up the lives of five children – if not more – and wonder what my daughter will think of me years from now…

I'd rather she see me as someone who followed his ideals, however foolhardy, who believed in passion and the creative spirit and who fought against injustice and resisted being a part of the status quo, rather than someone who surrendered my dreams to adopt a distorted concept of what it means to be middle class. Or a taxi driver. ◉

PART THREE

NAVIGATING THE UBER EFFECT

THE S.H.I.T.S.

We call them S.H.I.T.S.

Others may refer to these bandit cab companies as Uber and Lyft, but to San Francisco cab drivers, they'll just S.H.I.T.S.

If we must be technical, or polite, we'll use the term TNC – the designation given to them by the California Public Utilities Commission to justify their existence. But we'll never describe these Transportation Network Companies as "ride-hail" companies, or – god forbid – the most noxious misnomer of them all: "rideshare."

No, we prefer to label them as what they really are:

Smartphone

Hailed

Illegal

Taxi

Services

AKA, S.H.I.T.S.

And the people who use these services?

Why, SHIT-eaters, of course.

Unless we're trying to be civil. Then we just call them Phonies. ◉

JUST ANOTHER MANIC MANTRA

Istart my shift each day with the same mantra: I'm not going to let the thousands of Uber and Lyft drivers on the road get under my skin. I'm going to focus on making money and let the taxi winds take me wherever they may blow.

I leave the National yard ready to embrace the challenge of gridlock, reminding myself not to engage the swarm of Uber/Lyft drivers who pour into the city each day and flood the streets with their incompetence.

It doesn't take long, though, before that vow is put to the test.

Within the first hour of my shift, I'm outbound on Market Street when an Uber driver makes an illegal left onto Market from Seventh. Right in front of a cop.

I pull up beside the squad car at the next red light and roll down the passenger window.

"You didn't see that?" I ask the officer, pointing at the car idling in front of him. "He just made an illegal left."

The cop shrugs.

Just then, in full view, another Uber driver flips around on Market, cutting off oncoming traffic, including the 9R.

"What about that?" I yell out my window.

The cop rolls up his window and drives away.

Shortly thereafter, I pick up a fare at 555 Cal going to the Upper Haight. Head west on Sutter, bobbing and weaving to avoid double-parked Ubers and Lyfts using the designated bus and taxi lanes as their personal loading zones.

I coast through the lights at Van Ness and Franklin. Now I'm gunning for Gough. In the distance, I see the crosswalk numbers ticking down and push National 182 for all it's worth. Making this turn means catching the timed lights all the way down the hill to Turk.

Ahead of me is a gray Prius. Left indicator on. I'm coming in hot, certain we'll both get through on the yellow, but at the last second, the Prius comes to a complete stop. I lock up the brakes. Blow the horn.

"What the...?"

I glance in the rearview. My passenger is oblivious to the near collision, staring at his iPhone. I pull around to the side of the Prius to have a word with – yep, there's the phone on the dash, the ubiquitous placard in the right hand corner of the windshield, and a girl slumped down in the backseat – another confused Uber/Lyft driver.

I roll down my window and shrug my shoulders. "Really?"

The driver becomes enraged. "Don't 'really' me! You drive too fast! You always drive too fast! Why do you have to drive so fast?"

I want to shout, "Hey, I drive fast to save my passengers money!" But he doesn't seem to be in the mood to appreciate my witticisms. So I point out, "You could've made the light. We're transporting paying customers, you know."

This sets him off even more. "You're not supposed to turn left on red," he screams, pointing at the sign mounted prominently on the traffic light.

"Oh yeah? Watch this."

Poor bastard. I know what it's like to be an Uber/Lyft driver. It's not easy hauling self-entitled brats around town, working these mean streets with a tyrannical rating system hanging over your head for very little compensation. I wonder if his passenger will give him one less star for drawing the ire of a taxi driver… Oh, who am I kidding? Everyone knows cab drivers are disgruntled lunatics. She probably feels sorry for him.

She should feel sorry for me, though.

This is what driving in the city will do to you over time. I may not be as disgruntled as some of the cab drivers who've been at this for decades, but I'm getting close.

From the Upper Haight, I drive back downtown. I've been empty for over half an hour, stuck in traffic and getting more and more grumpy. Fighting my way down Post Street, my plan is to get into the St. Francis cabstand and regroup. Maybe catch a glimpse of a Victoria Secret mannequin through the partially boarded up windows.

Even though the line extends back to the corner, I squeeze in behind a Flywheel taxi. A Gold Star follows me, but ends up partially stuck in the busy crosswalk. There would be plenty of room for both of us all if the unmarked white Nissan, which isn't even supposed to be in the stand, pulled up some. I can tell the other cab drivers don't want to deal with the usurper, so I get out of my cab and rap on the person's window.

"You're in a taxi stand," I tell the guy who looks at me in complete shock. I see the Uber phone on his dash in driver mode. He's not even waiting for a passenger. "You need to move. Only taxis are allowed to park here."

I'm sure he's confused by the disruption, seeing as how no one enforces rules in San Francisco. The cops would certainly never chase somebody out of a cabstand.

As I walk away, the driver shouts something about my "sissy hair."

I turn heel and confront him.

"You need to get the fuck out of this cabstand, right the fuck now!"

Within inches of our altercation, a cable car is stopped, jam-packed with tourists hanging off the sides. They have a front row view of our profanity-laced contretemps.

I turn and implore them to pass judgment. I point to the sign that clearly states this is a taxi zone.

With so much evidence on my side, the driver begrudgingly pulls out.

I return to my cab and we all move forward into a nice and snug cabstand, hoping for a decent ride once we're summoned by the doorman's whistle.

The rousted driver, though, makes a U-turn and continues yelling at me.

Enraged by his arrogance, I get out of my cab again.

"I don't care who you represent!" he screams at me.

"What does that mean?" I laugh. "Are you high or just stupid?"

He keeps mouthing off.

"Look, motherfucker," I seethe at him. "You better drive the fuck away or I'm going to drag you out of that car and bash your dumb face into the asphalt."

Now, I'm not an intimidating guy. My look is hip graduate student, at best. Not the kind of guy who goes around starting brawls in public spaces. And yet, here I am, threatening to beat someone up while a crowd of tourists eggs me on.

"You tell 'em!" they holler in support.

"Yeah! Get that guy!"

Once the Uber driver finally peels off, the tourists applaud.

I walk back to my cab before anyone can see my hands shaking.

What is it with Uber drivers these days? For the past several months, I've noticed that Uber/Lyft drivers are getting way more aggressive, as if the two companies have finally exhausted the pool of eligible drivers in the Bay Area and now they're scraping the bottom of the barrel in order to sign up anyone who hasn't already fallen for their scam.

You see it on the streets. And not just the usual bad behavior: stopping wherever they please and blocking bike lanes. It's this increased sense of arrogance, that what they're doing is more important, and everyone else is in their way ...

The other night, I'm on Valencia, stopping to pick up a fare when the guy behind me keeps flashing his high beams at me. I flip around and block the lane. He rolls his window down, perhaps to yell at me, but I beat him to the punch.

"Don't you fucking flash your fucking high beams at me, you scumbag motherfucker! Learn how to fucking drive in San Francisco or get the fuck out, asshole!"

He quickly rolls up his window.

Besides the highbeam flashers and the outright psychos, there's an even more infuriating type of Uber driver: the kool-aid drinking, corporate apologist. ☉

FEAR AND LOATHING ON TALK RADIO

It was a bad idea from the get-go.

When the producer of the radio show "Your Call," broadcast on KALW 91.7, invited me to be an in-studio guest for a discussion on regulating Uber and Lyft, I agreed to participate right way. Even though it meant driving into the city at 9 a.m. – no easy feat for a night driver who lives in Oakland with an infant. Besides the prospect of a treacherous commute over the Bay Bridge, what little shuteye I would be able to

squeeze in between getting home from work and the time my alarm went off was sure to be erratic at best. Still, not a deal breaker, but then I realized the program was airing on the same day that former FBI director James Comey was testifying in front of Congress about his interactions with Donald Trump. Which explains why Rose Aguilar, the regular host of "Your Call," was taking the day off.

The Comey thing was a B.F.D.

Compared to his testimony, a discussion about Uber and Lyft was pretty insignificant.

So not only am I going to lose the precious commodity that sleep had become in my life, hardly anybody would even be listening to the show.

If that wasn't bad enough, things just kept getting worse …

Initial emails with the show's producer seemed to suggest there were going to be several drivers on the show. Both Uber/Lyft drivers, as well as taxi drivers. But the day before the show, she informed me there would be just one other guest besides myself: an Uber driver named Ron Childress.

Google didn't yield much about the guy. Just a few comments he'd made about insurance in a Facebook page for Uber drivers.

Despite a nagging impulseget to bail on the whole situation, I reminded myself that it would be good publicity for the column…

In order to make it to the radio station in Visitacion Valley on time, I had two options: either work my regular shift on Wednesday and just stay up, hoping the inevitable sleep deprivation and fatigue gave my voice an authoritative yet weary tone, or, skip work, go to bed early and start my shift on Thursday night instead.

The night before the show, we managed to get the baby to sleep at 2:47 a.m. At 4, I closed my eyes. Two hours later, the alarm went off. I jumped in the shower, got dressed and headed out across the Bay into the city, listening to the Comey testimony, which concluded right as I parked.

Inside the station, the producer informed me that Ron Childress would not be joining the host and me in the studio. He was calling in from his house in Vallejo because, apparently, driving to the city was too much of a schlep.

Discussing potential topics to cover during the show, I mentioned an article I'd written a while back about why Uber and Lyft drivers should support regulation, and how limiting on the number of cars on the road, proper background checks and standardized insurance would benefit the drivers more than the companies, and that the companies encouraged this false notion of independent contractors having all this freedom since it served their financial interests to lay no claim over their actions.

I wanted to talk about my experience switching from Lyft and Uber to taxi. As a way to establish a common ground and find some solidarity and point out that, under the current framework, all drivers were getting screwed over.

While setting up in the studio, the substitute host told me, given the media attention on the Comey interview, they thought about not doing the show at all. The Uber/Lyft topic was merely an offhand idea.

So much for feeling special.

After my usual spiel about how I ended up driving for Uber and Lyft and then becoming a taxi driver, it was Ron's turn to speak.

He could not have been more of a company man. While admitting that Uber has some "issues," he claimed that Uber was still a great deal for anyone who wanted to run "their own business." Despite a few attempts to sound like an expert on transportation in the city, he repeatedly attacked the taxi industry and challenged each of my comments. He was intentionally, it seemed, turning the discussion into an Uber vs taxi thing.

At one point, he referred to my column as a blog. When I tried to correct him, he threatened to hang up and end the interview.

I looked at the host in disbelief, but she kept asking him questions and letting him spew his misinformed opinions.

"Wow, I didn't know this subject was so volatile," the host said after another heated exchange.

"Hey, I don't have a problem with Uber drivers," I replied. "They seem to have a problem with me. But I used to drive for Uber, so I understand the frustration."

I left the studio feeling discomfited, as if I'd been broadsided. The host never mentioned my column, which is the only reason I agreed to do the radio show. Certainly not to prop up the taxi industry out of the goodness of my heart and get shit on by an idiotic Uber driver.

More than anything, though, I was left with this overwhelming sense of being one of "the others."

All the way home, I couldn't shake the alienation that came from aligning myself with the plight of taxi drivers. Which is something I've felt on numerous occasions since joining their ranks.

Who tries to understand the taxi driver? Most people assume a taxi driver is an immigrant, or someone who has failed at everything else. A loser. Not anyone worth consideration.

At one point during the show, a woman caller pointed out how many jobs Uber and Lyft have created and what a tragedy it would be if all those jobs went away.

But what about the hundreds of taxi drivers who've lost their livelihoods? Hardly any of the old-timers who were around when I first started driving a taxi are still on the streets.

That's different, of course. Taxi drivers are "the others."

Because the decision to drive a taxi doesn't fit their criteria of success, there must be something wrong with a person who choses that profession. Unlike Uber/Lyft drivers, who perceive the app as a bridge to another career. But how many Uber drivers are on the road to riches? And how many are stuck doing the same job as taxi drivers, day in and day out, hoping for that one ride that will lead to the promised land?

It's all a ruse. At least most taxi drivers know this. Unlike the nitwits who, no doubt, consider themselves progressive, but embrace authoritarianism by attributing value to the wealthy and powerful. They don't even try to challenge the myth that Uber must be doing something right because they're worth billions of dollars. Yet, how hard is it to see that Uber's success is based on eliminating the rights of workers and reducing their dignity and freedom so they won't resist the inequality that only benefits their corporate overlords?

It's easy to detest someone like Ron Childress, who acts as an unpaid shill for a morally bankrupt company like Uber. Instead of establishing a common ground to fight a shared enemy, his only real contribution to the discussion was sowing division and maintaining an Us vs. Them distraction, which prevents any kind of mutual understanding and, ultimately, perpetuates Uber's main objective: divide and conquer. ◉

THE POOR MAN'S TAXI DRIVER

S hortly after midnight, I'm rolling down Polk Street. It's been quiet since the Orpheum broke and the last of the autograph seekers lined up outside the stage door on Market have wandered off, making room for the homeless to bundle against the building.

My prospects for a fare are slim until I cross Bush and see a tall man in the middle of the street with his hand in the air. Just as I'm about to congratulate myself on taking a chance on Polk Street against my better judgment, I notice the front of his pants are soaked from crotch to hem, with his shoes, no doubt, a receptacle for what didn't spill onto the ground.

Before speeding away, I pause to consider the circumstances... It's likely that he's only pissed the front of his pants and his backside is relatively dry... And with the windows down it won't smell too bad... And he'll surely appreciate the ride home, since no other cab will pick him up anytime soon... Maybe he'll even reward me for my benevolence...

Then instinct kicks in. Keep driving. Sorry, buddy. If you're so drunk you can't control your bladder, it's the wingtip superhighway for you.

Later, I pick up a live one outside Martuni's. Middle-aged guy heading to Noe Valley.

your uber driver hates you
www.idrivesf.com

"How's business tonight?" he asks.

"Kinda slow," I say. "Been driving empty for almost an hour."

"Must be all the competition."

"Perhaps…"

I try to point out that there aren't many people out tonight, but he immediately goes off on a tirade about how taxis are relics of the past.

"Then why are you in one?" I laugh.

"I needed a ride and you were right there. I didn't feel like waiting."

He asks if I ever thought about going over to the dark side.

"I don't own a car," I tell him, adding that Uber and Lyft drivers aren't making money either. "There are too many of them on the road and they have to give so many more rides to earn what I do in a taxi."

"It's better than driving around empty, though, right?"

"Well, I prefer driving a cab." In an attempt to divert the conversation, I say, "Honestly, I'd rather deal with more than just one demographic of the city. Uber and Lyft only provide transportation for certain members of society, excluding the poor, elderly and disabled."

"What are you talking about?" he exclaims. "Taxis are way more expensive than Uber! And if you use the Pool option, it's even cheaper."

After making a bizarre argument that people who don't own smart phones can save money on rides to the airport by acquiring a burner at Walgreens, he tells me, "Part of what I love about Uber and Lyft is that they're affordable to everyone and not just the wealthy. Ask around. Most people could never dream of riding in a taxi regularly. Now they're riding in cars – nice cars, too – from their doorstep to work for only three to five bucks a pop."

As he continues making privileged judgments about how poor people should behave, I bite my tongue. This guy has no clue what it's like to live paycheck to paycheck. And just because the U.S. Department of Housing and Urban Development makes some announcement that Bay Area households earning six figures are now considered lower class, that doesn't mean the spoiled brats who find public transportation beneath them are actually broke. For most working class folks, taking a cab is a luxury, not a right.

The more I think about his nonsensical ideas the more my head feels like it's going to explode. There's just not enough time in the universe to explain all the many ways his viewpoint is fucked up.

Finally, I pull up to his location.

He concludes his rant with, "Taxis only serve the rich, Uber and Lyft are for everyone."

Whatever, dude. I point at the meter, which reads $16.70.

He hands me a $20 bill and says, "You really should consider switching over. You'd make a good Uber driver."

I'm tempted to roll down my window and tell him to shove his entitled opinions up his ass, but I fold the $20 into my shirt pocket and enjoy the peace and quiet of driving empty. ◉

THE UBER-IQUITY OF CONVENIENCE

The number one question I get asked while driving a taxi is always the same. Almost every day a passenger will bring it up.

"So, how's all this Uber stuff impacting your business?"

It often seems like they posit this question maliciously. As if they want to revel in the misfortunes of taxi drivers.

Over the years, I've tried to come up with a stock response to this perennial question. I'll say things like, "Well, since the taxi industry is so derided, I figured they must be on to something."

Or, "I always seem to constantly hitch my wagon to dying industries: print media, newspaper writing and taxi driving. Next up, I plan to get into coal mining."

Every once in a while, I'll fire back: "Is Uber impacting my business? Of course it is. When a new company enters an established marketplace and undercuts the competition by using a semantic loophole to break the law and skirt regulations, yeah, it's going to have a consequence on my bottom line."

Which leads the inevitable response: "Have you ever thought about switching to Uber?"

Like the first question, I try to field this one with a discussion-ending response: "I don't own a car."

I rarely tell people about my experience with Uber and Lyft prior to driving a taxi. It just confuses them. I prefer to act like some hapless kid who wandered into a cab by mistake.

The fact is, it doesn't matter whether you drive a taxi or do the Uber/Lyft thing, nobody's making much money on the streets of San Francisco. Oh, sure, you'll have the occasional good day. Maybe even a good week. But most of the time, you're competing for a limited number of fares with hundreds of taxis, thousands of Uber/Lyfts and the few remaining towncars and limos. As well as numerous private shuttles, Muni buses,

ID	1482		DESS AINUT KBW			GAS	Gals.	$ 12
Month/Day/Year		Vehicle License No. Cab No.		Medallion No.		GATES		$ 97
4/21/17			235	733				
Time Out		Total Miles	Paid Miles	Units	Trips	Company Revenue		$
3:30 PM	In					Driver Revenue		$ 132
Time In					25	Gross Turn In		$
3:15 AM	Out					Signature		
Hours Worked	Off							
1.5								

Trip	No. Pass.	TIME		FROM	TO	AMOUNT	
		IN	OUT				
1				CALTRAIN	FLOOD BUILDING	16	00
2				S/MARKET	HUNTINGTON	8	00
3				STANFORD COURT	S/MARKET	20	00
4				NEW MONTGOMERY	CENTERFOLDS	10	00
5				555 CAL	PINE/GOUGH	11	00
6				FAIRMONT	1700 FILLMORE	10	00
7		1:15		SW MARRIOTT	UNION GARDEN SC	40	00
8				CALTRAIN		15	00
9				GEARY/LEAN	18/CASTRO	14	00
10				PIER 27	BROADWAY/COLUMBUS	9	00
11				UNION/COLUMBUS	POST/POLK	11	00
12		1:74		BROADWAY/COL	WASH/POLK	10	00
13				14/MISSION	30/AVE PEDRO	13	00
14				14/MISSION	ELLIS/LARKIN	12	00
15				DRUMONT/GEARY	SHERATON PW	11	00
16				SUTTER/POWELL	BROADWAY/COL	10	00
17		2:12		FOLSOM/ JACKSON	SW ACM/ 22	22	00
18							
19							
20				15-DINNER	$ 242		
21				5 - DRINK			
22				11-GIGS	$ 102		
23							

DRIVE CAREFULLY   **DRESS NEATLY**   **BE COURTEOUS**

streetcars, light rail trains and BART.

If you drive a 10 to 14 hour shift, you might get an airport or a ride to the East Bay or Marin County. Or get lucky with a big tipper, or a meter and a half fare to someplace like San Jose or Livermore.

The same is true with Uber and Lyft. Keep the app open long enough and you could score a long haul during surge. Or get a bonus for doing over 100 rides in a week. Or whatever carrot they're dangling in front of drivers that month.

Even though driving for hire is a total crap job, unlike other crap jobs with regular paychecks, there's this delusion you'll eventually hit pay dirt. That's what keeps you on the road.

Several months back, a National driver had a fare to Salt Lake City. Yeah. The one in Utah. Apparently, the passenger lost his wallet and had to be in court the next day or face jail. With limited travel options, he took a taxi. I think they settled on two grand. Just thinking about what the actual fare would have been on the meter, at $2.75 a mile is enough to make any driver salivate. Forget meter and a half.

Of course, the ability to negotiate flat rates, accept cash payments and use manual taximeters that won't lose an internet connection over long distances are exclusive to real taxis. The minute an Uber driver takes a cash fare, he's no longer an Uber driver. He's just some guy with a car driving you for money. Kind of like the roller coaster at a carnival that popped up one day on the side of the highway outside town.

Unlike Uber/Lyft vehicles, no matter where a taxi goes, it remains a taxi. It still has a toplight, a phone number and a name on the side panels, or some indication that it's a licensed and insured vehicle for hire.

While it may seem baller to ride in the back of an unmarked Accord like when your mom drove you home from soccer practice, things like safety and liability can be beneficial at times.

Not only are real taxicabs fully insured and held accountable to city regulations, taxi drivers are able to actually determine their own earning potential. Unlike Uber and Lyft drivers, they aren't beholden to an app to connect them to paying fares.

Just look at what happened during the SXSW Ride-Hail Disaster of 2017, when the demand for rides during a storm overwhelmed the servers for the three ride-hailing apps that served the city at that point. (None of which were Uber or Lyft, because they didn't want to play by the rules and the citizens of Austin voted them out.) So you had all these riders incapable of getting drivers, and all these drivers incapable of getting riders, without an app to make the connection. As if the only way to get

laid is through Tinder.

Unlike Uber and Lyft, cabs don't need algorithms to determine what a ride is worth. They have taximeters that calculate the city-regulated rates based on time and distance. But the meter is only a guide. All fares are negotiable. Which means that a taxi driver truly is his own boss. He can drive you to Oakland for $20, or Salt Lake City from San Francisco for $2,000.

And yet, the question remains: "So what made you decide to drive a taxi, as opposed to…"

These days, there are only three reasons why anyone would drive a taxi. They're either bound to the industry financially, like medallion holders. They don't have any other opportunities. Or they're motivated by an ideology.

For me, driving a taxi is a form of resistance – a refusal to accept this notion that the world is supposed to be a particular way.

As an aspiring Luddite, I crave authenticity. I'm not opposed to technology, but I refuse to buy into the rampant pursuit of convenience and this need to avoid friction. Life is what happens when we deal with conflict and overcome obstacles. Without hassles, life would be boring and pointless. If there are no more problems to deal with, what's left to do but embrace hedonism?

I'm not interested in all these gadgets and apps that are supposed to simplify our lives but only seem to make things more complicated. Most new tech doesn't benefit humankind or offer anything significant to the human experience. It just enriches tech companies and their investors.

As people allow technology to take over their lives, they willingly surrender their freedom and privacy. They hand over their identities to these corporate-minded entities that "promise" to protect them from the "bad guys," even though they are the ones who created the "bad guys."

The "One Percenters" use these same tactics to pit poor people against each other by convincing one group that their problems aren't caused by a system that only serves the wealthy but the result of too many immigrants taking all the jobs.

Like the bullshit spewed by the ruling elite, tech companies succeed by capitalizing on the public's fears and laziness.

So in a way, driving a cab is my way of saying, "Fuck you!" to the dominant paradigm.

Although, lately, when people ask why I don't drive Uber, I just cut to chase and tell them, "Because I'm allergic to yuppies and assholes." ◉

PART FOUR

THE DEATH OF CAB CULTURE

THE TAXI DRIVER'S WORST ENEMY

During shift change last Saturday morning, a bunch of drivers are standing around the National office, chewing the fat and spitting out the gristle of a beef shank night.

In the mix of the conversational bouillabaisse, someone adds a dash of Costco.

Colin brings it up. "I need a battery charger for 1434," he says, sipping on a bottle of craft beer. "Every single morning, I go to start the cab and it's been promoted to Glory."

While National provides roadside assistance, you're better off pushing the cab across the Bay Bridge than waiting for the tow truck to arrive in Oakland.

Colin is hoping Jesse can acquire him a portable battery charger through his Costco membership.

As the discussion meanders, a few drivers begin exulting the big box store for their cutthroat business tactics. They recount with admiration how several years ago Costco took Coca-Cola to task when the soda company wouldn't lower their wholesale rates. As retaliation, Costco put large displays of Pepsi products in the front of the store and informed shoppers that Coca-Cola refused to provide "competitive pricing so that we may pass along the value our members deserve."

"They did this in all their stores across the country," Jesse says with chuckle. "To fuck Coke over."

"How long did it take before they caved?" Bobby wonders.

It's a rhetorical question, obviously, but I can't help but interject: "You do realize that's the same tactic Uber uses, right?"

"What? No..." Another driver tries to explain the story to me, as if I missed the point.

"No. I get it. Just like Costco, Amazon, Wal-Mart, or any other discount company," I explain, "the Uber and Lyft business model is designed to save people money. They promote themselves as heroes of the working class by boosting their bottom lines. And if anyone gets in their way – whether it's vendors, regulators, workers, laws, etc. – they act like martyrs. 'Boohoo! We're tying to save folks money but this ballot measure will force us to raise prices.' Or, 'If we have to train drivers, rates will go up.'"

"He's right, you know," Colin says. "That's why Uber and Lyft are so popular. It's the exact same business model."

"Come on, man," Bobby says. "It's just Costco! People with families are trying to save money."

"I have a family too!" I declare. "But I'm not willing to sacrifice my daughter's future to save 50 cents. Personally, I look for the highest price available and that's the price I want to pay!" I laugh.

"Kelly, you're always talking crazy." Bobby snorts.

"All these companies promote lies," adds Colin, subtly flexing that Econ degree from Cal. "They deceive consumers into thinking the only way to save money is through absolute freedom. Like Costco taking advantage of cheap products bought in bulk, Uber bases their low rates on the lack of accountability with an unregulated workforce."

"But Uber isn't that cheap," Boris points out. "They lie all the time. Have you seen the app? You see how much it says a taxi costs versus what an UberX costs? It's lies!"

"Costco isn't cheap either," Jesse says. "Unless you buy in bulk."

"Yeah, you gotta buy a case of ten jars of peanut butter to save five bucks," adds Lee.

"What are you gonna do with ten jars of peanut butter?" wonders Boris.

"Eat a lot a peanut butter and jelly sandwiches."

"Then you gotta buy ten jars of jelly." Lee says.

"And what about bread?" I include.

"Nobody's gonna buy that much bread in bulk," quips Lee.

"Regardless, you can't have it both ways," Colin states. "If you support evil conglomerations determined to destroy small business, of which you are a part, you can't bitch and moan about the consequences. You have to pick a side. Or be your own worst enemy. And with that…" Colin stands up, drains his bottle of 21st Amendment and belches. "It's past my bedtime."

"Can I hitch a ride east?" I ask, quickly grabbing my bag.

"Sure."

"All of a sudden I'm craving a peanut butter and jelly sandwich." ◉

HELL IS OTHER CAB DRIVERS

Somehow, I seem to have spawned a budding little socialite. Whenever we're in public, Baby Girl is all smiles, making eyes at strangers and shouting "Hey!" at anyone in earshot, from the stoop jockeys across the street to old ladies in Trader Joe's.

My daughter's quest for attention can get a little unnerving after a while. Especially after several taxi shifts when I'm really not in the mood to interact with some random person who wants to know her age and name.

As much as I'd like to go to the store without answering a bunch of stupid questions (Why do they want to know her name anyway? To write her a letter?) it's hard to be a sourpuss when there's a gleeful baby strapped to your chest. So I play along.

While she's usually an angel out in the world, at home, she's like a drunken sorority girl. Since she learned to screech at the top of her lungs, that's how she expresses excitement, frustration and when she's really not in the mood for a diaper change. Much to the neighbor's delight, I'm sure.

The shrieking of an infant reminds me of those impatient taxi drivers who use their horns to communicate…

A few weeks ago, I was lining up on Market Street waiting for the Orpheum to break.

Several cabs have already queued. I pull behind an unmarked SUV with its hazards on. I don't know if it's an Uber so I keep my distance. A Flywheel cab gets behind me and starts blowing his horn. Several taps at first, but then he really lays on it.

Is he honking at me? I wonder. And if so, why?

Finally, the guy gets out walks to the front of my cab. He starts gesturing at the space between the SUV and me. In broken English, he tells me to pull up. I try to explain that I don't know what the SUV is going to do and want to avoid getting stuck. But he keeps shouting at me, so I just move up grudgingly.

He bellyaches all the way back to his cab.

A few minutes go by and the show lets out. People start getting in cabs.

The Flywheel driver, who doesn't seem to know how to work the theaters, starts blowing his horn again and trying to get around me on the left. I see people get into the taxis in front of the SUV, which, predictably, doesn't move. As a couple heads for my cab, the Flywheel is angled on my left so that when a lady tries to get into his cab, he's too far away and she gets into the Fog City behind him. I hit reverse to move around the SUV to escape the mêlée.

When it comes to an eight-month-old, screaming pretty much gets the desired result. According to baby experts, she doesn't understand "No!" yet and well, we really don't want our neighbors to hate us too much. For taxi drivers who use their horns to communicate, though, it doesn't always pay…

The other day I'm turning left onto Drumm to work the Hyatt Regency taxi stand. As I wait for the flow of pedestrian traffic to cross the street, I hear someone blowing their horn behind me.

It's a cab from my own company, Veterans cab 1151. I guess he disagrees with my decision not to plow down half a dozen pedestrians.

Whatever, dude. I ignore him. But a few seconds later, he makes the turn anyway, maneuvering between the people in the crosswalk and then accelerating towards the red light at California without stopping.

He comes to a screeching halt in the middle of the intersection and when the light turns green, swerves in front of me and pulls behind a Luxor.

I'm not sure what he hopes to gain, but think to myself, if this asshole gets an SFO, it'll confirm my suspicion that the universe is designed to shit on those who don't screw over their comrades.

Once he's on the throne, though, a couple approaches his cab and he takes off towards the Wharf.

As I chuckle to myself, a guy knocks on my window. I look over my shoulder and see that he's got a suitcase…

I laugh all the way back to the city. For a brief moment, my faith in humanity is restored. It's still early in the day, though. I have a few hours of working around taxi drivers until heading home to hang out with someone way more civilized. ☉

CANARY IN THE COALMINE

I was talking with a journalist the other day about the inevitable death of the taxi industry. He seemed surprised by my response: taxis aren't going anywhere.

"They may not look the same in the future," I said, "or function the same, but when the day comes that a retired couple from Omaha flying into SFO is required to not only possess a smartphone but also download an app, surrender their personal information and have their movements tracked and then sold to a third party for marketing purposes just to get a ride into the city… Well, that's the day you can officially say San Francisco has lost its soul."

We were at The Orbit Room and while he wrote down my comment, one of those old streetcars from Milan clattered past on Market Street.

No, taxis aren't going anywhere. And automated vehicles are a long, long way off. In San Francisco, anyway. Unless the city invests millions of dollars in public infrastructure.

Several months ago, I drove two guys who picked my brain about which San Francisco streets were the worst to drive on. As soon as I found out they worked for Ford, I challenged them on the issue of self-driving cars.

"You know they'll never work here, don't you?" I demanded. "It's hard enough for a human to drive in this city, much less a computer. Besides potholes the size of Lake Merritt, many streets don't even have clearly marked lanes. How are lasers supposed to detect something that's not there? It's impossible, right?"

Both guys nodded.

No, taxis aren't going anywhere.

Sure, this isn't the popular opinion. Even my shrink has referred to me as a canary in the coal mine, implying that my experience driving a taxi, as documented in these pages, is some kind of barometer of the industry.

Now, if we're being honest, things aren't so great for me personally these days. I've reached a level of poverty that is absolutely terrifying. I've never been this broke with so much at stake. Each month I struggle to pay the rent without accruing late fees or bank charges from bounced checks. I have holes in my pants, holes in shoes and holes in my teeth. I need new glasses. I need a new phone. And, according to my wife, I need a new job.

Driving a taxi isn't getting better. It's getting worse. I wouldn't recommend this career to anyone I didn't hate.

But what does my experience say about the industry as a whole?

Three years ago I stopped driving for Uber and Lyft because it was no longer sustainable for me. After a year of fulltime driving for the two companies, my car was ragged out, my bank account was overdrawn and my morale was at an all time low. I wouldn't have recommended that gig to anyone I didn't hate. Full stop.

Yet, today Uber and Lyft are still flourishing. Why? Because a sucker is born every minute. There will always be someone desperate enough to work for less than another person.

The same thing is happening with taxis. There are essentially three types of drivers left: the indentured servants, those who bought medallions and can't give up without declaring bankruptcy; the old timers too stubborn to admit defeat who continue to drive a taxi as a form of resistance; and those who can't, for whatever reason, do the Uber/Lyft thing.

The sad thing about all this, though, is the false analogy between taxis and coal mines. How are the two similar? Do people really believe that Uber and Lyft exist in some magical realm where they don't operate the same as taxicabs?

Uber and Lyft drivers transport people in a vehicle from Point A to Point B for money. Same as a taxi. The only thing innovative about Uber and Lyft (since taxis had apps before Uber and Lyft existed) is their ability to run cab companies without owning a single car or being required to adhere to the same laws and regulations due to corrupt backroom dealings and semantic subterfuge. And a public more than willing to accept a cut-rate alternative as long as it's cheap. Who cares that someone else has to make up the difference?

No, taxis aren't going anywhere.

As far as being a lucrative form of employment... Oh yeah, that ship has sailed. How many dead canaries do you need to prove that? ☉

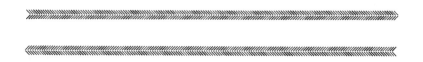

PART FIVE

SAN FRANCISCO HAS NEVER BEEN WHAT IT USED TO BE

THE NEW SCOURGE

ROUND 4 A.M., I wake up with a headache. I pop a Benadryl and chase four Advils with the abandoned vodka drink on my desk that's mostly three parts melted ice and one part San Pellegrino. Rather than lie in bed thinking about how I can't stop thinking about anything other than having a headache, I grab my hoodie, my pipe and head out back for a cigarette and a few puffs of weed.

It's not easy smoking in a breezeway on a windy, cold night. As leaves rustle across the concrete like cackling maidens, I flick my Bic repeatedly, trying to maintain a flame. In between squalls, I finally get a hit.

With a satisfying glow at the end of my American Spirit, I smoke and browse Twitter.

Puff, puff, scroll. Puff, scroll, pass.

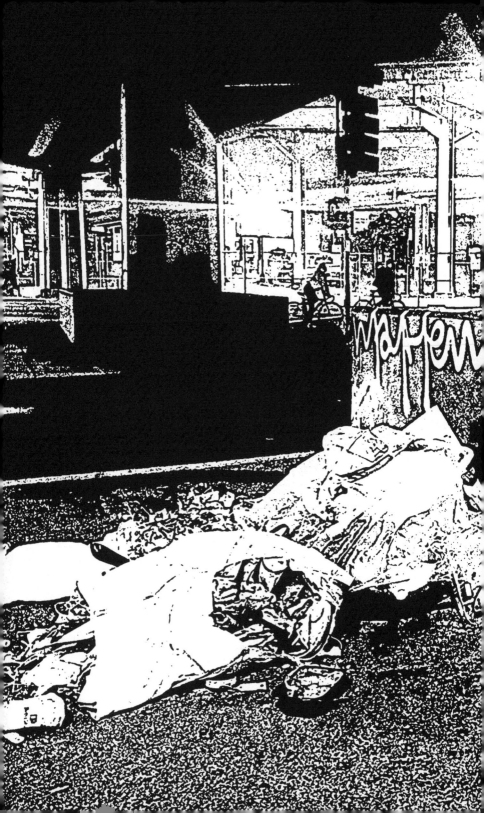

Several minutes later, just when it dawns on me that I've almost forgotten my headache, I hear footsteps at the back gate that leads to the sidewalk outside our building. The knob twists back and forth.

At this hour, I'm in no mood for an encounter with a neighbor, however brief. I scurry around the side of the building and wait for them to pass, taking the last drag from my cigarette. Nobody comes through the gate, though. I leave my hiding place and head inside.

Opening the back door, I hear footsteps on the landing above me. To avoid making any noise, I leave the back door slightly ajar and walk down the hallway towards my apartment.

Through the glass front door, I notice flashing police lights on the street. I quickly go into my apartment and surreptitiously peer through the window. Five OPD cruisers are in tactical position around my building, with a sixth one pulling up.

Several officers are creeping along the side towards the back with guns out and flashlights aimed down the driveway and foyer. I pull aside the curtain so they can see me watching them.

One of the cops waves at me. I flash him an okay hand gesture while shrugging my shoulders.

He nods. I continue to monitor their activity until a different cop sees me and points towards the front door. I open the window and whisper, "Is everything alright?"

"Can you open the front gate?"

Before I can heed his request, an officer out of view opens it and the cop says, "Never mind."

Now they're in the building.

I look in the hallway anyway and see flashlights through the back door I'd left slightly ajar. The door opens and a cop with his gun out in a defensive position enters. He ignores me and says to the cops behind him, "It's just another hallway." I close the door to my apartment and go back to the window. A few minutes later they all drive away.

Needless to say, it takes a while before I'm able to fall back asleep, with all the possible scenarios running through my head… What if the cops had encountered me skulking around the building? I could have been shot.

The next morning, I run into a guy who moved in upstairs a few months ago. As we're talking, I tell him about the police incident.

"No!" he gasps.

"What?"

"I'm the one who called the police" he says. "I heard a suspicious noise and saw someone in a hoodie."

"That was me."

"No."

Since I'm still wearing my hoodie, I pull it over me head. "Yeah. It was me."

"But it sounded like someone was using a tool of some sort."

I flick my lighter a few times. "Did it sound like this?"

"Uhhh."

"Man, I could've been shot!" I tell him.

"No!" He looks ashen, the reality of his actions becoming clear.

Uh, yeah.

What's with this new breed of urbanite? These busybodies looking out the window at night for suspicious figures? In Oakland? People overly sensitive to loud noises? In Oakland? Where do they think they moved to? Mayberry? This is fucking Oakland!

As this reverse White Flight continues, I feel less safe living around suburbanites than I ever have with the so-called "element." These kids just don't know how to exist in cities. They don't know how to walk in cities. They don't know how to drive in cities. And they don't know how to coexist with other people in cities. ☉

TUB-THUMPING FOR A LOST CAUSE

That evening, just as the Golden Gate Theater is about to break, the sky fills with rain clouds. I'm pulled over on Sixth Street, when my backdoor opens. A middle-aged, well-dressed lady climbs in, followed by a young guy and a middle-aged man.

"Uh, where to?" I ask the misguided family.

"Tell him your address," the lady prompts the young guy.

"1056 Fell," he responds.

"And if you don't mind, after dropping him off we need to return to the St. Francis," she tells me.

"Not a problem," I say, making a U-turn.

As I wait for the light to change at Mission, a bedraggled woman on the corner is flailing her arms and bitching out the sky.

"Oh my god." The lady behind me gasps. "What's wrong with her?"

Continuing down, she points out the motley cast of characters hanging

out on the sidewalks and expresses shock at the various displays of mental illness.

"How close are we to your neighborhood?" she asks her son. "I'm really not comfortable with you living around all this squalor."

"This isn't my neighborhood," he replies with obvious annoyance.

"This area doesn't look safe at all," she intones.

"Mom, I never even come down here!"

As they go back and forth on how much danger she thinks he's being exposed to, despite his protestations, I'm inclined to interrupt. Not that I'm feeling like much of a booster for San Francisco these days, but someone has to do it.

"It's not as bad as it seems," I say, adding a good-natured chuckle.

"What do you mean?" she asks.

"Homeless people aren't necessarily dangerous. The most you have to worry about, really, is aggressive panhandling."

"I don't think I've been asked for money so much in my life," the man says, chiming in for the first time.

I take Ninth Street towards Hayes and try to explain the income disparity that's plaguing the Bay Area and how, even people with normal jobs can barely afford to live here anymore. "All it takes is one bad decision or a greedy landlord and you lose the roof over your head."

"I just don't understand why they choose to live on the streets."

"Most people don't want to live on the streets. There's just not enough available housing. And they need to stay close to where the outreach services are, which is why you see so many people concentrated in certain areas of the city."

"Well, it's been everywhere we've gone so far. Yesterday, right outside our hotel, I saw a man... defecate in the street."

"We live in a society that doesn't provide a safety net for its most vulnerable citizens. There's no protection for people with mental illness, which isn't limited to schizophrenia. People with bipolar disorder or PTSD are just as likely to end up homeless. As well as those suffering from drug addiction and people trying to escape abusive relationships."

When I pull up to the brick apartment building, the guy's parents get out to say goodbye. On our way back to Union Square, they tell me their son is interning at a tech company for the summer.

"He really likes San Francisco but I don't know..."

"Well, if he's anything like the other young folks here, he exists in a bubble, where he's shielded from the harsh realities of city life. He's certainly not wandering the streets looking for trouble."

As I turn onto Powell, the man jokes that I've made a valiant effort to assuage his wife's concerns.

"How can I not worry?" she says, emphatically. "He's my baby!"

"It's understandable that you're shocked by all this poverty and despair. Everyone should be shocked. Shocked that these people are being forced to live in these circumstances should offend us all. But you can't be afraid of it. Or feel threatened by it. What you see on the streets are the consequences of a city that's growing so fast it can't keep up with all the changes. And in a city as small as San Francisco, it's impossible to hide the consequences."

When I pull up to their hotel, the doorman opens the back door.

"Thank you for talking to me. I feel... a little better."

"Everything's going to be okay," I tell her with a smile. "He's lucky to have a mom who worries so much."

"Tell him that!"

After she exits the vehicle, the man hands me a folded $20 bill and shakes my hand. "Thanks so much!"

"Just doing my part," I say, while pulling away.

On the corner, a man covered in filthy rags is shouting profanities while barging into oncoming traffic, scattering a group of tourists in his way. ◉

THE WORLD'S A MESS – IT'S IN MY CAB

When a hard rain is falling, it's time to complain. As if, once the waterworks start, you can't contain the deluge …

Heading to The Dogpatch down 16th Street, I take full advantage of the new taxi/bus lane, while the girl behind me talks about growing up in San Francisco.

"I remember being a kid and going to my grandparents' house," she says. "Right where you're taking me now. 16th was a completely different street back then. My grandfather built the house after the earthquake and fire in 1906. Over the years, the neighborhood got worse, but he never left. Since then, it's all changed and I often wonder what he would think of what's become of this area…"

She takes a long pause. I don't know what to say. As the windshield wipers scrape across the glass, I look around at the ultramodern condos, the state-of-the-art UCSF medical center and children's hospital, and looming in the distance, the menacing shell of the new Warriors stadium in mid-construction… What do you say about unbridled progress?

"I'm sure he would have hated it," she asserts.

Later that night, I'm rushing across town to grab a burger from Sam's on Broadway before they close. But as fate would have it, a block away, I see an arm in the air. She's just going to the Tenderloin. A short ride, but it'll pay for my dinner.

"I live on Ada Toilet," the woman tells me. "You know where that is? On O'Farrell between Hyde and Leavenworth. I usually walk or take the bus," she continues. "But not is this weather."

"It's really nasty out there," I concede. "At least the streets are getting rinsed off."

"It'll take more than a little rain to clean these streets."

"That reminds me of a line in *Taxi Driver*," I point out. "'Someday a real rain will come and wash all the scum off the streets.'"

"So the yuppies can take over? Shit, the TL is the only part of the city left that still feels like San Francisco. If only there was a rain hard enough to wash away the layers of whitewash and bring back the filth."

It's such a common refrain, from natives to long-term residents who can't imagine a life outside San Francisco, from teachers and bartenders and food servers and 9-1-1 operators and civil servants… Anyone who doesn't work in tech, fighting to stay in the city, as armies of suburbanites abandon their planned communities, tree-lined avenues, cul-de-sacs

and white picket fences to embrace the urban existence. Even though the harsh realities of city life seems to offend them and they try to recreate the complacent lives they left behind...

My next fare is the bartender from Public Works. Listening to her cringe-worthy tales of serving drinks to Millennials, all I can do is laugh. At 3:30 a.m., it's a welcome change of pace to deal with a sober person.

I've actually driven her home twice before. Her boyfriend used to drive for Luxor. Eventually, we change the subject. Talk about collecting LPs and end the night on a positive note...

While taxi driving can be a demoralizing act of futility most of the time, there are still plenty of enjoyable encounters with cool people. Those rides sustain you. For hours, days... Sometimes even weeks.

Sadly, though, the best rides are often the least noteworthy.

A couple months ago, I drove this guy from Cole Valley to downtown. We talked the whole time. One of those truly invigorating taxi encounters that's like a B-12 shot on a crappy night.

For the life of me, though, I can't remember what we talked about. It was nothing negative. I remember thinking afterwards, Wow, we didn't complain once! Not about San Francisco. Not about how the tech industry has ruined the city. No talk of millennials. Or sexual assault. No Uber or Trump. No hurricanes. No homeless. No opioid epidemic.

It had to have been something cool though...

Probably our families. Or music. Favorite Victorians. Local history.

It was one of those conversations that didn't feel like a jeremiad on the installment plan. You know, those rants that go on for days, as you go through your daily life, bitching about the same thing from one person to the next.

Who knows? Maybe we just talked about the weather. ⊙

REQUIEM FOR VALENCIA STREET

T he city is dead.
Even though the rain has dissipated, half the bars in the Mission are already shuttered. Most of the late night taquerias as well. Even the line at El Farolito is barely out the door.

There isn't much left to do but ride the green wave down Valencia Street and blast Galaxie 500 as an Uber tailgates me. Probably wants to race up to the red light, slam on his brakes and then speed off to the next intersection. Cause that's what they do.

I could easily pull over and let him get on with his exercise in futility while I practice my own, but the lo-fi psychedelia pouring out of my speakers has me in a tranquil headspace. Ah, who am I kidding? I just really love annoying Uber drivers.

Not that I should harbor so much animosity towards these poor schmucks who don't know they're getting screwed yet. One day, they might figure out the system is rigged against them.

Slowly, the public is becoming aware that taxi drivers aren't the only ones getting fucked by Uber. As the wave of anti-Uber/Lyft backlash continues to surge, the people of San Francisco are realizing they're also getting the proverbial big one up the you-know-what.

It seems the only people benefiting from the proliferation of scab cabs are the passengers who use these services. Of course, they're usually skulked down in the backseat with their phones in front of their faces, willfully oblivious to the problems their transportation choices create, so who knows what they think…

As 1 a.m. approaches, I've been empty for over an hour.

What am I doing? I should go home and hang out with my baby girl, who's certainly still awake now that she's four and a half months old and

has decided sleep is for suckers. Even though I try to remind her how happy she gets after a good night's rest – so full of smiles and giggles and pure joy – she just blows raspberries and insists I dance her around the room to the Talking Heads. Which is more fun than trying to squeeze one last fare out of these empty streets. Or pissing off Uber drivers...

Where the fuck is everyone anyway?

Nobody goes out anymore. Who can afford it? The cost of living in San Francisco is so outrageous, it's cheaper to stay at home, watch Netflix and order delivery. Which is why it's no surprise that white tablecloth restaurants are going out of business while take-out places proliferate and beloved bars are getting torn down to build more condos.

That's the new San Francisco: Be sure to put some flowers on your bedroom walls ...

Sometimes it's hard to be a booster for this place when there's not much to be excited about anymore, and the traces of the past are few and far between. Then I pass the Elbo Room, and even though there are only a few smokers on the sidewalk, the guy playing piano out of the back of his van in front of Good Vibrations is pounding the keys as if it the smoking section were twenty times the size.

And in the next block, there's the guitar hero and his one-man band performing in an alcove next to the Curtis Hotel. His expansive rig includes a drum machine, samplers, multiple effects and a DVD player. From dusk to dawn, seven days a week, his Dan Armstrong axe reverberates against the buildings, infuriating everyone within earshot.

If there is one constant in the Mission these days that harkens back to the old, it is this guy and his heavy noodling.

Not many people are feeling nostalgic at 3 a.m., however, when he's in the midst of another meth-drenched shredding frenzy.

Petitions have circulated to get him to stop playing his music on the street. And during a recent altercation with the cops, a sergeant from the SFPD Mission Station pleaded with him to at least limit his aural assault on the residents, business owners and visitors of Valencia Street to normal waking hours.

"Every day I have multiple complaints about your music," the sergeant yelled at him. "Every single day!"

When confronted with the harsh reality of his critics, our axe man was all apologies, but once they left, he just shouted, "Fuck the police!" and turned it up even louder. "No one stands in the way of my art!"

The city may be dead, but the heart of rock and roll is...

Uhm... Well, it's still bleating.

ID 1482	Driver DESSAINT				GAS		15
Month Day Year 09/13/17	Vehicle License No./Cab No. 233		Medallion No. 233		GATES		97
Time Out 12:15 pm	Total Miles In 245,698	Paid Miles 5	Units 170/65	Trips	Company Returns		112
Time In 1:30 AM	Out 245,828	145		4	Driver Returns 789		33
Hours Worked 13	In 130	($14 KC)		TOTAL	Credit Tips In 145		10
							181

No. Pass.	TIME IN	OUT	FROM	TO	AMOUNT	
1	12:30		825	Pier 39	10	65
2			Pier 39	Cannery	9	55
3			600 Lombard	Commercial/Ferry	11	75
4			Sam/Bush	Pier 33	10	10
5			Pier 39	Vasc/Baker	25	50
6			Lyon/Market	Beach/Griffin	21	00
7			Columbus Village	Ferry Village	5	90
8			Mint/Sac	15/Folsom	22	20
9			40 1st	20th/Valencia	23	30
10			5/Market	Pier 39	13	85
11			Pier 39	100 VN	17	80
12			743 Highway	25/Alabama	8	45
13			Grant/Post	712 Bayberry	6	80
14	8PM		EC1	Bay Club	5	15
15	DINNER		EC5	8/Lake	9	65
16			Lucy B	HK8/Divis	7	40
17			Opera	19/De Haro	11	20
18			AT&T	6th/Fell More	14	90
19			AT&T		9	55
20			4/Market	2/Carmel	14	50
21	1:30		Fillmore	William/Innes	10	60
22					336	

DRIVE CAREFULLY   DRESS NEATLY $33 89 BE COURTEOUS

SPECIAL THANKS TO:

Colin Marcoux, Joe Fitzgerald Rodriquez, Michael Howerton, Denise Sullivan, V. Vale, Gregory Anderson, Deborah Peterson, Sara Gaiser, Ivy at City Lights, Colin Fowler, Thomas Canne, Trevor Johnson, Jacob Black, Leonski Slomovic, John Han, Peter Juneaux, Beth Powder, Irina Borisovna, Breezy at Needles and Pens, Christian Lewis, Austin Peterson, Anthony Karr, Barry Taranto, Chucky Johnson, Larry Sturgis, Ben Valis, Barry Taranto, Artur Lyubelskiy, Simone Nevraumont, Joshua Duford, Lauren Smiley, Andy and Patrick at Green Arcade Books, Jon Kessler, Apollo Kahl, Meghan Roberts, Abel Soria, Mary McGuire, David Smith Dias, Jesse Shatara, Brent Johnson, Heather Rosner, Douglas O'Connor, Maya Archer Doyle, Bill Doyle, Urban, Carol Osorio, Ruach Graffis, Barry Korengold, Charles Rotter, Rich Koury, Stuart Shuffman, Mark Gruberg and Jen Joseph.

For more dispatches from
behind the wheel, visit:

www.idrivesf.com

or pick your poison:

facebook.com/idrivesf
@piltdownlad
idrivesf.tumblr.com

PILTDOWNLAD

A PERSONAL NARRATIVE ZINE

WWW.PILTDOWNLAD.COM